SUICIDE RISK™

VOLUME ONE • GRUDGE WAR

ROSS RICHIE CEO & Founder • MATT GAGNON Editor-in-Chief • FILIP SABLIK VP-Publishing & Marketing • LANCE KREITER VP-Licensing & Merchandising • PHIL BARBARO Director of Finance • BRYCE CARLSON Managing Editor
DAFNA PLEBAN Editor • SHANNON WATTERS Editor • ERIC HARBURN Editor • CHRIS ROSA Assistant Editor • ALEX GALER Assistant Editor • WHITNEY LEOPARD Assistant Editor • JASMINE AMIRI Assistant Editor
STEPHANIE GONZAGA Graphic Designer • MIKE LOPEZ Production Designer • DEVIN FUNCHES E-Commerce & Inventory Coordinator • BRIANNA HART Executive Assistant • AARON FERRARA Operations Assistant

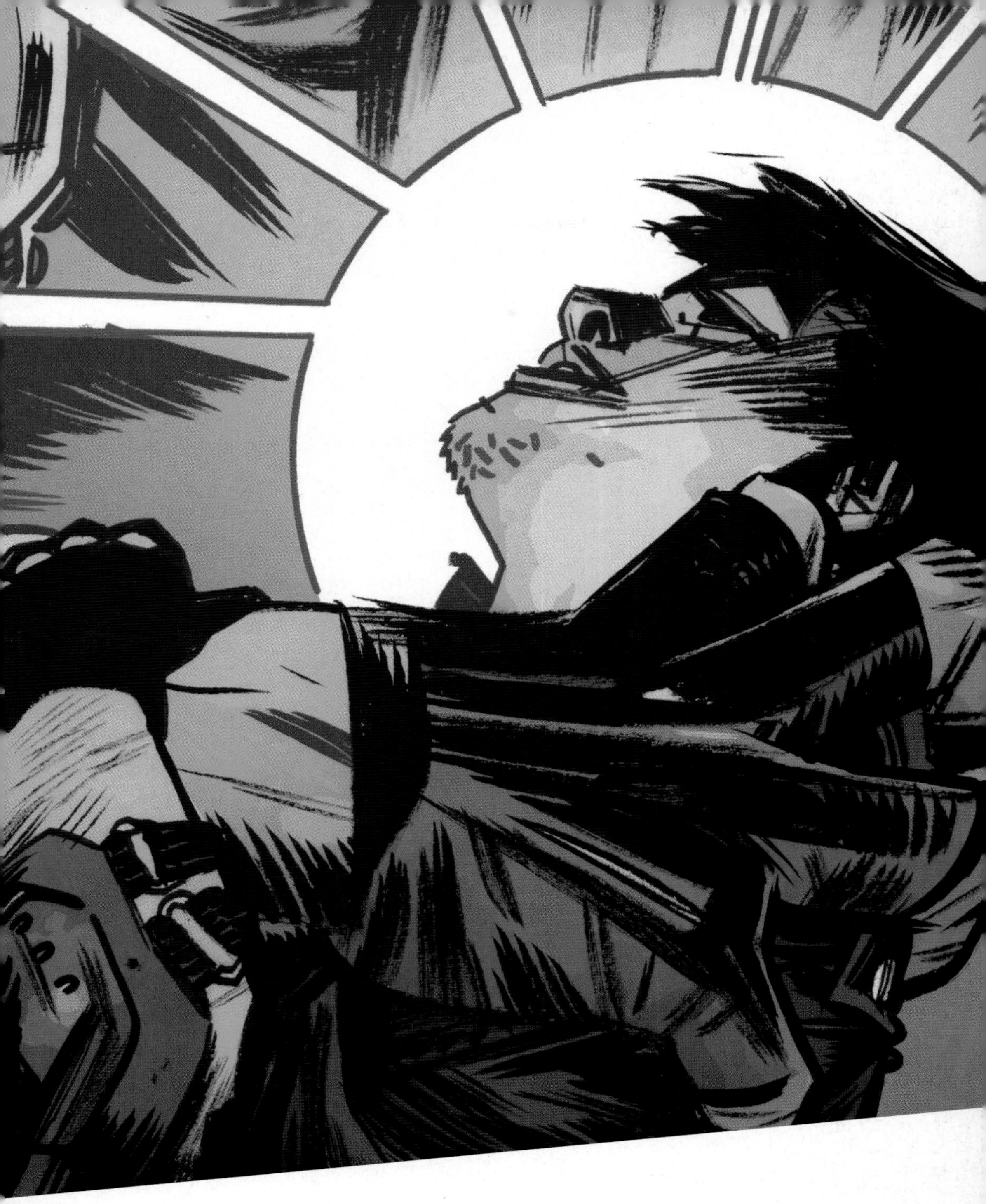

Created & Written By
MIKE CAREY
Art By
ELENA CASAGRANDE
Colors By
ANDREW ELDER
Letters By
ED DUKESHIRE
Editors
DAFNA PLEBAN
MATT GAGNON
Cover By
TOMMY LEE EDWARDS
Trade Design By
HANNAH NANCE PARTLOW

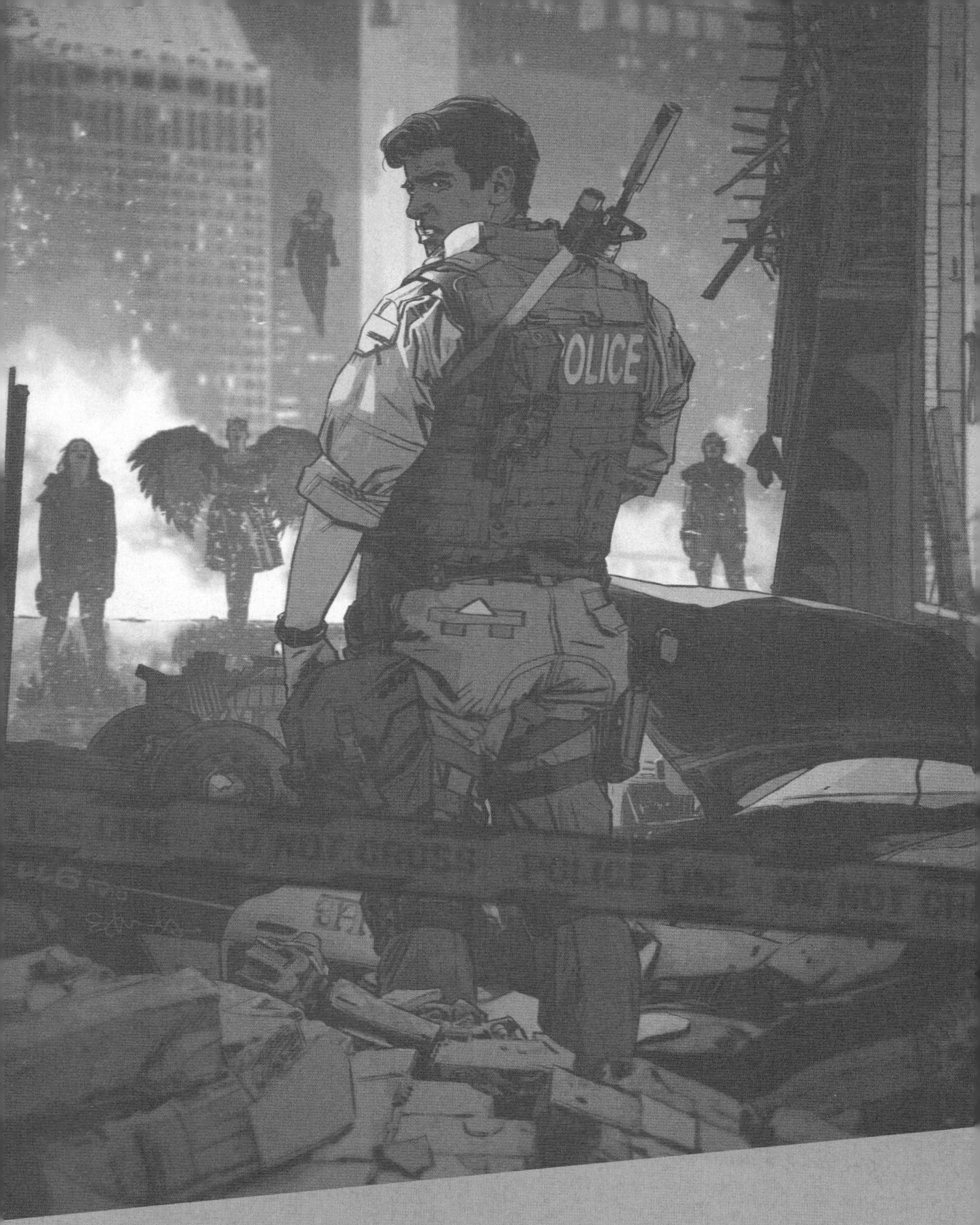
POLICE

"NO ONE COMES THROUGH SOMETHING LIKE THAT WITHOUT **TRAUMA**."

Chapter 1

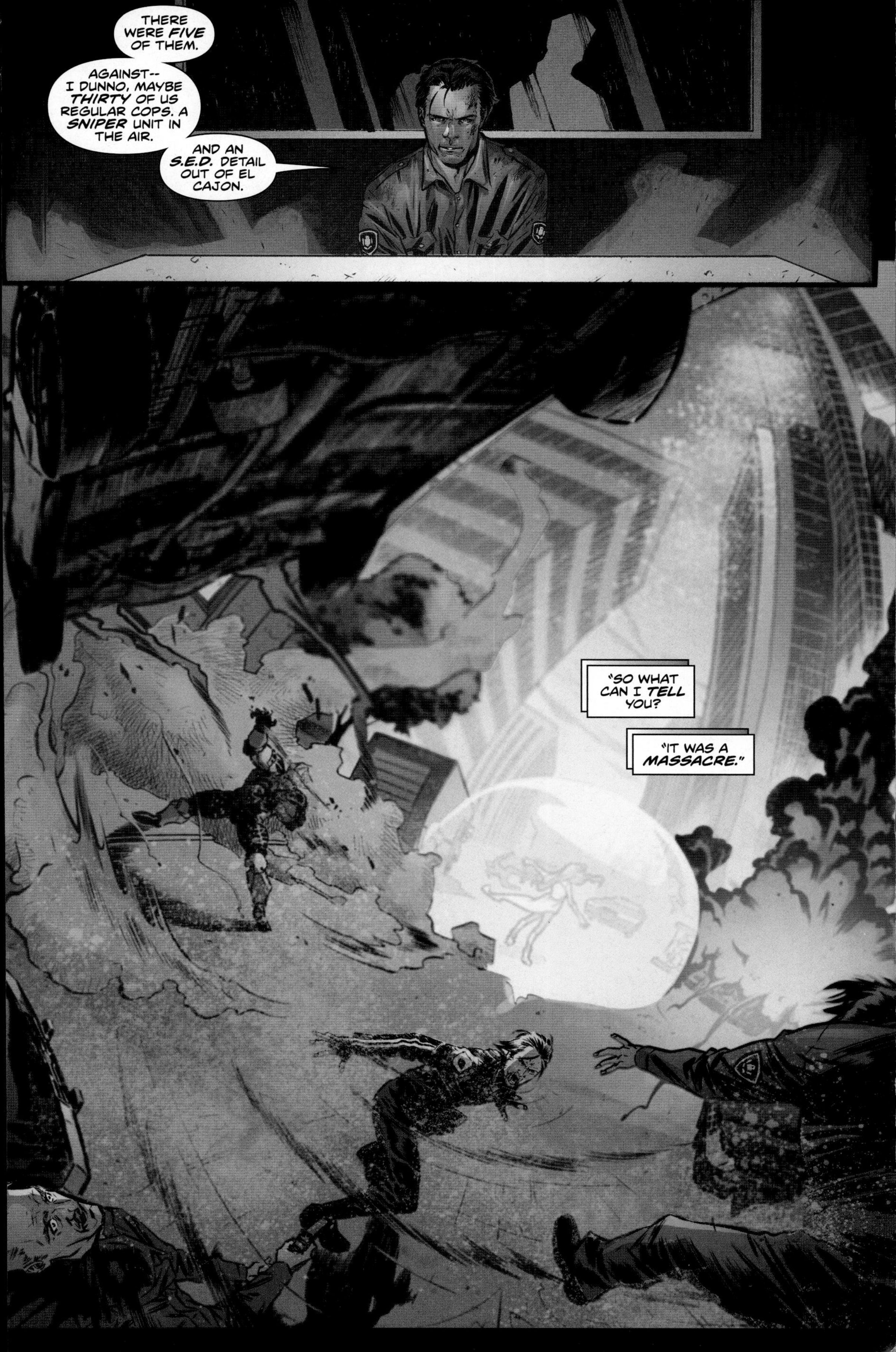
THERE WERE *FIVE* OF THEM.
AGAINST-- I DUNNO, MAYBE *THIRTY* OF US REGULAR COPS. A *SNIPER* UNIT IN THE AIR.
AND AN *S.E.D.* DETAIL OUT OF EL CAJON.
"SO WHAT CAN I *TELL* YOU?
"IT WAS A *MASSACRE*."

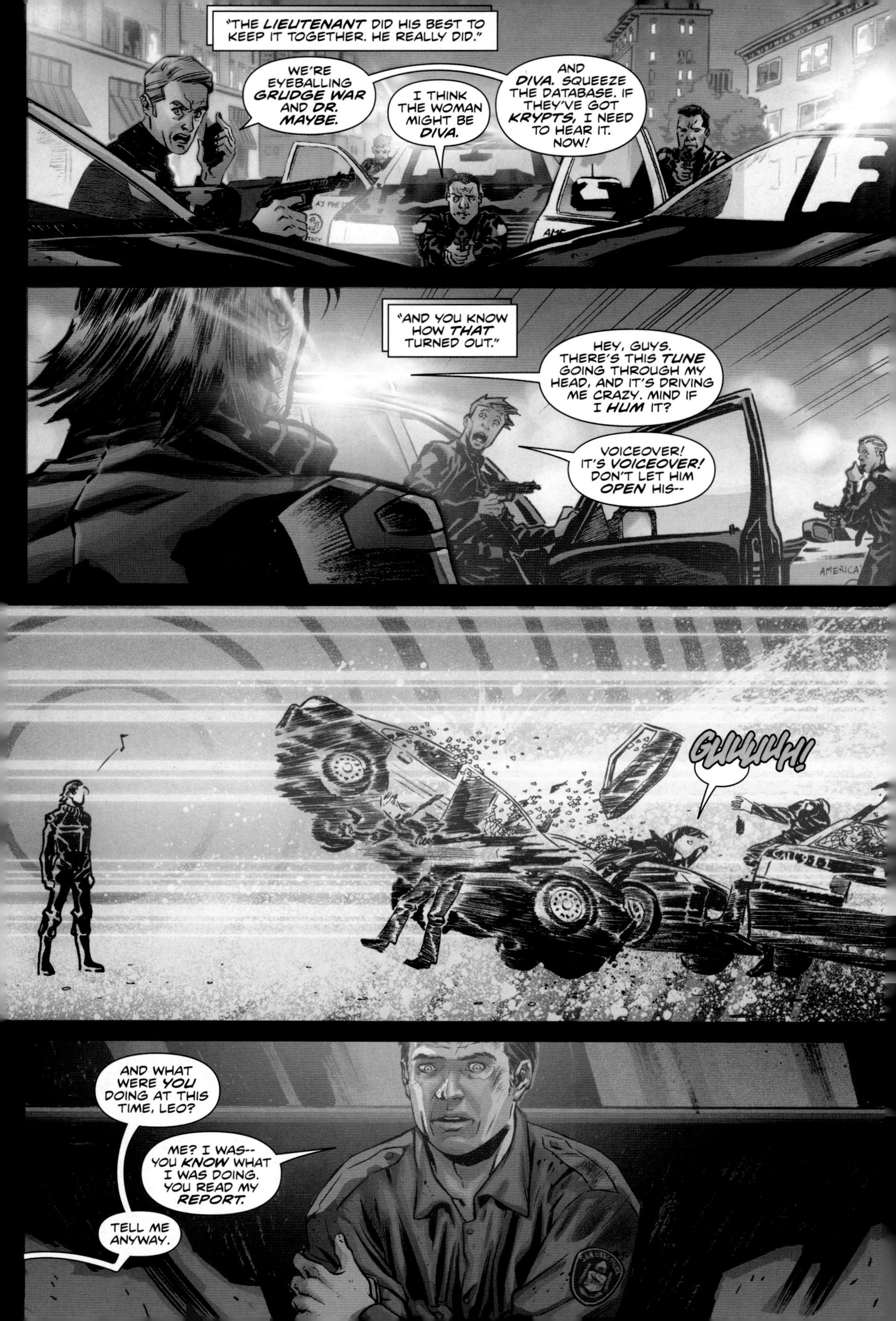
"THE LIEUTENANT DID HIS BEST TO KEEP IT TOGETHER. HE REALLY DID."
WE'RE EYEBALLING GRUDGE WAR AND DR. MAYBE.
I THINK THE WOMAN MIGHT BE DIVA.
AND DIVA. SQUEEZE THE DATABASE. IF THEY'VE GOT KRYPTS, I NEED TO HEAR IT. NOW!
"AND YOU KNOW HOW THAT TURNED OUT."
HEY, GUYS. THERE'S THIS TUNE GOING THROUGH MY HEAD, AND IT'S DRIVING ME CRAZY. MIND IF I HUM IT?
VOICEOVER! IT'S VOICEOVER! DON'T LET HIM OPEN HIS--
AMERICA
GUUUUH!
AND WHAT WERE YOU DOING AT THIS TIME, LEO?
ME? I WAS-- YOU KNOW WHAT I WAS DOING. YOU READ MY REPORT.
TELL ME ANYWAY.

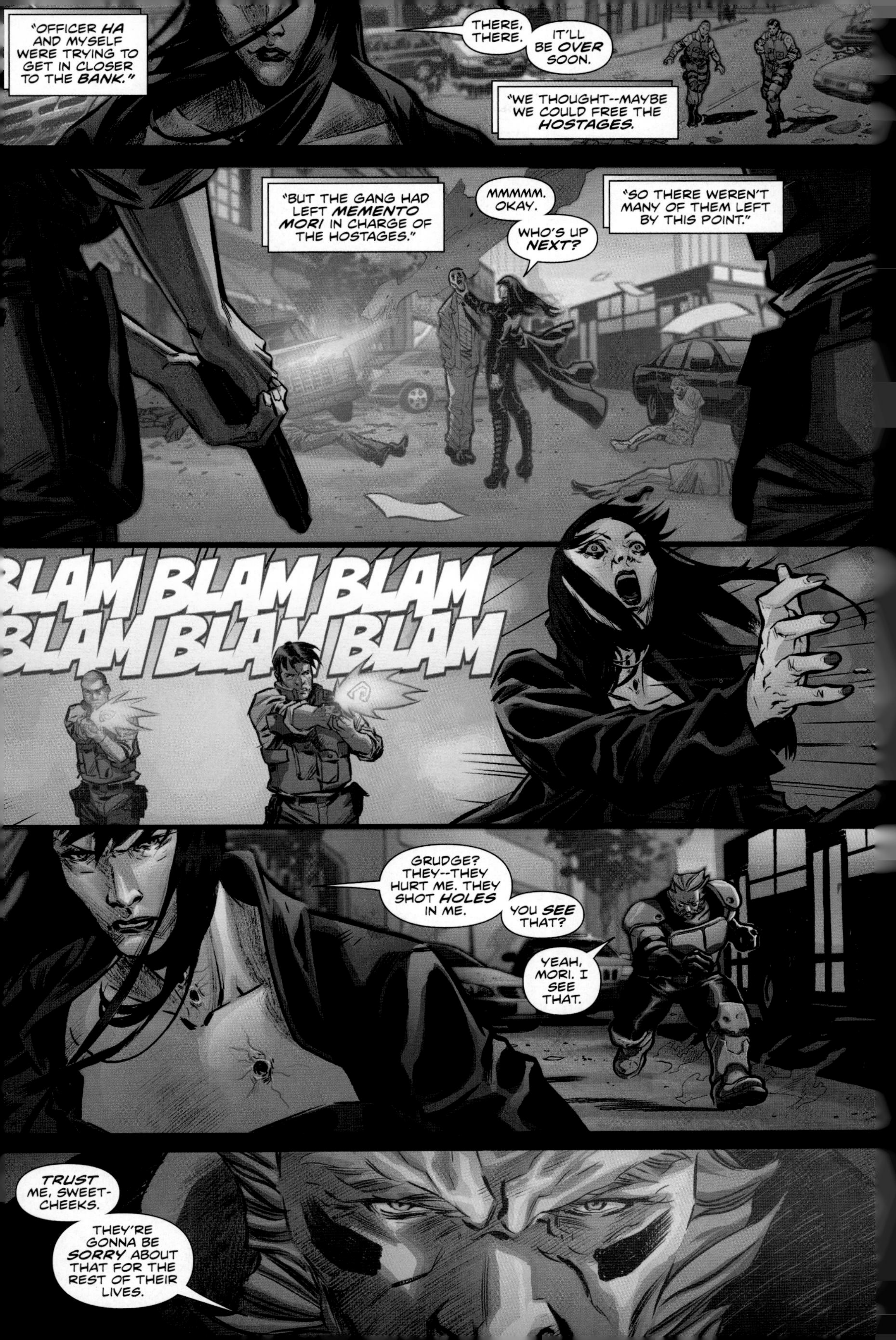
"OFFICER HA AND MYSELF WERE TRYING TO GET IN CLOSER TO THE BANK."
THERE, THERE.
IT'LL BE OVER SOON.
"WE THOUGHT--MAYBE WE COULD FREE THE HOSTAGES.
"BUT THE GANG HAD LEFT MEMENTO MORI IN CHARGE OF THE HOSTAGES."
MMMMM. OKAY.
WHO'S UP NEXT?
"SO THERE WEREN'T MANY OF THEM LEFT BY THIS POINT."
BLAM BLAM BLAM
BLAM BLAM BLAM
GRUDGE? THEY--THEY HURT ME. THEY SHOT HOLES IN ME.
YOU SEE THAT?
YEAH, MORI. I SEE THAT.
TRUST ME, SWEET-CHEEKS.
THEY'RE GONNA BE SORRY ABOUT THAT FOR THE REST OF THEIR LIVES.

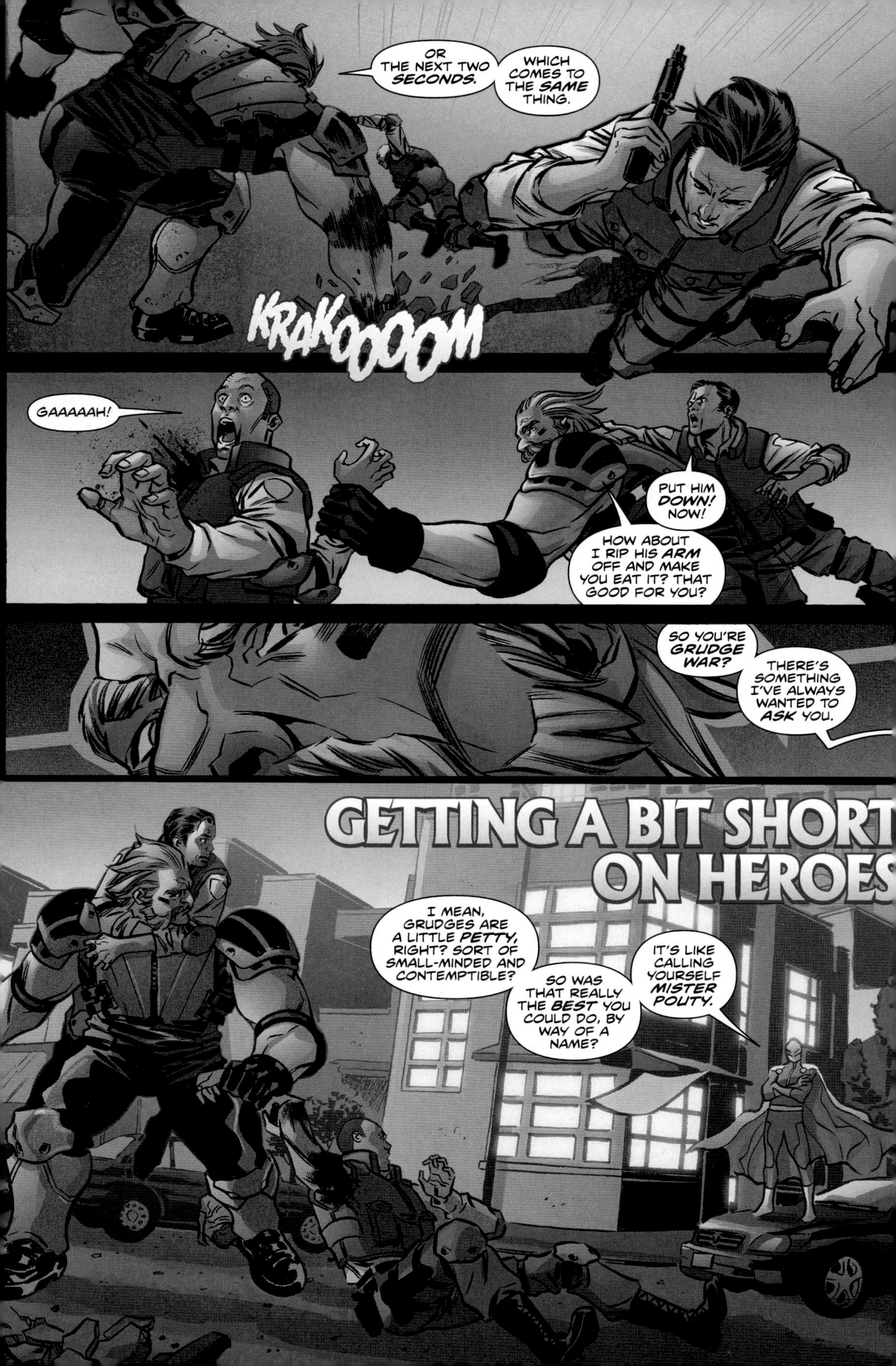

OR THE NEXT TWO SECONDS.
WHICH COMES TO THE SAME THING.
KRAKOOOOM
GAAAAAH!
PUT HIM DOWN! NOW!
HOW ABOUT I RIP HIS ARM OFF AND MAKE YOU EAT IT? THAT GOOD FOR YOU?
SO YOU'RE GRUDGE WAR?
THERE'S SOMETHING I'VE ALWAYS WANTED TO ASK YOU.
GETTING A BIT SHORT ON HEROES
I MEAN, GRUDGES ARE A LITTLE PETTY, RIGHT? SORT OF SMALL-MINDED AND CONTEMPTIBLE?
SO WAS THAT REALLY THE BEST YOU COULD DO, BY WAY OF A NAME?
IT'S LIKE CALLING YOURSELF MISTER POUTY.

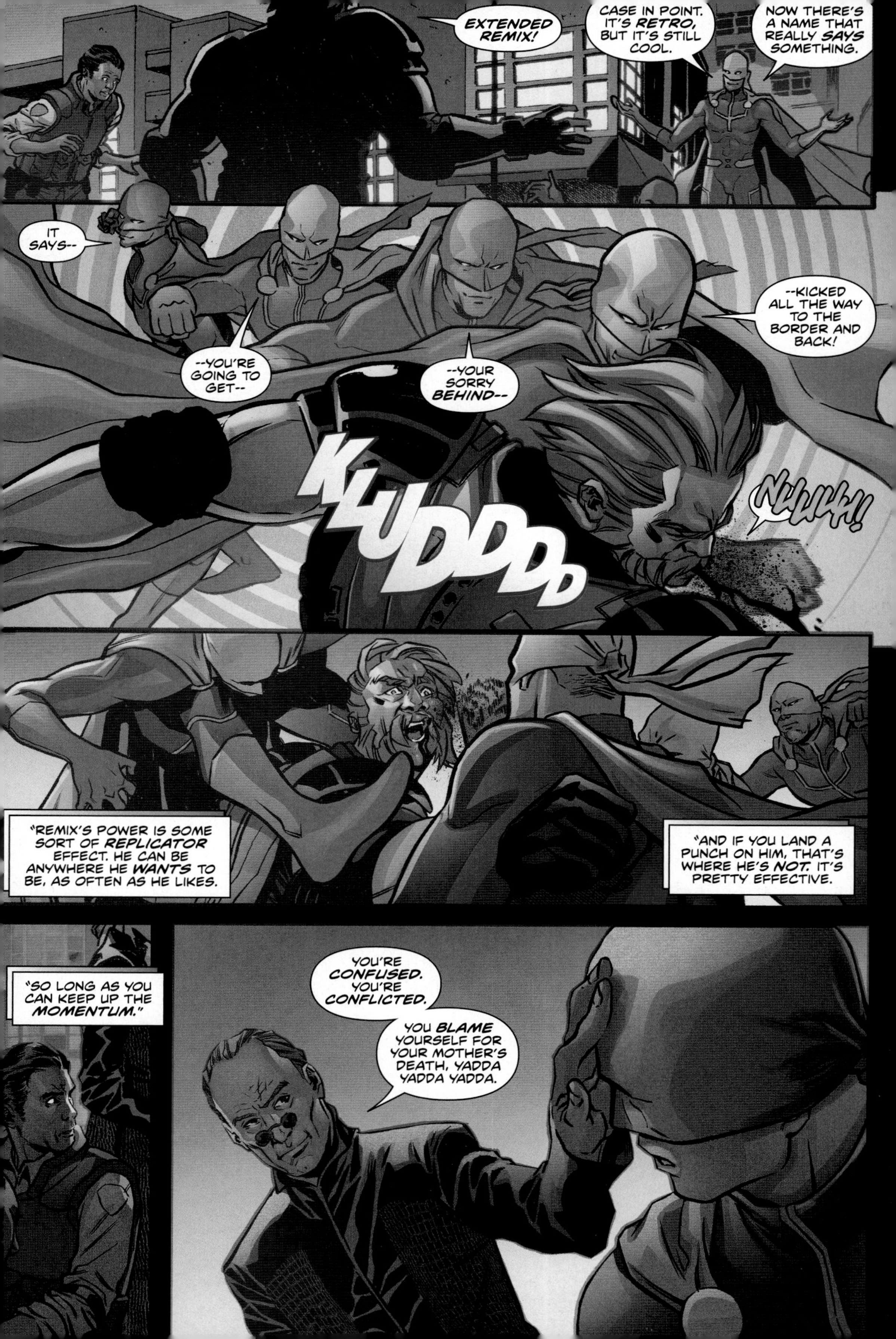
EXTENDED REMIX!
CASE IN POINT. IT'S RETRO, BUT IT'S STILL COOL.
NOW THERE'S A NAME THAT REALLY SAYS SOMETHING.
IT SAYS--
--YOU'RE GOING TO GET--
--YOUR SORRY BEHIND--
--KICKED ALL THE WAY TO THE BORDER AND BACK!
KLUDDDD
NUUUH!!
"REMIX'S POWER IS SOME SORT OF REPLICATOR EFFECT. HE CAN BE ANYWHERE HE WANTS TO BE, AS OFTEN AS HE LIKES.
"AND IF YOU LAND A PUNCH ON HIM, THAT'S WHERE HE'S NOT. IT'S PRETTY EFFECTIVE.
"SO LONG AS YOU CAN KEEP UP THE MOMENTUM."
YOU'RE CONFUSED. YOU'RE CONFLICTED.
YOU BLAME YOURSELF FOR YOUR MOTHER'S DEATH, YADDA YADDA YADDA.

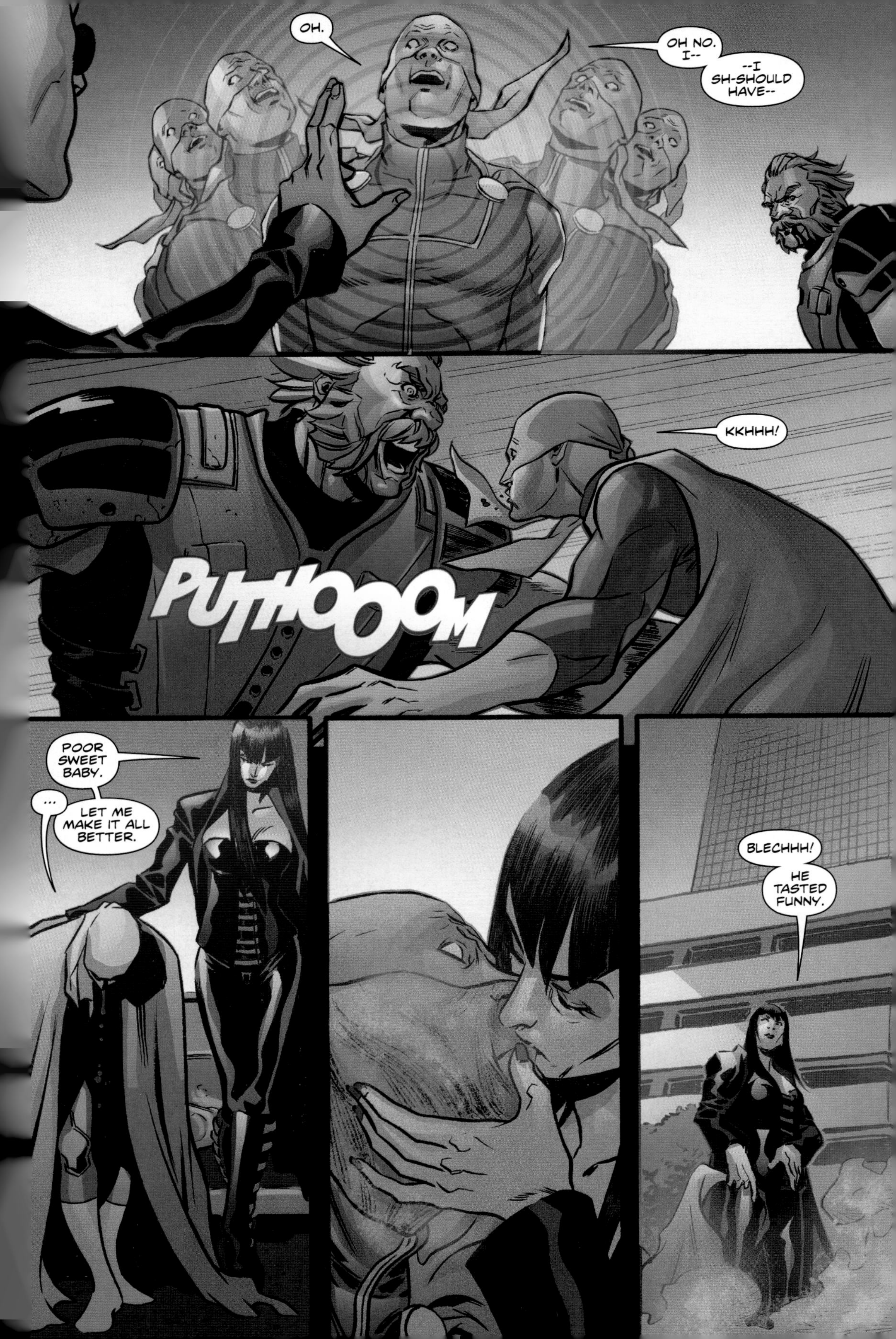
OH.
OH NO. I--
--I SH-SHOULD HAVE--
KKHHH!
PUTHOOOM
POOR SWEET BABY.
...
LET ME MAKE IT ALL BETTER.
BLECHHH!
HE TASTED FUNNY.

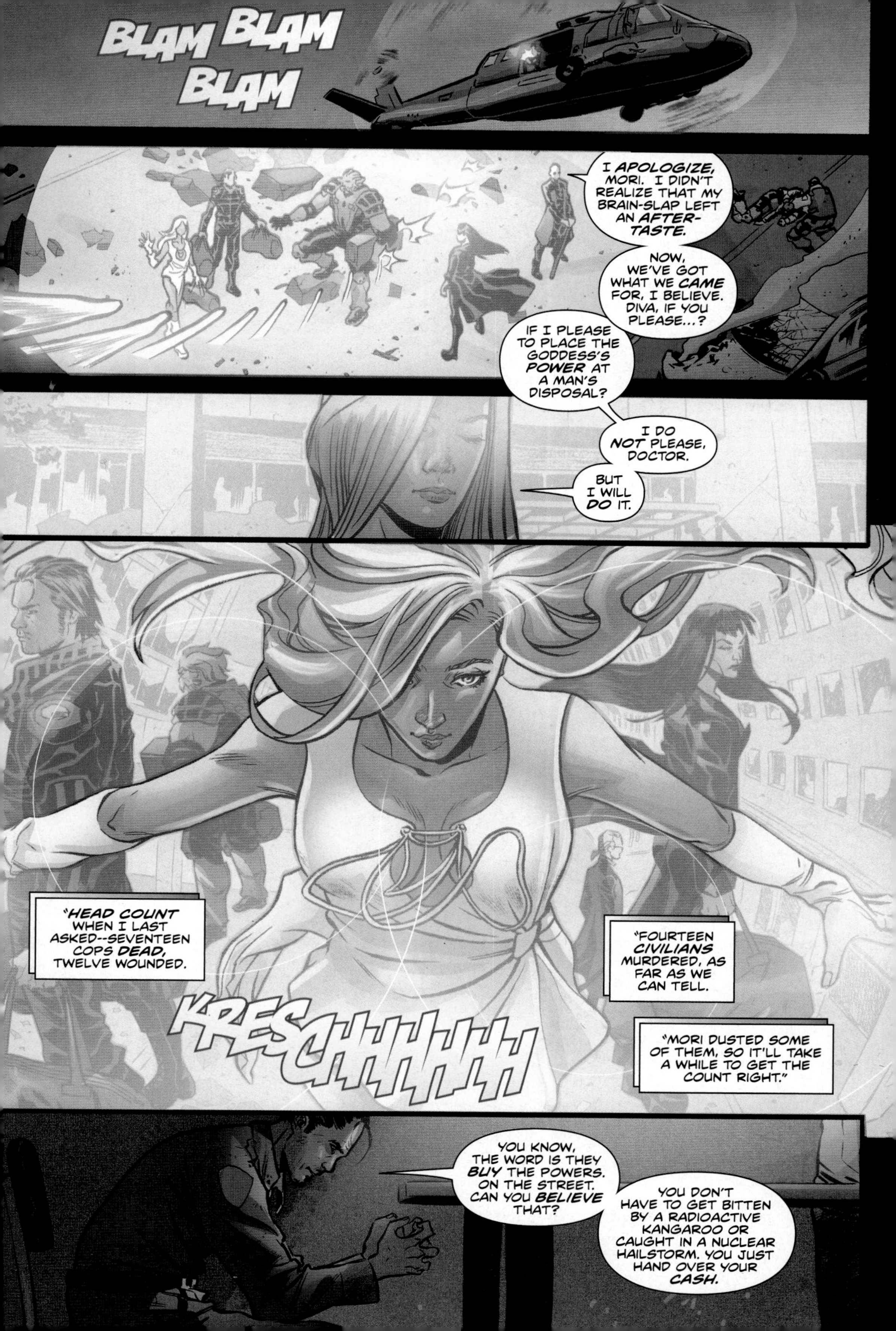
BLAM BLAM BLAM
I APOLOGIZE, MORI. I DIDN'T REALIZE THAT MY BRAIN-SLAP LEFT AN AFTER-TASTE.
NOW, WE'VE GOT WHAT WE CAME FOR, I BELIEVE. DIVA, IF YOU PLEASE...?
IF I PLEASE TO PLACE THE GODDESS'S POWER AT A MAN'S DISPOSAL?
I DO NOT PLEASE, DOCTOR.
BUT I WILL DO IT.
"HEAD COUNT WHEN I LAST ASKED--SEVENTEEN COPS DEAD, TWELVE WOUNDED.
"FOURTEEN CIVILIANS MURDERED, AS FAR AS WE CAN TELL.
KRESCHHHHHH
"MORI DUSTED SOME OF THEM, SO IT'LL TAKE A WHILE TO GET THE COUNT RIGHT."
YOU KNOW, THE WORD IS THEY BUY THE POWERS. ON THE STREET. CAN YOU BELIEVE THAT?
YOU DON'T HAVE TO GET BITTEN BY A RADIOACTIVE KANGAROO OR CAUGHT IN A NUCLEAR HAILSTORM. YOU JUST HAND OVER YOUR CASH.

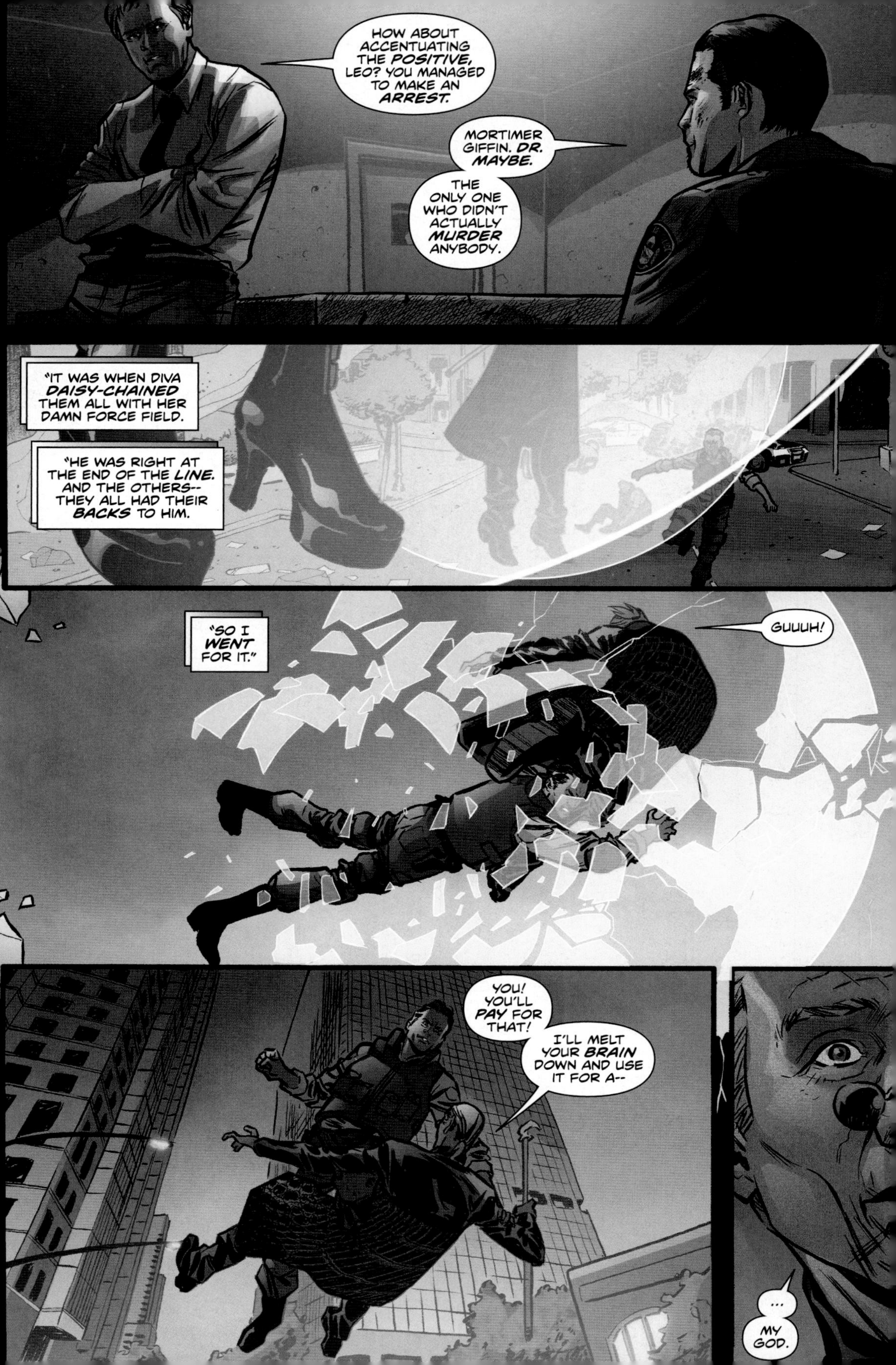

HOW ABOUT ACCENTUATING THE *POSITIVE*, LEO? YOU MANAGED TO MAKE AN *ARREST.*
MORTIMER GIFFIN. *DR. MAYBE.*
THE ONLY ONE WHO DIDN'T ACTUALLY *MURDER* ANYBODY.
"IT WAS WHEN DIVA *DAISY-CHAINED* THEM ALL WITH HER DAMN FORCE FIELD.
"HE WAS RIGHT AT THE END OF THE *LINE*. AND THE OTHERS-- THEY ALL HAD THEIR *BACKS* TO HIM.
"SO I *WENT* FOR IT."
GUUUH!
YOU! YOU'LL *PAY* FOR THAT!
I'LL MELT YOUR *BRAIN* DOWN AND USE IT FOR A--
... MY GOD.

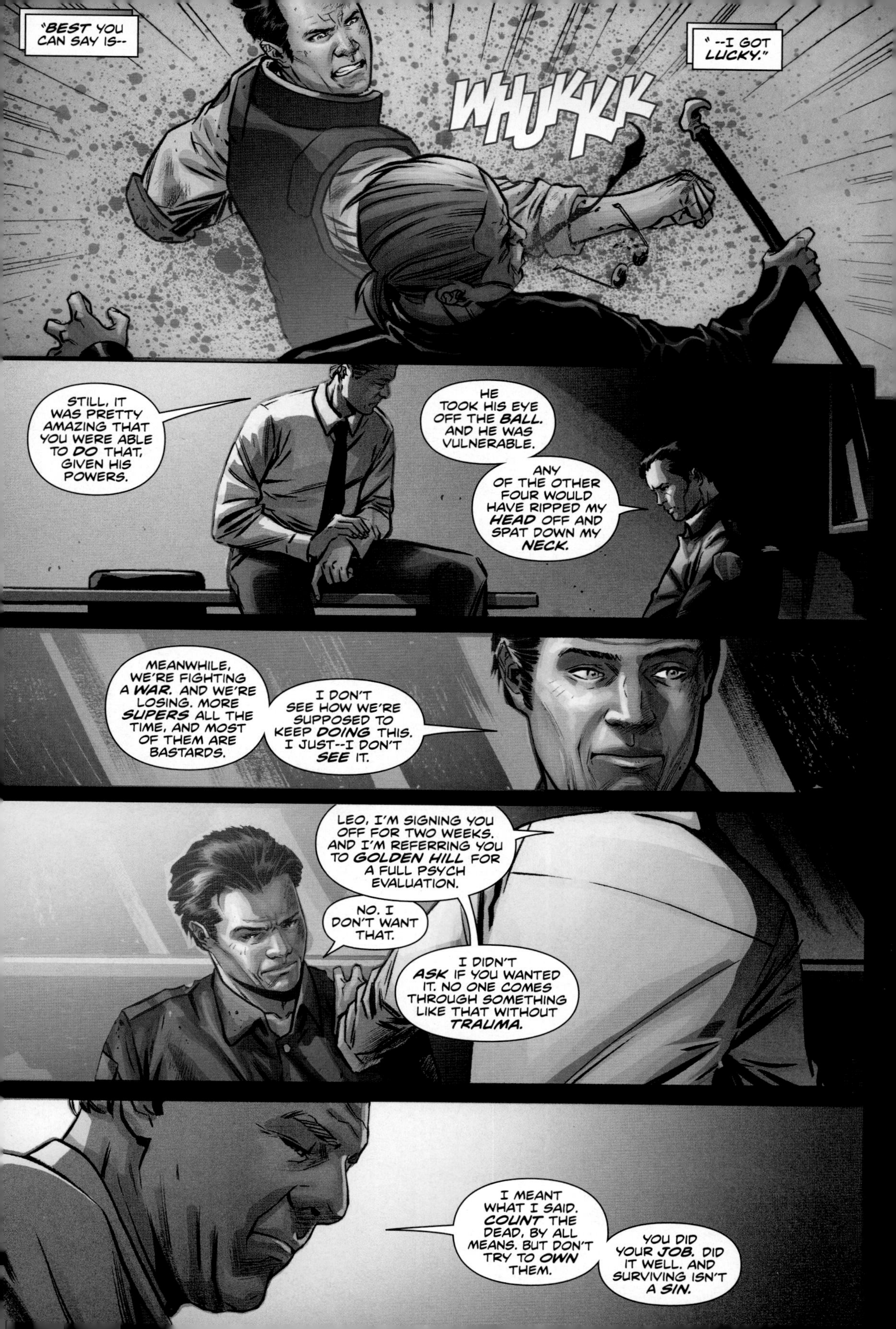
"BEST YOU CAN SAY IS--
"--I GOT LUCKY."
WHUKKK
STILL, IT WAS PRETTY AMAZING THAT YOU WERE ABLE TO DO THAT, GIVEN HIS POWERS.
HE TOOK HIS EYE OFF THE BALL. AND HE WAS VULNERABLE.
ANY OF THE OTHER FOUR WOULD HAVE RIPPED MY HEAD OFF AND SPAT DOWN MY NECK.
MEANWHILE, WE'RE FIGHTING A WAR. AND WE'RE LOSING. MORE SUPERS ALL THE TIME, AND MOST OF THEM ARE BASTARDS.
I DON'T SEE HOW WE'RE SUPPOSED TO KEEP DOING THIS. I JUST--I DON'T SEE IT.
LEO, I'M SIGNING YOU OFF FOR TWO WEEKS. AND I'M REFERRING YOU TO GOLDEN HILL FOR A FULL PSYCH EVALUATION.
NO. I DON'T WANT THAT.
I DIDN'T ASK IF YOU WANTED IT. NO ONE COMES THROUGH SOMETHING LIKE THAT WITHOUT TRAUMA.
I MEANT WHAT I SAID. COUNT THE DEAD, BY ALL MEANS. BUT DON'T TRY TO OWN THEM.
YOU DID YOUR JOB. DID IT WELL. AND SURVIVING ISN'T A SIN.

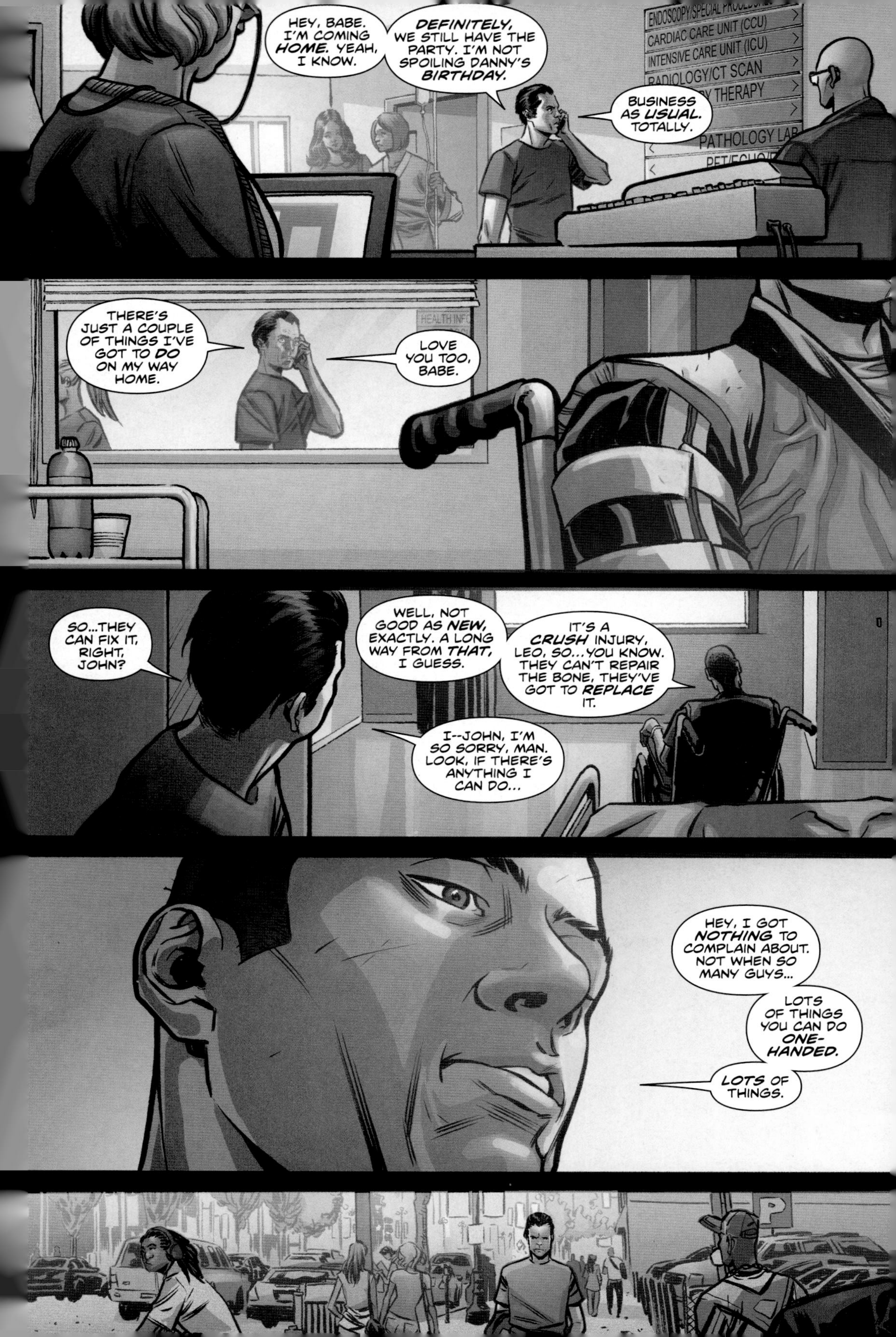
ENDOSCOPY/SPECIAL PROCEDURES
CARDIAC CARE UNIT (CCU)
INTENSIVE CARE UNIT (ICU)
RADIOLOGY/CT SCAN
THERAPY
PATHOLOGY LAB
HEY, BABE. I'M COMING HOME. YEAH, I KNOW.
DEFINITELY, WE STILL HAVE THE PARTY. I'M NOT SPOILING DANNY'S BIRTHDAY.
BUSINESS AS USUAL. TOTALLY.
THERE'S JUST A COUPLE OF THINGS I'VE GOT TO DO ON MY WAY HOME.
LOVE YOU TOO, BABE.
SO...THEY CAN FIX IT, RIGHT, JOHN?
WELL, NOT GOOD AS NEW, EXACTLY. A LONG WAY FROM THAT, I GUESS.
IT'S A CRUSH INJURY, LEO, SO...YOU KNOW. THEY CAN'T REPAIR THE BONE, THEY'VE GOT TO REPLACE IT.
I--JOHN, I'M SO SORRY, MAN. LOOK, IF THERE'S ANYTHING I CAN DO...
HEY, I GOT NOTHING TO COMPLAIN ABOUT. NOT WHEN SO MANY GUYS...
LOTS OF THINGS YOU CAN DO ONE-HANDED.
LOTS OF THINGS.
P

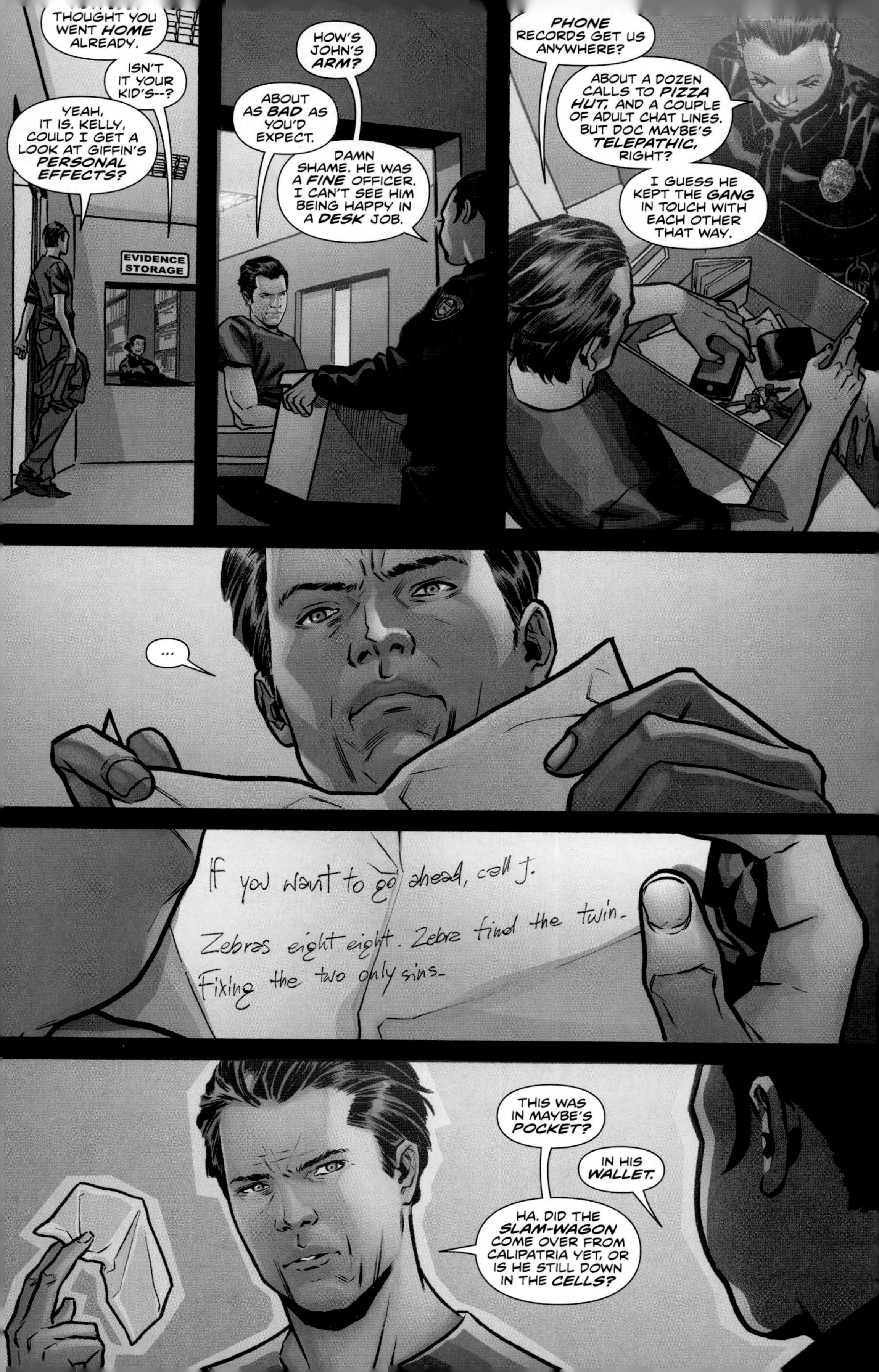
THOUGHT YOU WENT HOME ALREADY.
ISN'T IT YOUR KID'S--?
YEAH, IT IS. KELLY, COULD I GET A LOOK AT GIFFIN'S PERSONAL EFFECTS?
EVIDENCE STORAGE
HOW'S JOHN'S ARM?
ABOUT AS BAD AS YOU'D EXPECT.
DAMN SHAME. HE WAS A FINE OFFICER. I CAN'T SEE HIM BEING HAPPY IN A DESK JOB.
PHONE RECORDS GET US ANYWHERE?
ABOUT A DOZEN CALLS TO PIZZA HUT, AND A COUPLE OF ADULT CHAT LINES. BUT DOC MAYBE'S TELEPATHIC, RIGHT?
I GUESS HE KEPT THE GANG IN TOUCH WITH EACH OTHER THAT WAY.
...
If you want to go ahead, call J.
Zebras eight eight. Zebra find the twin.
Fixing the two only sins.
THIS WAS IN MAYBE'S POCKET?
IN HIS WALLET.
HA. DID THE SLAM-WAGON COME OVER FROM CALIPATRIA YET, OR IS HE STILL DOWN IN THE CELLS?

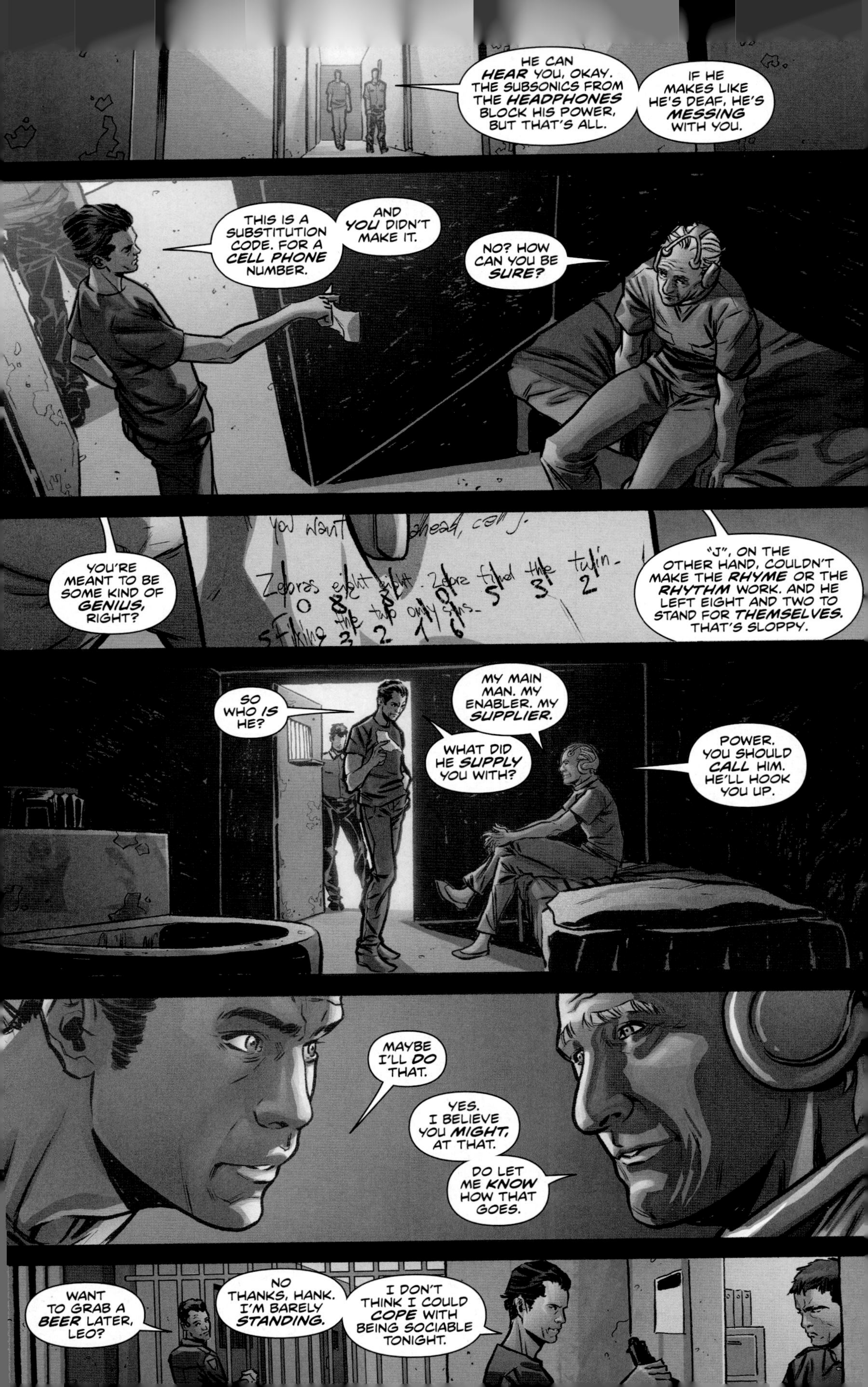
HE CAN HEAR YOU, OKAY. THE SUBSONICS FROM THE HEADPHONES BLOCK HIS POWER, BUT THAT'S ALL.
IF HE MAKES LIKE HE'S DEAF, HE'S MESSING WITH YOU.
THIS IS A SUBSTITUTION CODE. FOR A CELL PHONE NUMBER.
AND YOU DIDN'T MAKE IT.
NO? HOW CAN YOU BE SURE?
YOU'RE MEANT TO BE SOME KIND OF GENIUS, RIGHT?
"J", ON THE OTHER HAND, COULDN'T MAKE THE RHYME OR THE RHYTHM WORK. AND HE LEFT EIGHT AND TWO TO STAND FOR THEMSELVES. THAT'S SLOPPY.
SO WHO IS HE?
MY MAIN MAN. MY ENABLER. MY SUPPLIER.
WHAT DID HE SUPPLY YOU WITH?
POWER. YOU SHOULD CALL HIM. HE'LL HOOK YOU UP.
MAYBE I'LL DO THAT.
YES. I BELIEVE YOU MIGHT, AT THAT.
DO LET ME KNOW HOW THAT GOES.
WANT TO GRAB A BEER LATER, LEO?
NO THANKS, HANK. I'M BARELY STANDING.
I DON'T THINK I COULD COPE WITH BEING SOCIABLE TONIGHT.

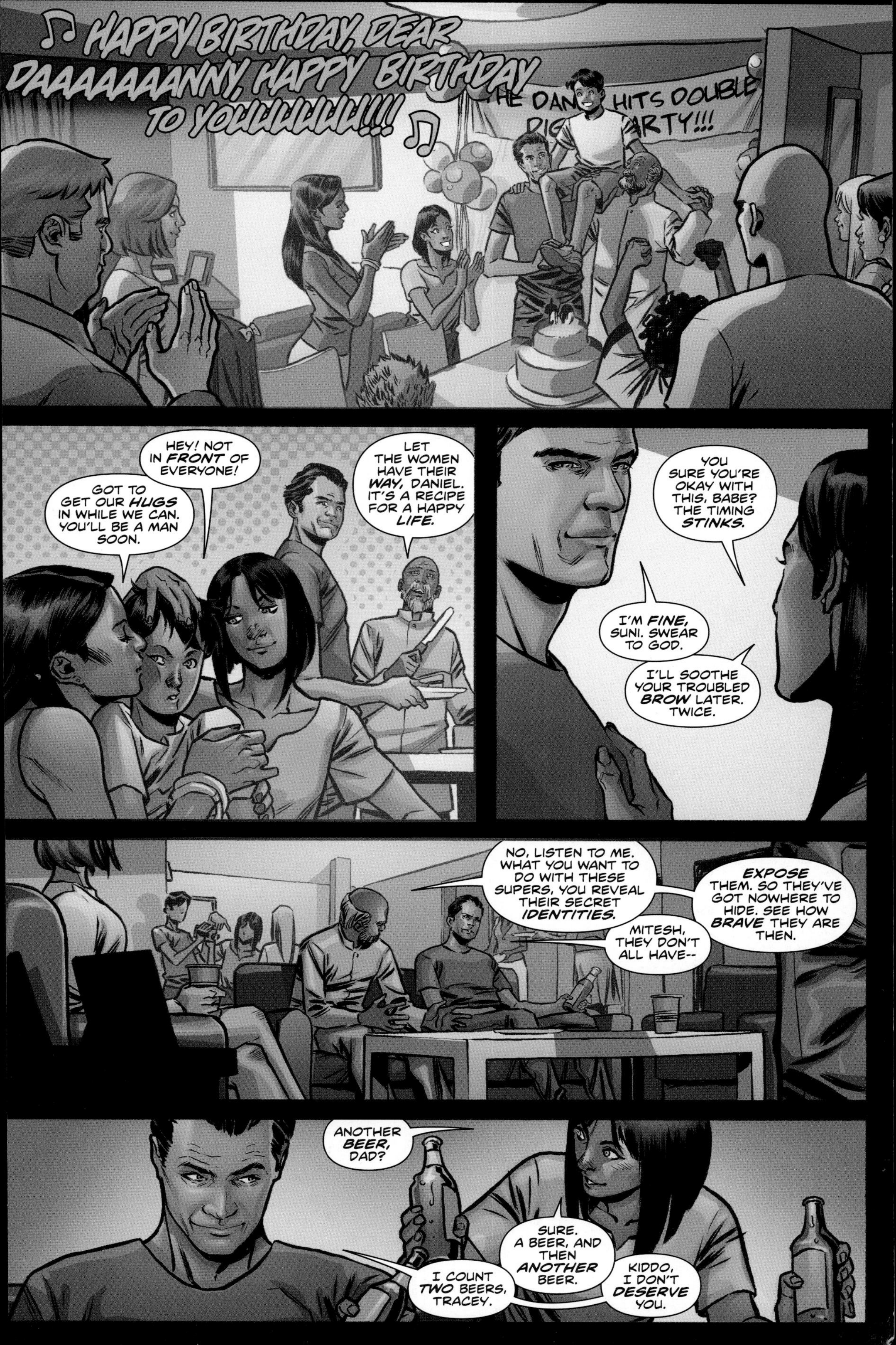
♫ HAPPY BIRTHDAY, DEAR DAAAAAAANNY, HAPPY BIRTHDAY TO YOUUUUUU!!! ♫
THE DAN HITS DOUBLE DIG ARTY!!!
HEY! NOT IN FRONT OF EVERYONE!
GOT TO GET OUR HUGS IN WHILE WE CAN. YOU'LL BE A MAN SOON.
LET THE WOMEN HAVE THEIR WAY, DANIEL. IT'S A RECIPE FOR A HAPPY LIFE.
YOU SURE YOU'RE OKAY WITH THIS, BABE? THE TIMING STINKS.
I'M FINE, SUNI. SWEAR TO GOD.
I'LL SOOTHE YOUR TROUBLED BROW LATER. TWICE.
NO, LISTEN TO ME. WHAT YOU WANT TO DO WITH THESE SUPERS, YOU REVEAL THEIR SECRET IDENTITIES.
EXPOSE THEM. SO THEY'VE GOT NOWHERE TO HIDE. SEE HOW BRAVE THEY ARE THEN.
MITESH, THEY DON'T ALL HAVE--
ANOTHER BEER, DAD?
SURE. A BEER, AND THEN ANOTHER BEER.
I COUNT TWO BEERS, TRACEY.
KIDDO, I DON'T DESERVE YOU.

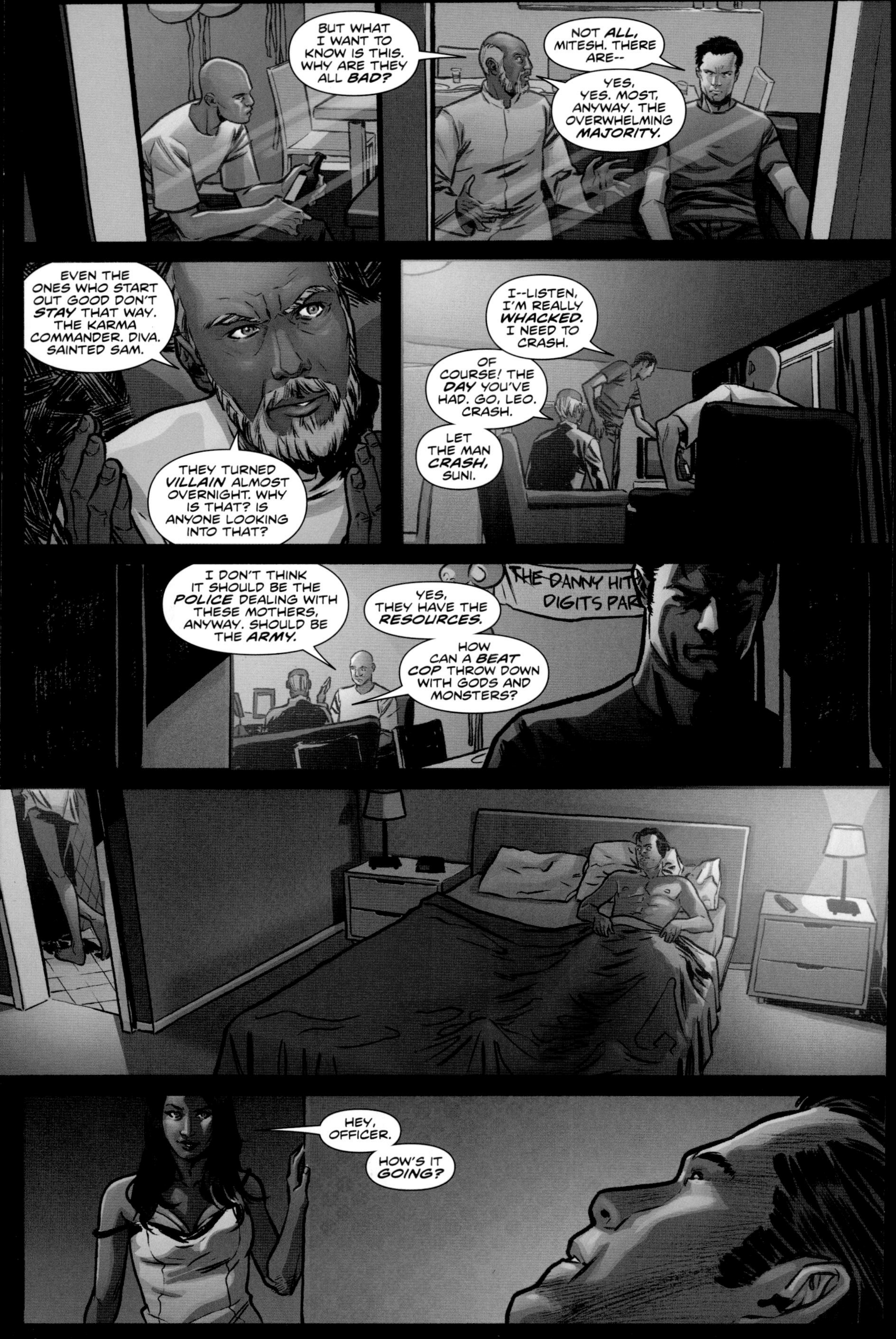
BUT WHAT I WANT TO KNOW IS THIS. WHY ARE THEY ALL BAD?
NOT ALL, MITESH. THERE ARE--
YES, YES. MOST, ANYWAY. THE OVERWHELMING MAJORITY.
EVEN THE ONES WHO START OUT GOOD DON'T STAY THAT WAY. THE KARMA COMMANDER. DIVA. SAINTED SAM.
THEY TURNED VILLAIN ALMOST OVERNIGHT. WHY IS THAT? IS ANYONE LOOKING INTO THAT?
I--LISTEN, I'M REALLY WHACKED. I NEED TO CRASH.
OF COURSE! THE DAY YOU'VE HAD. GO, LEO. CRASH.
LET THE MAN CRASH, SUNI.
I DON'T THINK IT SHOULD BE THE POLICE DEALING WITH THESE MOTHERS, ANYWAY. SHOULD BE THE ARMY.
YES, THEY HAVE THE RESOURCES.
HOW CAN A BEAT COP THROW DOWN WITH GODS AND MONSTERS?
THE DANNY HIT
DIGITS PAR
HEY, OFFICER.
HOW'S IT GOING?

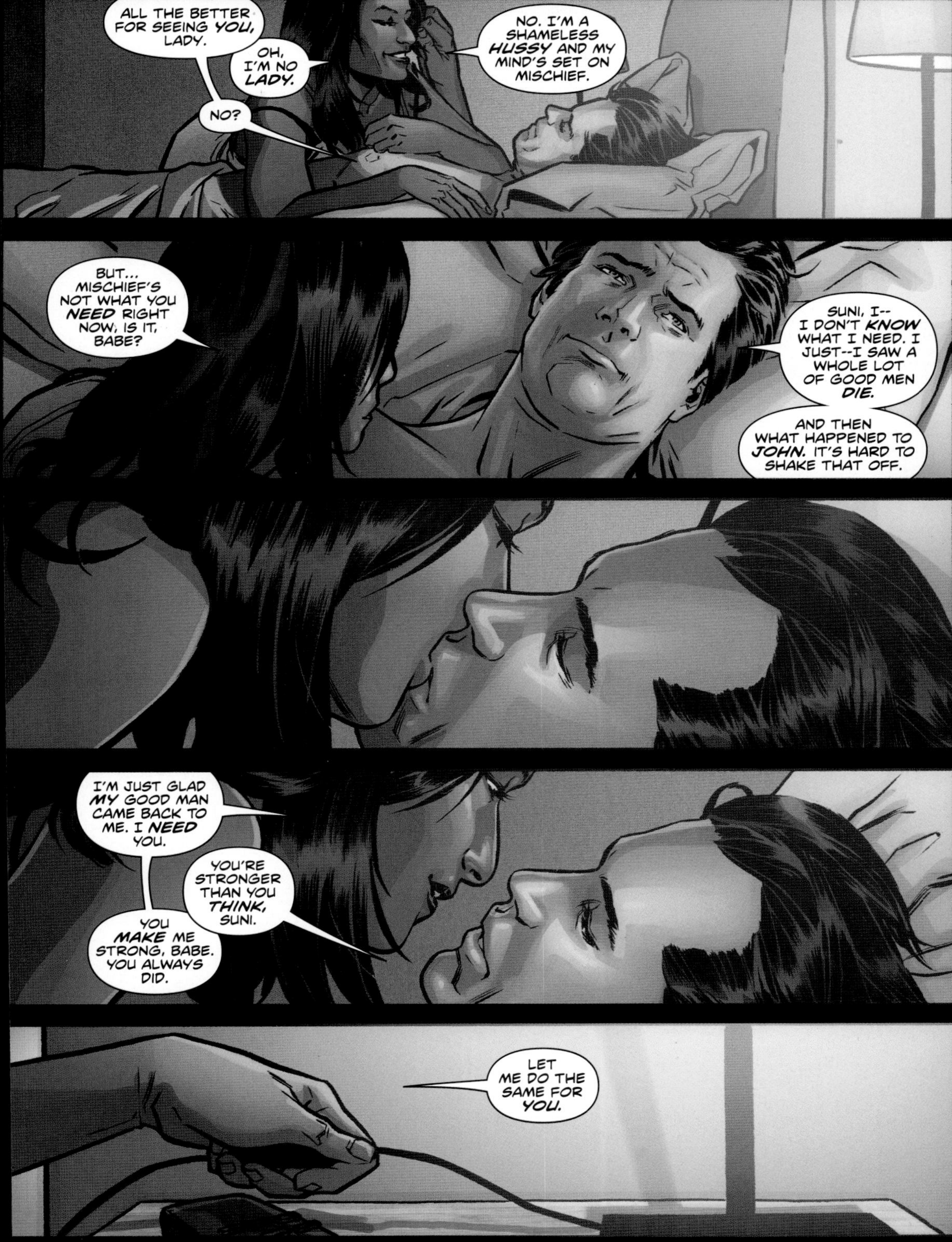

ALL THE BETTER FOR SEEING YOU, LADY.
OH, I'M NO LADY.
NO?
NO. I'M A SHAMELESS HUSSY AND MY MIND'S SET ON MISCHIEF.
BUT... MISCHIEF'S NOT WHAT YOU NEED RIGHT NOW, IS IT, BABE?
SUNI, I-- I DON'T KNOW WHAT I NEED. I JUST--I SAW A WHOLE LOT OF GOOD MEN DIE.
AND THEN WHAT HAPPENED TO JOHN. IT'S HARD TO SHAKE THAT OFF.
I'M JUST GLAD MY GOOD MAN CAME BACK TO ME. I NEED YOU.
YOU'RE STRONGER THAN YOU THINK, SUNI.
YOU MAKE ME STRONG, BABE. YOU ALWAYS DID.
LET ME DO THE SAME FOR YOU.

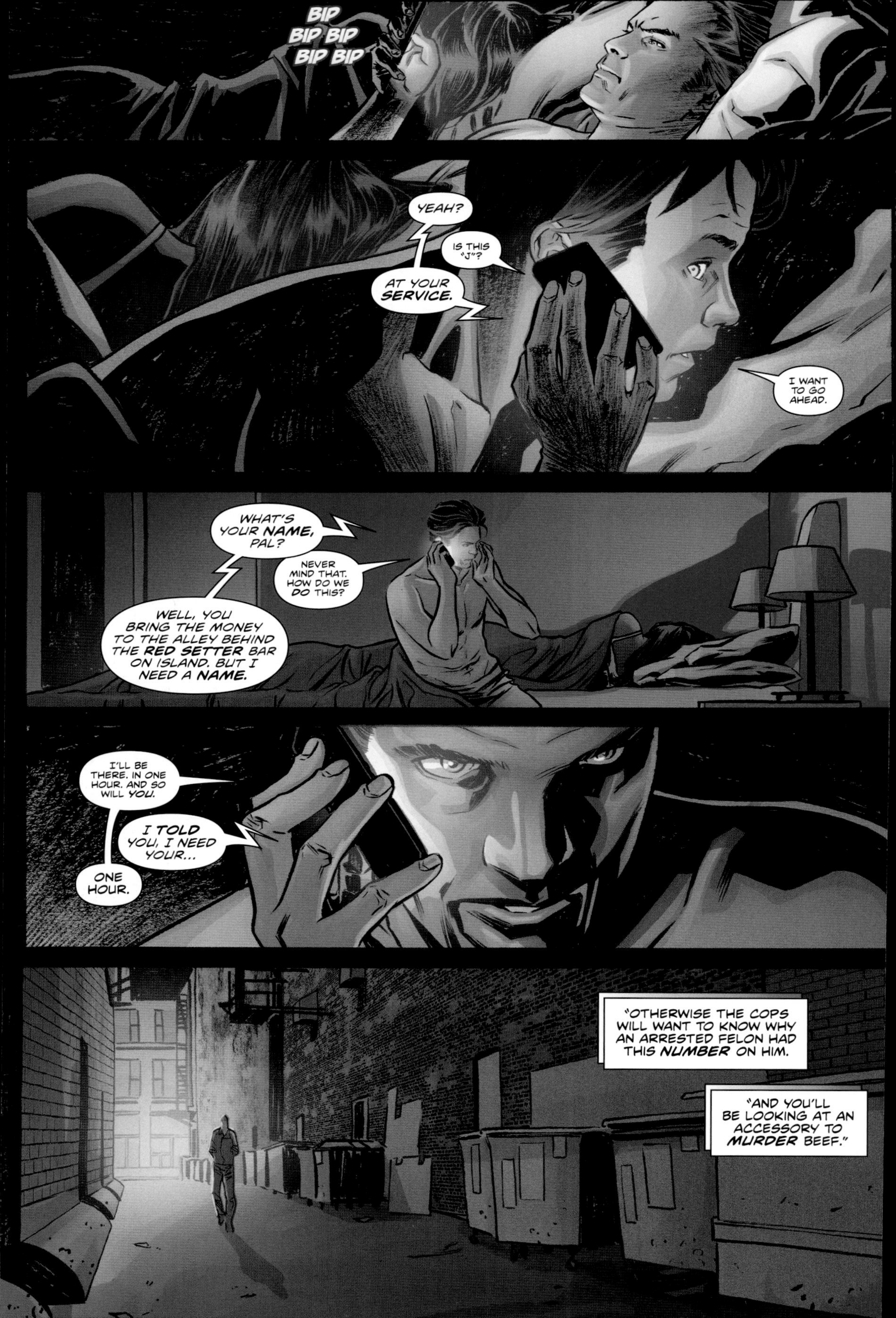
BIP
BIP BIP
BIP BIP
YEAH?
IS THIS "J"?
AT YOUR SERVICE.
I WANT TO GO AHEAD.
WHAT'S YOUR NAME, PAL?
NEVER MIND THAT. HOW DO WE DO THIS?
WELL, YOU BRING THE MONEY TO THE ALLEY BEHIND THE RED SETTER BAR ON ISLAND. BUT I NEED A NAME.
I'LL BE THERE. IN ONE HOUR. AND SO WILL YOU.
I TOLD YOU, I NEED YOUR...
ONE HOUR.
"OTHERWISE THE COPS WILL WANT TO KNOW WHY AN ARRESTED FELON HAD THIS NUMBER ON HIM.
"AND YOU'LL BE LOOKING AT AN ACCESSORY TO MURDER BEEF."

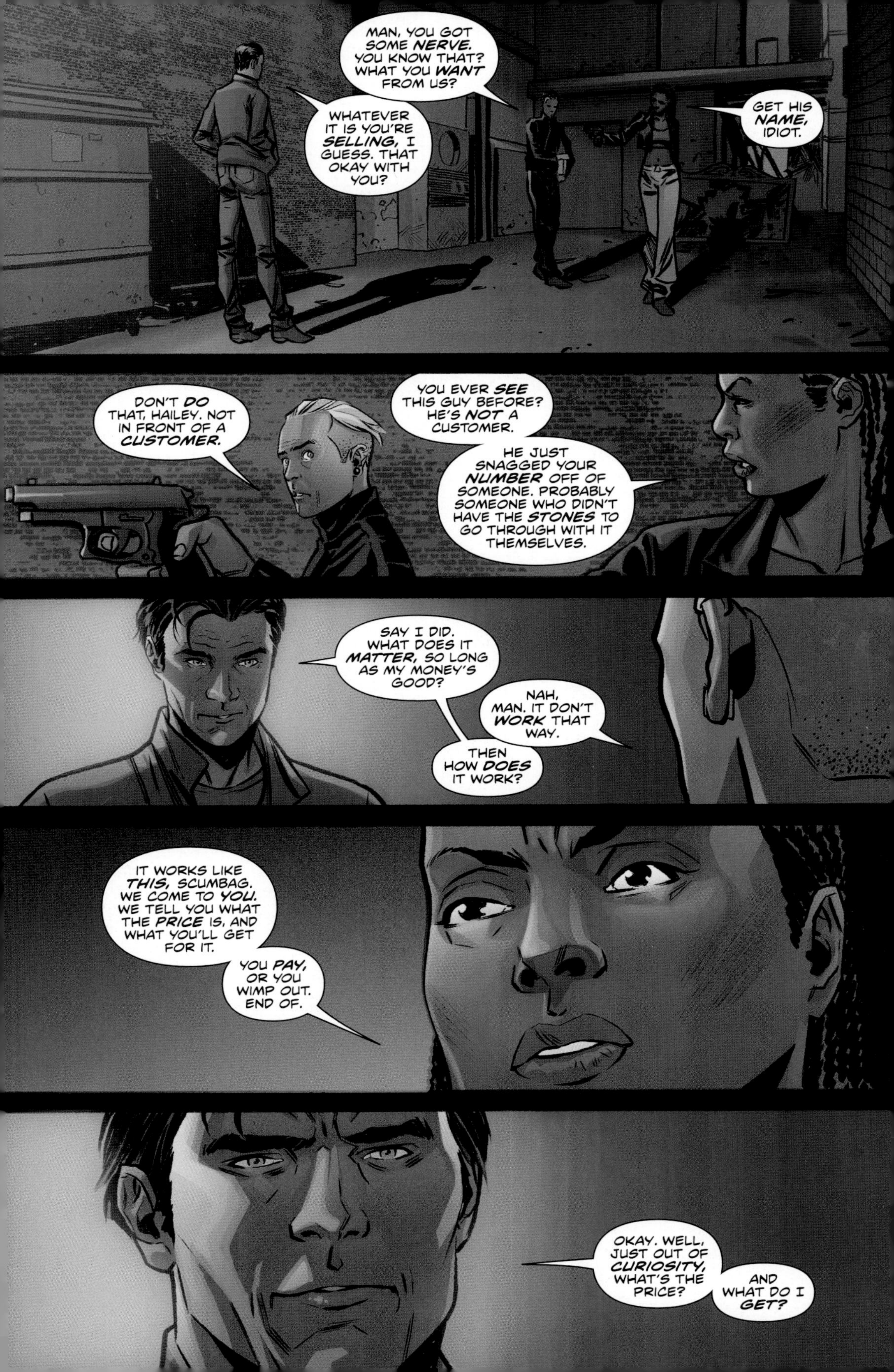
MAN, YOU GOT SOME NERVE. YOU KNOW THAT? WHAT YOU WANT FROM US?
WHATEVER IT IS YOU'RE SELLING, I GUESS. THAT OKAY WITH YOU?
GET HIS NAME, IDIOT.
DON'T DO THAT, HAILEY. NOT IN FRONT OF A CUSTOMER.
YOU EVER SEE THIS GUY BEFORE? HE'S NOT A CUSTOMER.
HE JUST SNAGGED YOUR NUMBER OFF OF SOMEONE. PROBABLY SOMEONE WHO DIDN'T HAVE THE STONES TO GO THROUGH WITH IT THEMSELVES.
SAY I DID. WHAT DOES IT MATTER, SO LONG AS MY MONEY'S GOOD?
NAH, MAN. IT DON'T WORK THAT WAY.
THEN HOW DOES IT WORK?
IT WORKS LIKE THIS, SCUMBAG. WE COME TO YOU. WE TELL YOU WHAT THE PRICE IS, AND WHAT YOU'LL GET FOR IT.
YOU PAY, OR YOU WIMP OUT. END OF.
OKAY. WELL, JUST OUT OF CURIOSITY, WHAT'S THE PRICE?
AND WHAT DO I GET?

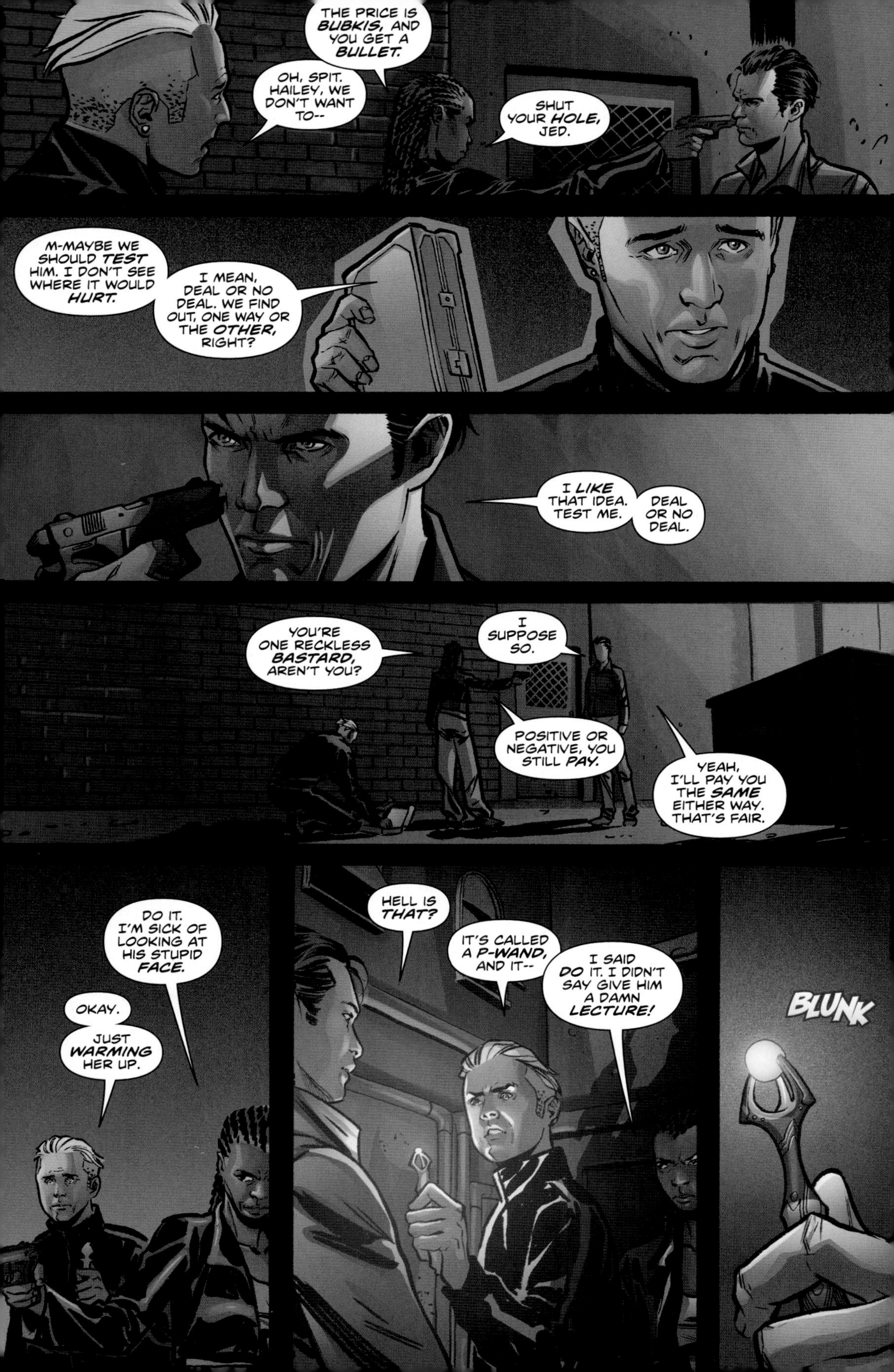
THE PRICE IS BUBKIS, AND YOU GET A BULLET.
OH, SPIT. HAILEY, WE DON'T WANT TO--
SHUT YOUR HOLE, JED.
M-MAYBE WE SHOULD TEST HIM. I DON'T SEE WHERE IT WOULD HURT.
I MEAN, DEAL OR NO DEAL. WE FIND OUT, ONE WAY OR THE OTHER, RIGHT?
I LIKE THAT IDEA. TEST ME.
DEAL OR NO DEAL.
YOU'RE ONE RECKLESS BASTARD, AREN'T YOU?
I SUPPOSE SO.
POSITIVE OR NEGATIVE, YOU STILL PAY.
YEAH, I'LL PAY YOU THE SAME EITHER WAY. THAT'S FAIR.
DO IT. I'M SICK OF LOOKING AT HIS STUPID FACE.
OKAY.
JUST WARMING HER UP.
HELL IS THAT?
IT'S CALLED A P-WAND, AND IT--
I SAID DO IT. I DIDN'T SAY GIVE HIM A DAMN LECTURE!
BLUNK

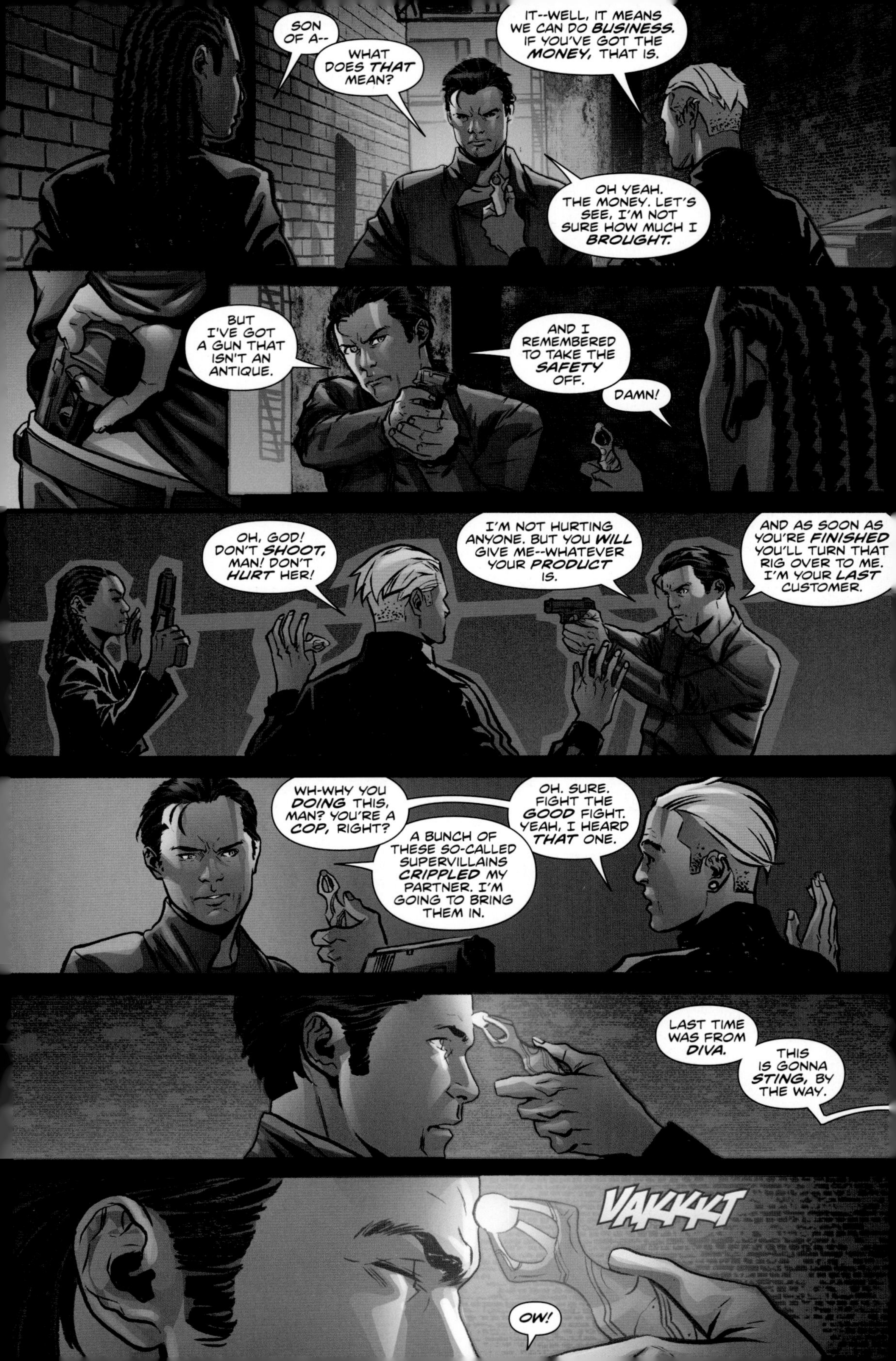
SON OF A--
WHAT DOES THAT MEAN?
IT--WELL, IT MEANS WE CAN DO BUSINESS. IF YOU'VE GOT THE MONEY, THAT IS.
OH YEAH. THE MONEY. LET'S SEE, I'M NOT SURE HOW MUCH I BROUGHT.
BUT I'VE GOT A GUN THAT ISN'T AN ANTIQUE.
AND I REMEMBERED TO TAKE THE SAFETY OFF.
DAMN!
OH, GOD! DON'T SHOOT, MAN! DON'T HURT HER!
I'M NOT HURTING ANYONE. BUT YOU WILL GIVE ME--WHATEVER YOUR PRODUCT IS.
AND AS SOON AS YOU'RE FINISHED YOU'LL TURN THAT RIG OVER TO ME. I'M YOUR LAST CUSTOMER.
WH-WHY YOU DOING THIS, MAN? YOU'RE A COP, RIGHT?
A BUNCH OF THESE SO-CALLED SUPERVILLAINS CRIPPLED MY PARTNER. I'M GOING TO BRING THEM IN.
OH. SURE. FIGHT THE GOOD FIGHT. YEAH, I HEARD THAT ONE.
LAST TIME WAS FROM DIVA.
THIS IS GONNA STING, BY THE WAY.
VAKKKT
OW!

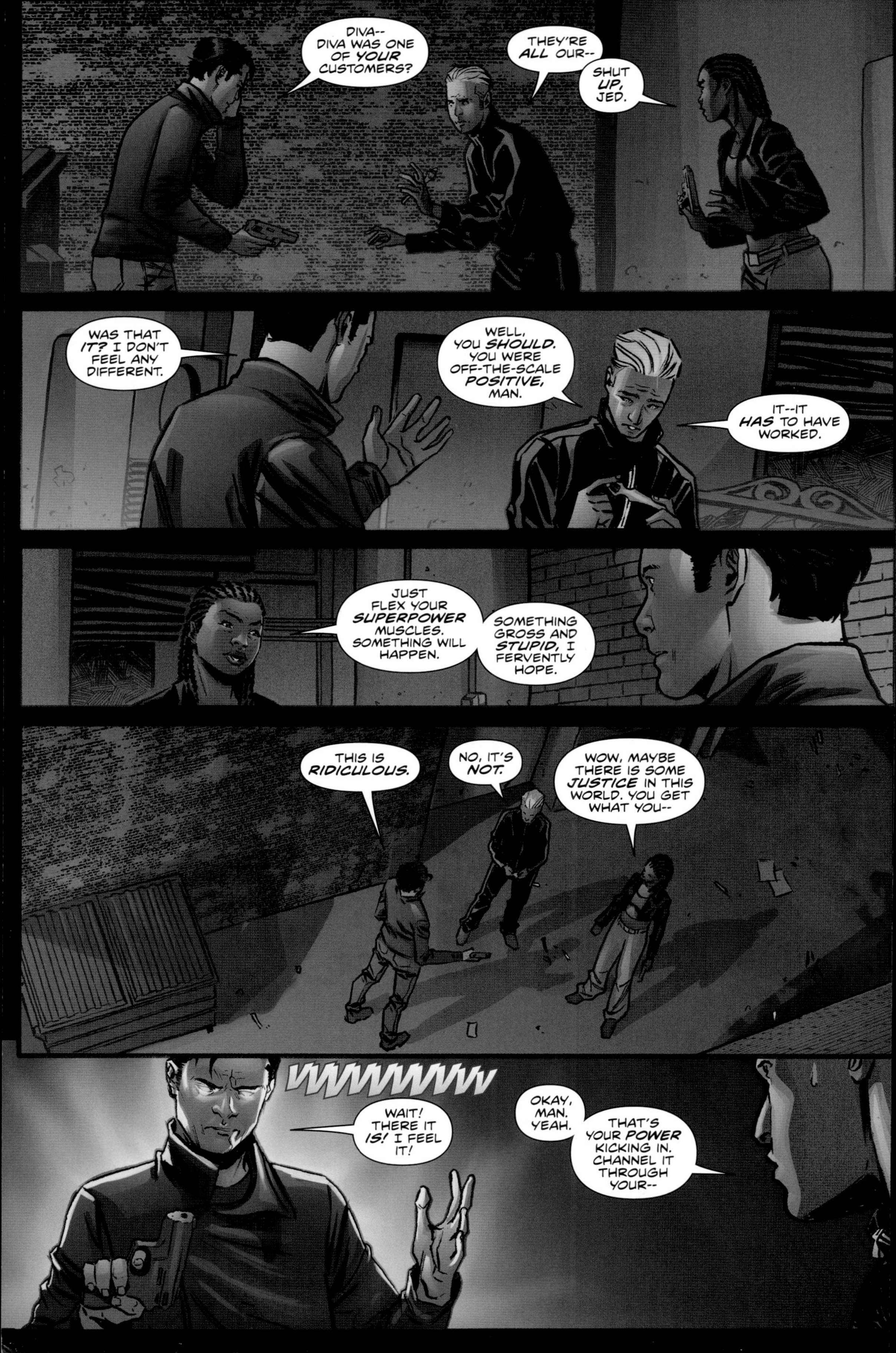
DIVA-- DIVA WAS ONE OF YOUR CUSTOMERS?
THEY'RE ALL OUR--
SHUT UP, JED.
WAS THAT IT? I DON'T FEEL ANY DIFFERENT.
WELL, YOU SHOULD. YOU WERE OFF-THE-SCALE POSITIVE, MAN.
IT--IT HAS TO HAVE WORKED.
JUST FLEX YOUR SUPERPOWER MUSCLES. SOMETHING WILL HAPPEN.
SOMETHING GROSS AND STUPID, I FERVENTLY HOPE.
THIS IS RIDICULOUS.
NO, IT'S NOT.
WOW, MAYBE THERE IS SOME JUSTICE IN THIS WORLD. YOU GET WHAT YOU--
VVVVVVVVVVVV
WAIT! THERE IT IS! I FEEL IT!
OKAY, MAN. YEAH.
THAT'S YOUR POWER KICKING IN. CHANNEL IT THROUGH YOUR--

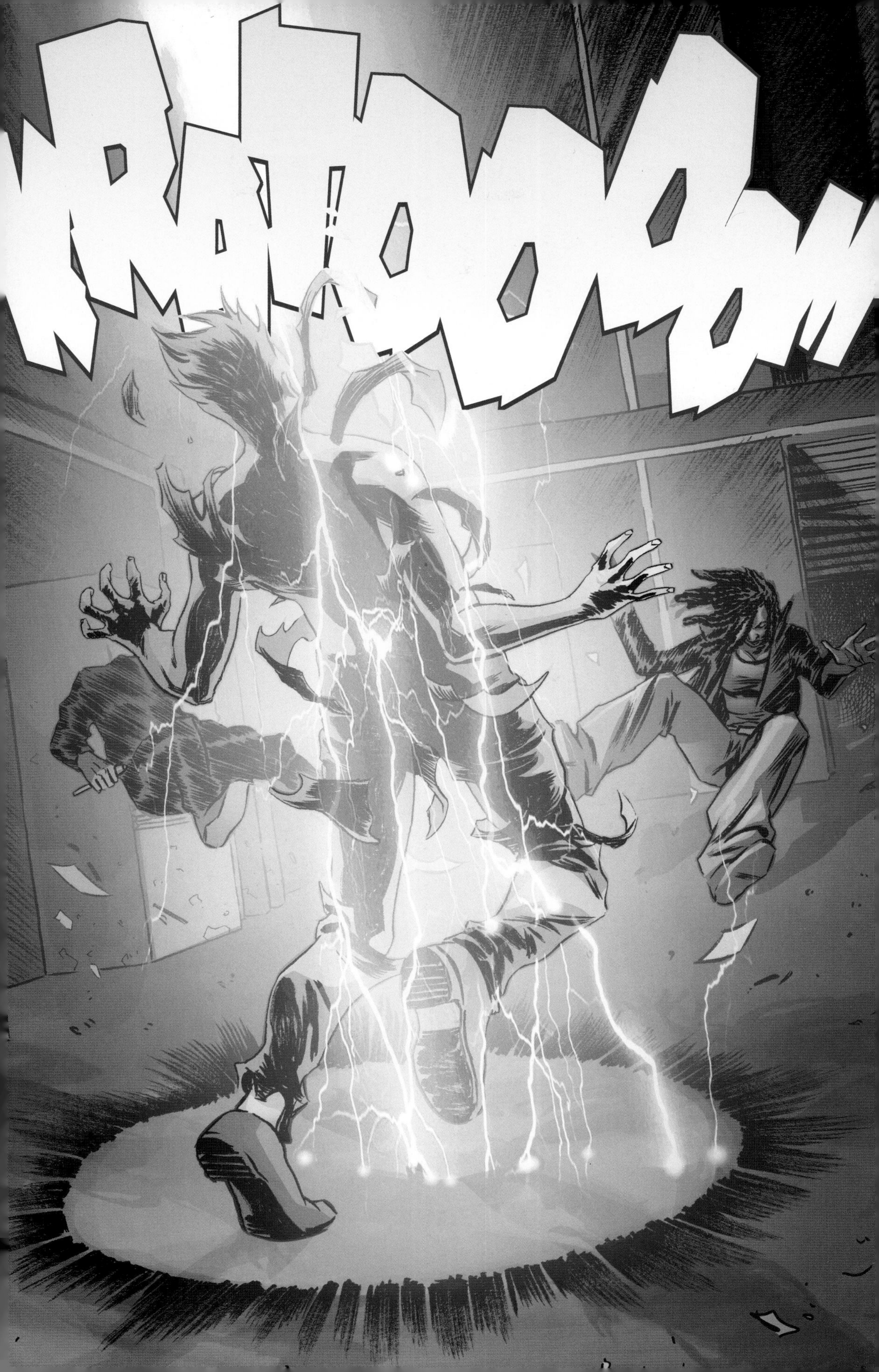

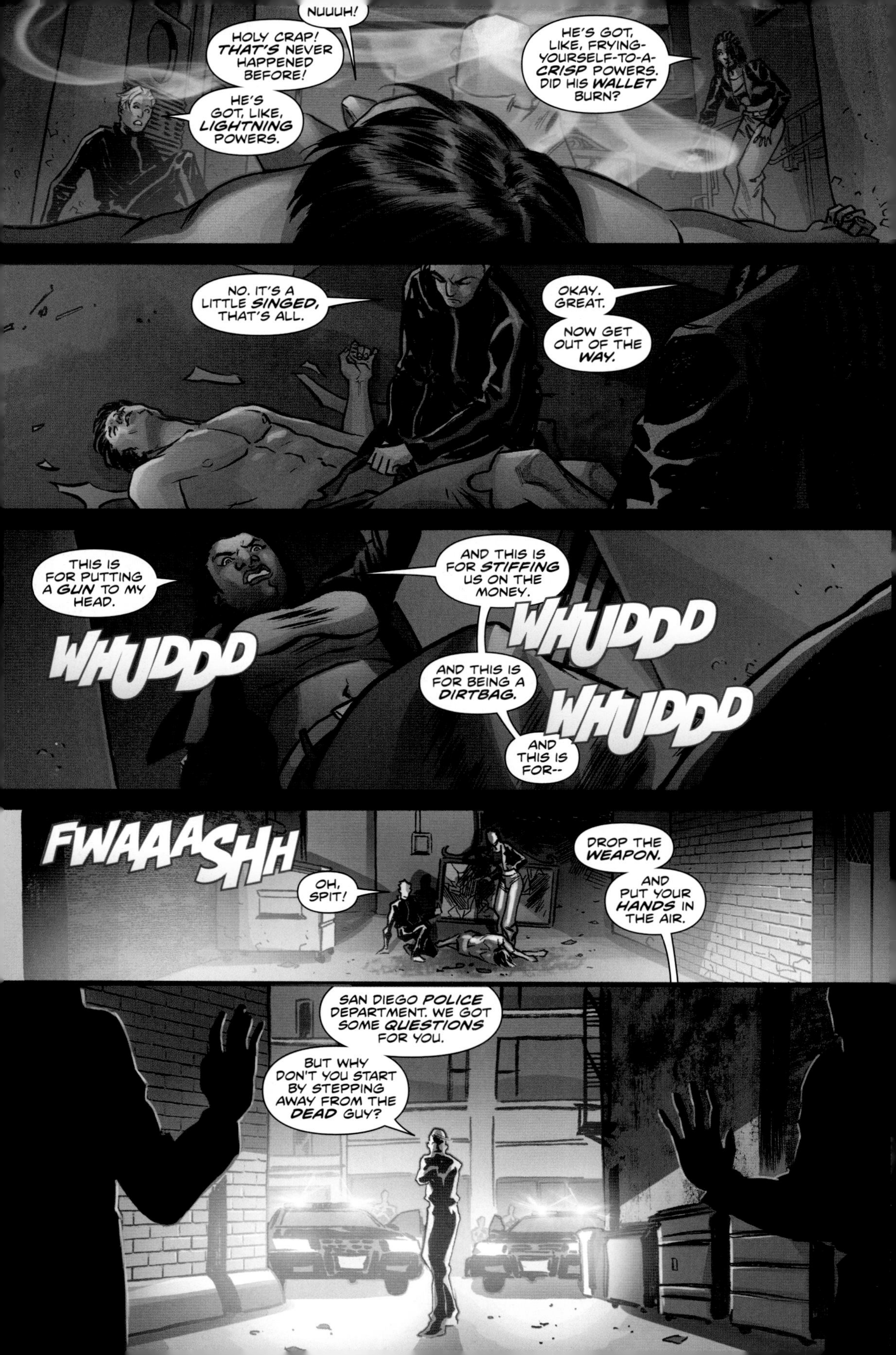
NUUUH!
HOLY CRAP! THAT'S NEVER HAPPENED BEFORE!
HE'S GOT, LIKE, LIGHTNING POWERS.
HE'S GOT, LIKE, FRYING-YOURSELF-TO-A-CRISP POWERS. DID HIS WALLET BURN?
NO. IT'S A LITTLE SINGED, THAT'S ALL.
OKAY. GREAT.
NOW GET OUT OF THE WAY.
THIS IS FOR PUTTING A GUN TO MY HEAD.
WHUDDD
AND THIS IS FOR STIFFING US ON THE MONEY.
WHUDDD
AND THIS IS FOR BEING A DIRTBAG.
WHUDDD
AND THIS IS FOR--
FWAAASHH
OH, SPIT!
DROP THE WEAPON.
AND PUT YOUR HANDS IN THE AIR.
SAN DIEGO POLICE DEPARTMENT. WE GOT SOME QUESTIONS FOR YOU.
BUT WHY DON'T YOU START BY STEPPING AWAY FROM THE DEAD GUY?

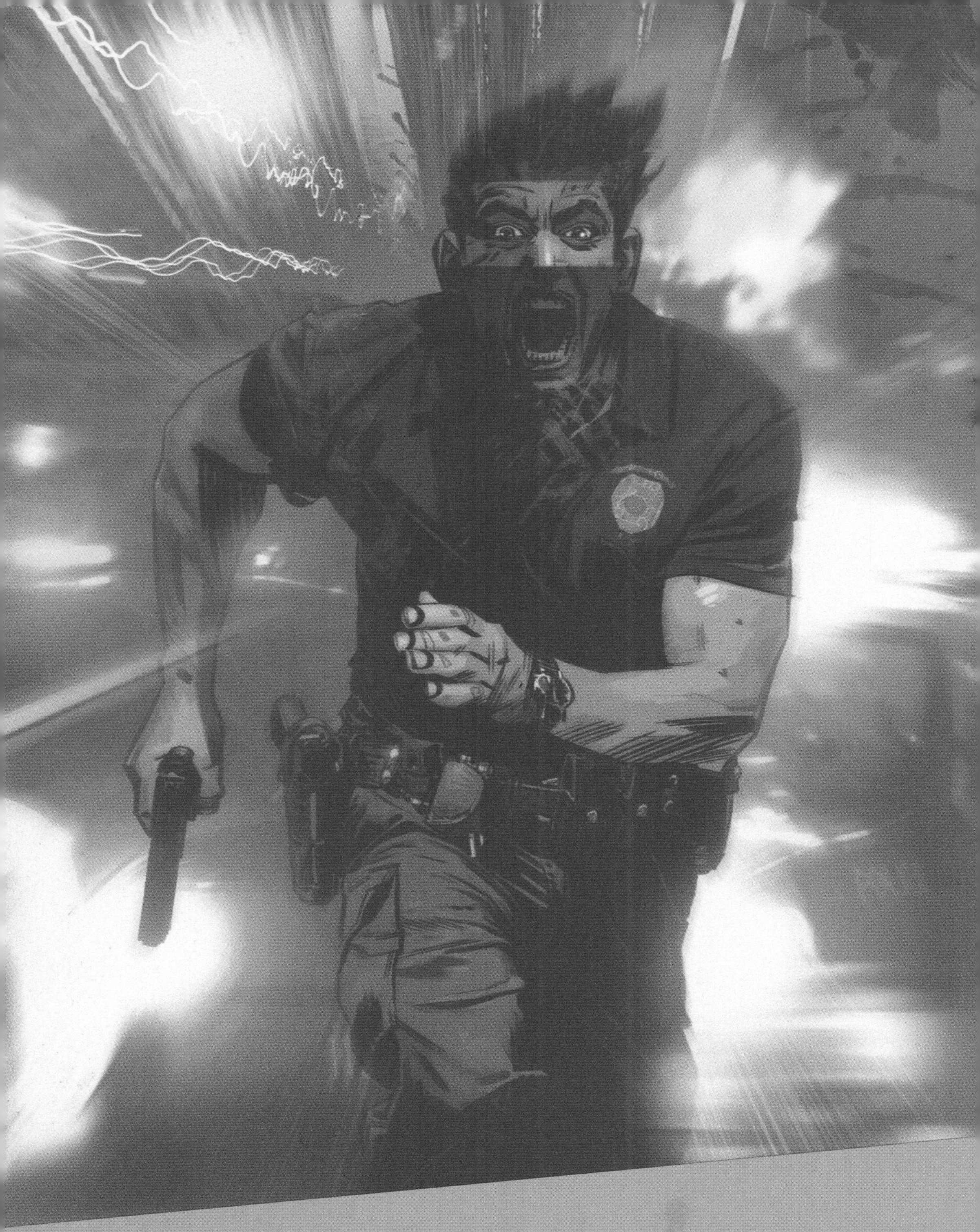

"THAT WAS WHEN I KNEW I WAS
A **SUPERHERO**."

Chapter 2

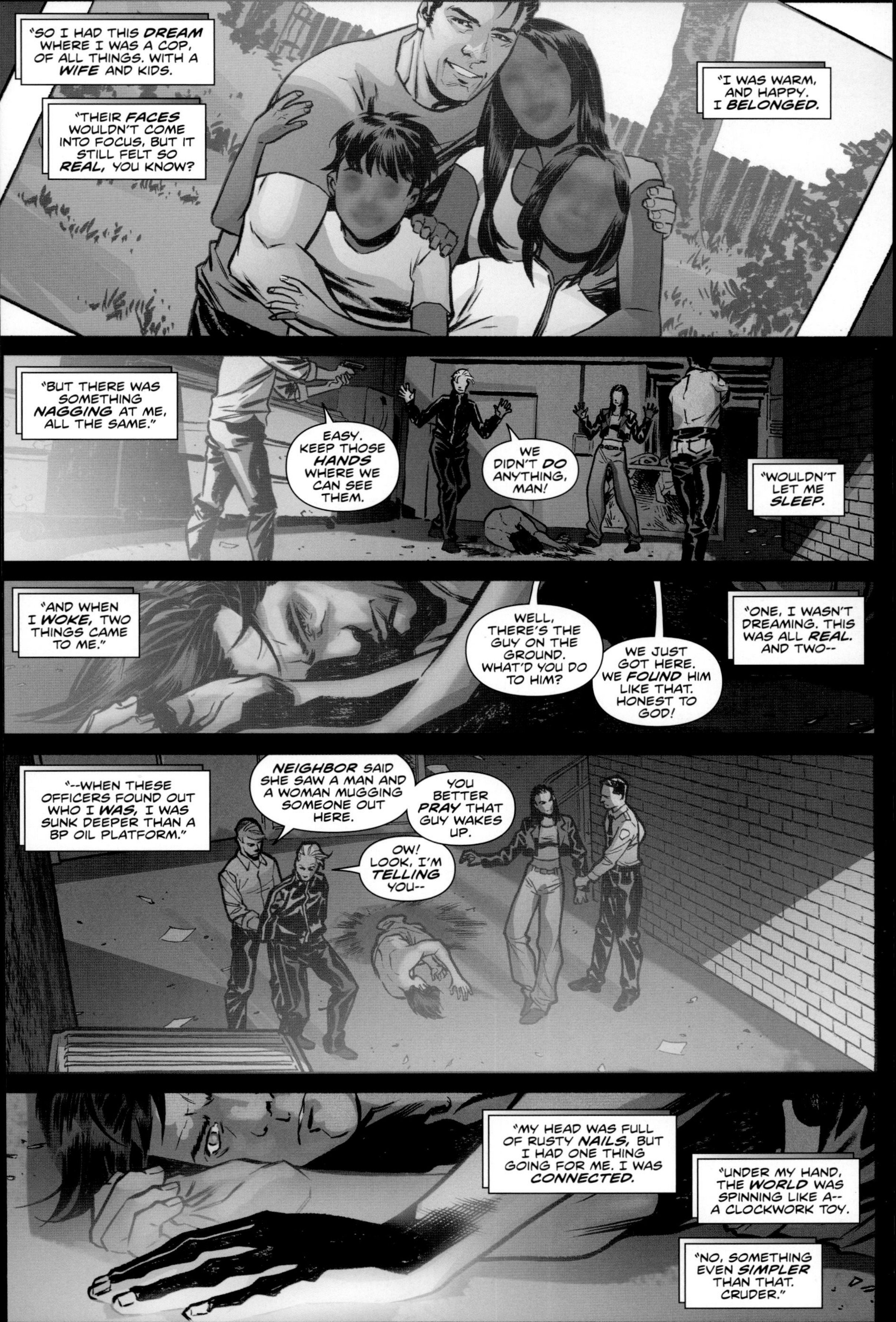
"SO I HAD THIS DREAM WHERE I WAS A COP, OF ALL THINGS. WITH A WIFE AND KIDS.
"THEIR FACES WOULDN'T COME INTO FOCUS, BUT IT STILL FELT SO REAL, YOU KNOW?
"I WAS WARM, AND HAPPY. I BELONGED.
"BUT THERE WAS SOMETHING NAGGING AT ME, ALL THE SAME."
EASY. KEEP THOSE HANDS WHERE WE CAN SEE THEM.
WE DIDN'T DO ANYTHING, MAN!
"WOULDN'T LET ME SLEEP.
"AND WHEN I WOKE, TWO THINGS CAME TO ME."
WELL, THERE'S THE GUY ON THE GROUND. WHAT'D YOU DO TO HIM?
WE JUST GOT HERE. WE FOUND HIM LIKE THAT. HONEST TO GOD!
"ONE, I WASN'T DREAMING. THIS WAS ALL REAL. AND TWO--
"--WHEN THESE OFFICERS FOUND OUT WHO I WAS, I WAS SUNK DEEPER THAN A BP OIL PLATFORM."
NEIGHBOR SAID SHE SAW A MAN AND A WOMAN MUGGING SOMEONE OUT HERE.
YOU BETTER PRAY THAT GUY WAKES UP.
OW! LOOK, I'M TELLING YOU--
"MY HEAD WAS FULL OF RUSTY NAILS, BUT I HAD ONE THING GOING FOR ME. I WAS CONNECTED.
"UNDER MY HAND, THE WORLD WAS SPINNING LIKE A-- A CLOCKWORK TOY.
"NO, SOMETHING EVEN SIMPLER THAN THAT. CRUDER."

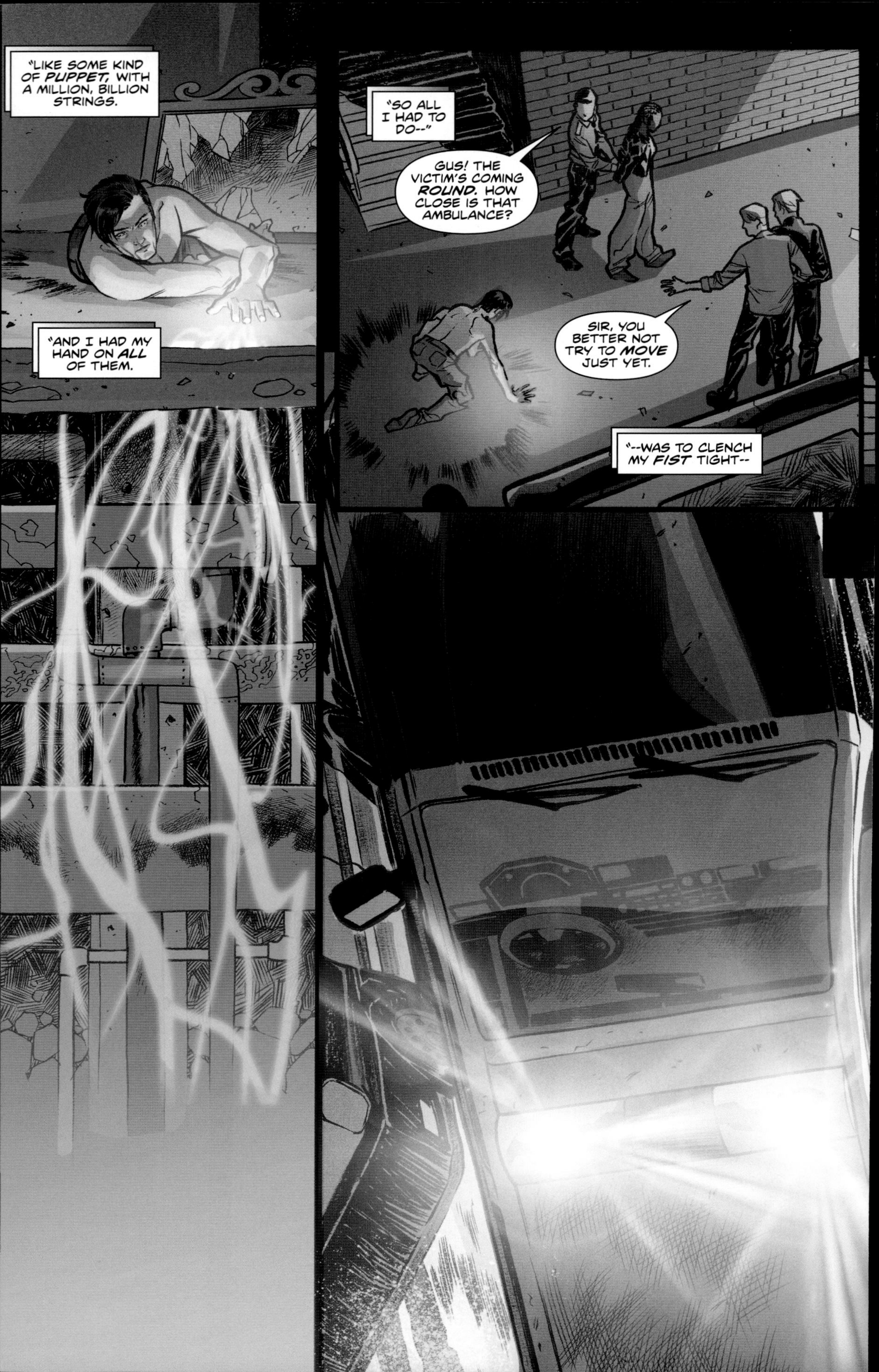
"LIKE SOME KIND OF PUPPET, WITH A MILLION, BILLION STRINGS.
"AND I HAD MY HAND ON ALL OF THEM.
"SO ALL I HAD TO DO--"
GUS! THE VICTIM'S COMING ROUND. HOW CLOSE IS THAT AMBULANCE?
SIR, YOU BETTER NOT TRY TO MOVE JUST YET.
"--WAS TO CLENCH MY FIST TIGHT--

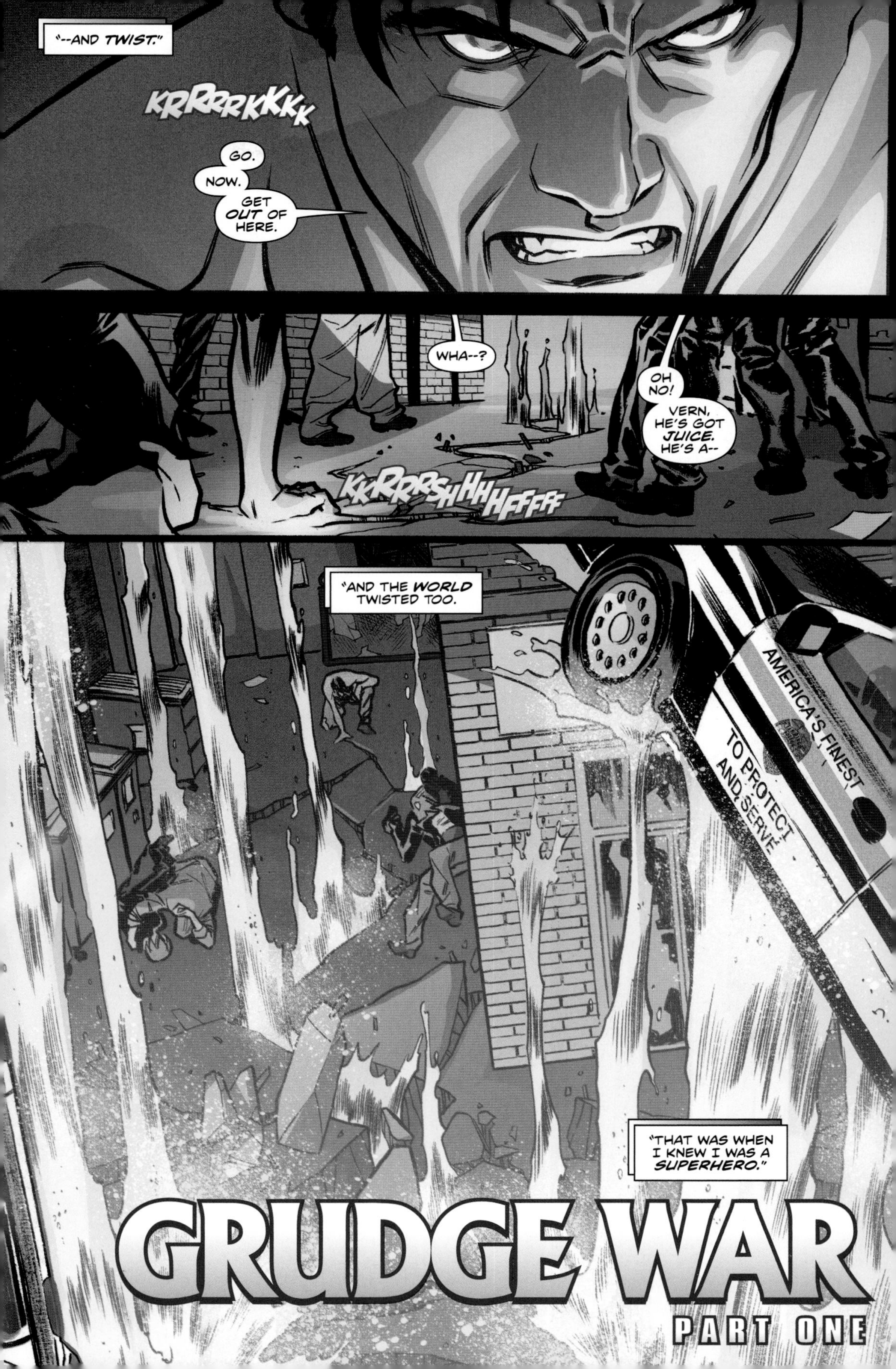
"--AND TWIST."
KRRRRKKKK
GO.
NOW.
GET OUT OF HERE.
WHA--?
OH NO!
VERN, HE'S GOT JUICE. HE'S A--
KKRRRSHHHHFFFFF
"AND THE WORLD TWISTED TOO.
AMERICA'S FINEST
TO PROTECT AND SERVE
"THAT WAS WHEN I KNEW I WAS A SUPERHERO."
GRUDGE WAR
PART ONE

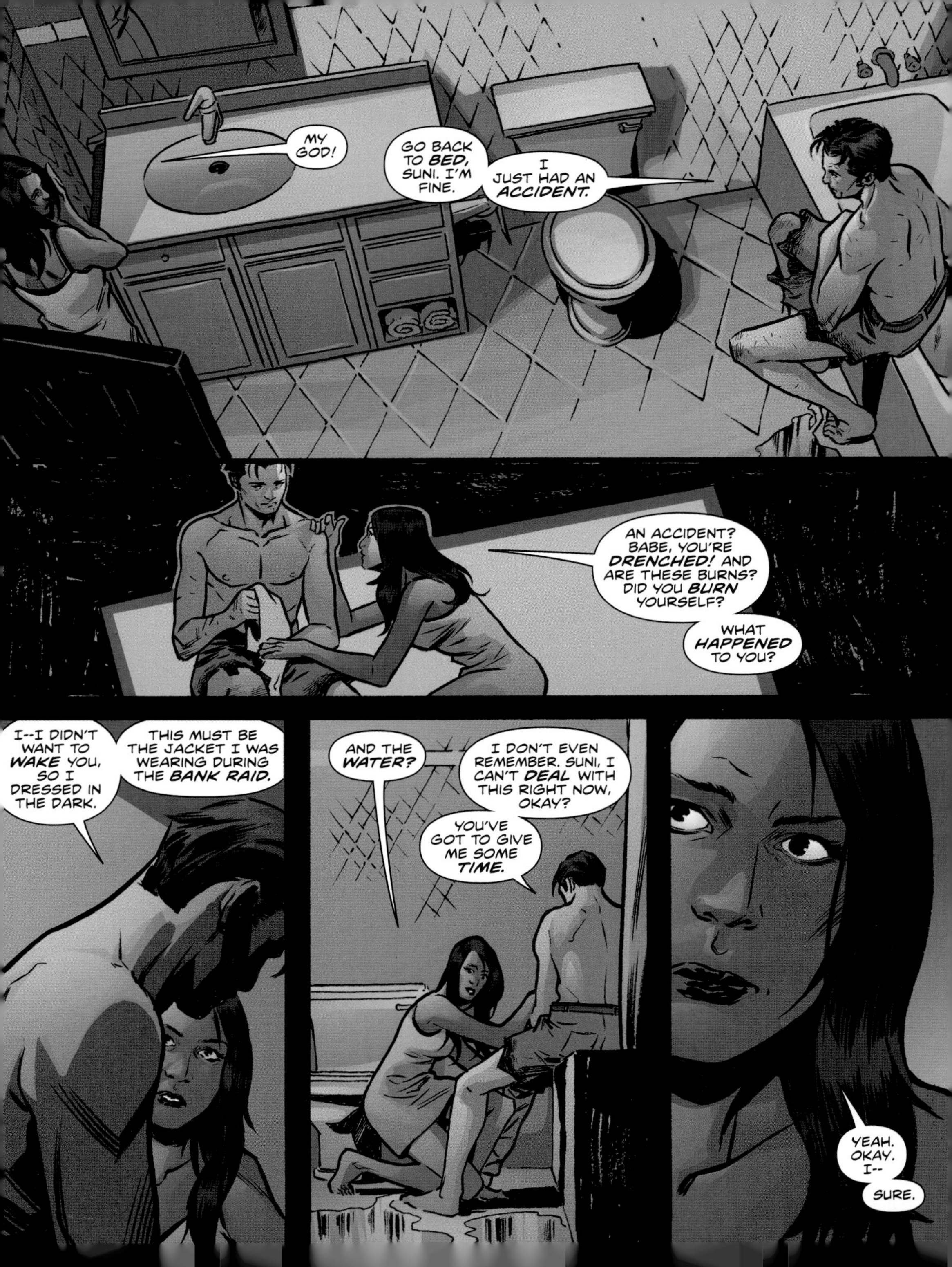
MY GOD!
GO BACK TO BED, SUNI. I'M FINE.
I JUST HAD AN ACCIDENT.
AN ACCIDENT? BABE, YOU'RE DRENCHED! AND ARE THESE BURNS? DID YOU BURN YOURSELF?
WHAT HAPPENED TO YOU?
I--I DIDN'T WANT TO WAKE YOU, SO I DRESSED IN THE DARK.
THIS MUST BE THE JACKET I WAS WEARING DURING THE BANK RAID.
AND THE WATER?
I DON'T EVEN REMEMBER. SUNI, I CAN'T DEAL WITH THIS RIGHT NOW, OKAY?
YOU'VE GOT TO GIVE ME SOME TIME.
YEAH. OKAY. I--
SURE.

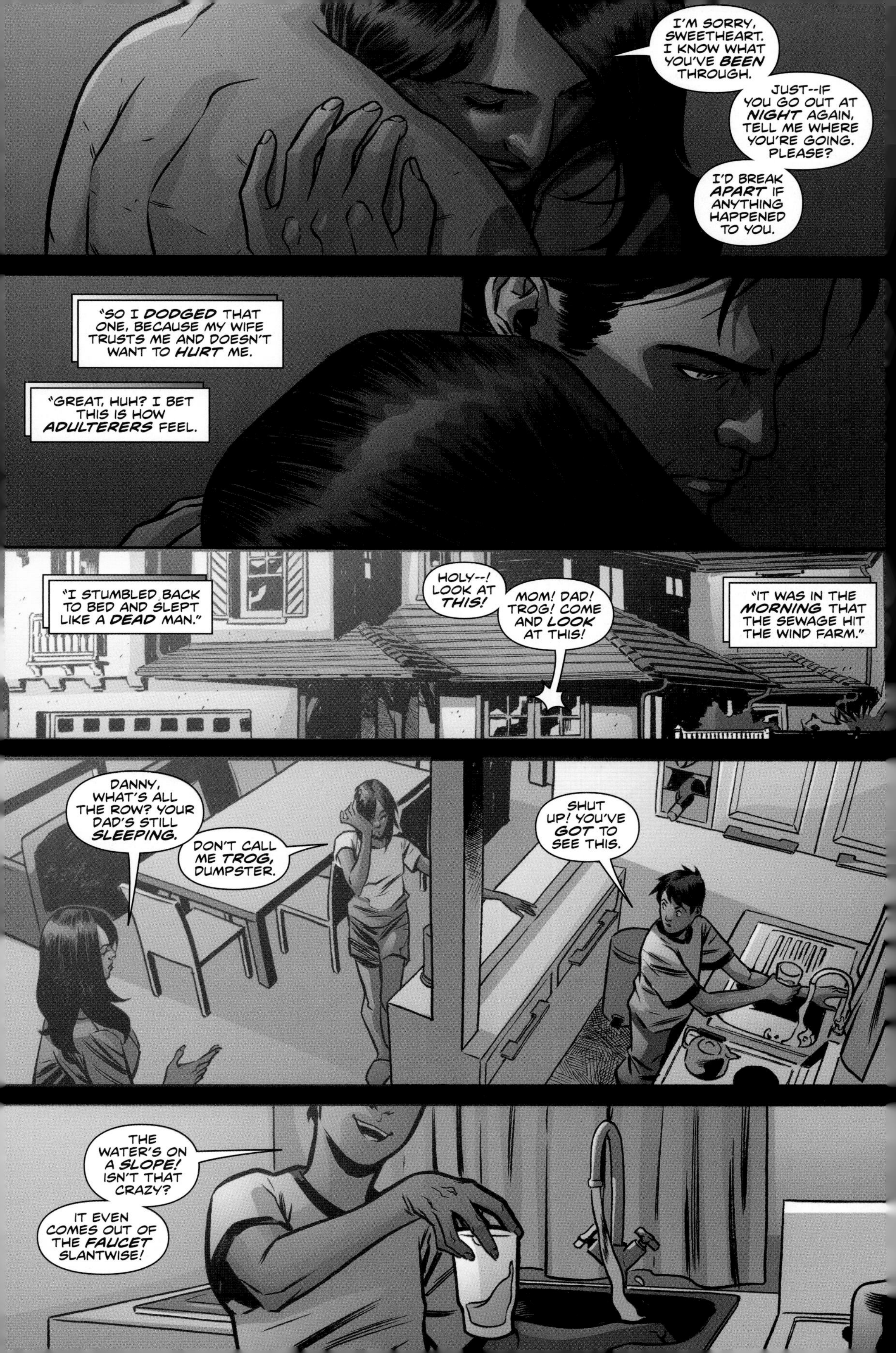
I'M SORRY, SWEETHEART. I KNOW WHAT YOU'VE BEEN THROUGH.
JUST--IF YOU GO OUT AT NIGHT AGAIN, TELL ME WHERE YOU'RE GOING. PLEASE?
I'D BREAK APART IF ANYTHING HAPPENED TO YOU.
"SO I DODGED THAT ONE, BECAUSE MY WIFE TRUSTS ME AND DOESN'T WANT TO HURT ME.
"GREAT, HUH? I BET THIS IS HOW ADULTERERS FEEL.
"I STUMBLED BACK TO BED AND SLEPT LIKE A DEAD MAN."
HOLY--! LOOK AT THIS!
MOM! DAD! TROG! COME AND LOOK AT THIS!
"IT WAS IN THE MORNING THAT THE SEWAGE HIT THE WIND FARM."
DANNY, WHAT'S ALL THE ROW? YOUR DAD'S STILL SLEEPING.
DON'T CALL ME TROG, DUMPSTER.
SHUT UP! YOU'VE GOT TO SEE THIS.
THE WATER'S ON A SLOPE! ISN'T THAT CRAZY?
IT EVEN COMES OUT OF THE FAUCET SLANTWISE!

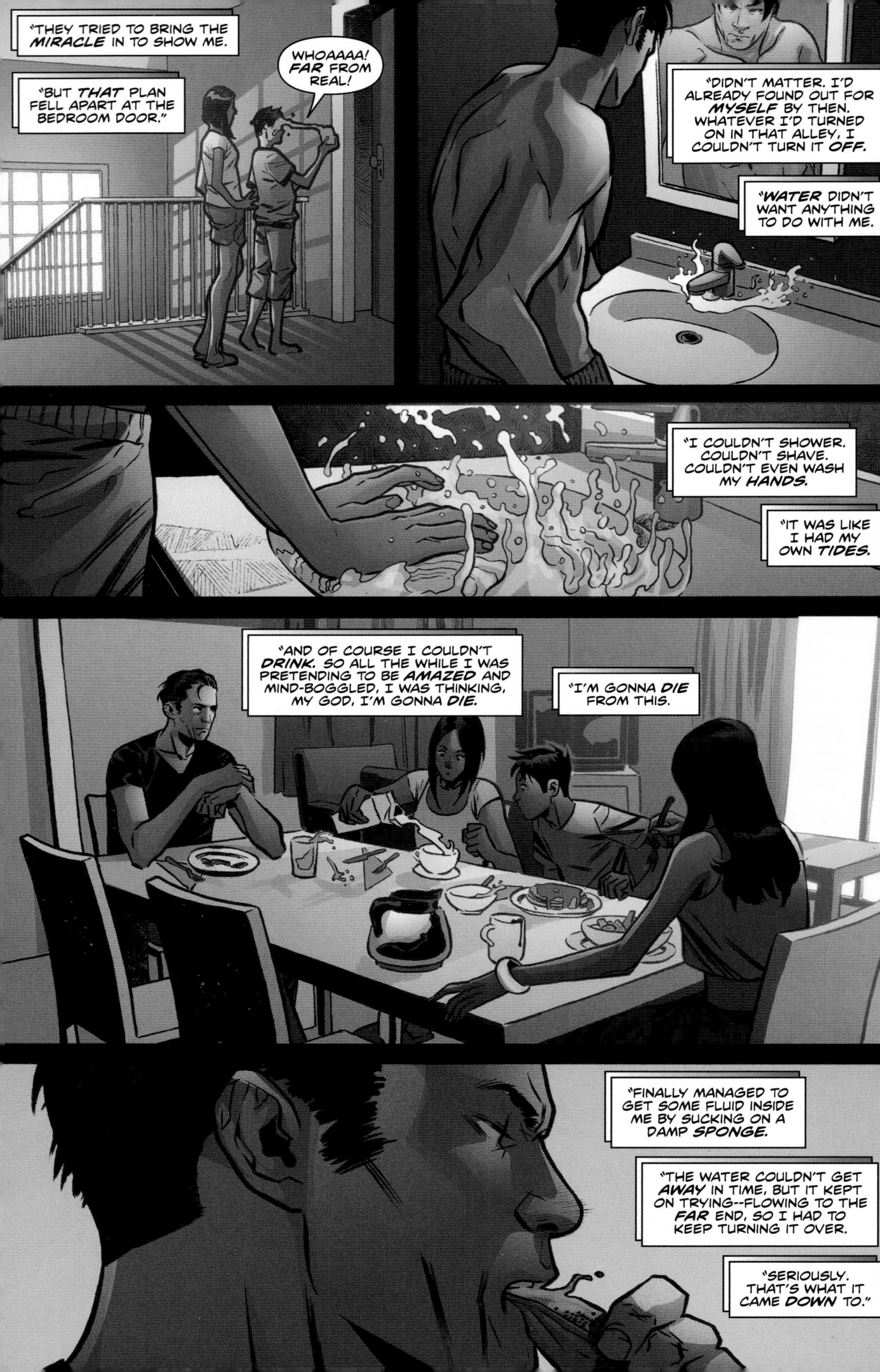
"THEY TRIED TO BRING THE MIRACLE IN TO SHOW ME.
"BUT THAT PLAN FELL APART AT THE BEDROOM DOOR."
WHOAAAA! FAR FROM REAL!
"DIDN'T MATTER. I'D ALREADY FOUND OUT FOR MYSELF BY THEN. WHATEVER I'D TURNED ON IN THAT ALLEY, I COULDN'T TURN IT OFF.
"WATER DIDN'T WANT ANYTHING TO DO WITH ME.
"I COULDN'T SHOWER. COULDN'T SHAVE. COULDN'T EVEN WASH MY HANDS.
"IT WAS LIKE I HAD MY OWN TIDES.
"AND OF COURSE I COULDN'T DRINK. SO ALL THE WHILE I WAS PRETENDING TO BE AMAZED AND MIND-BOGGLED, I WAS THINKING, MY GOD, I'M GONNA DIE.
"I'M GONNA DIE FROM THIS.
"FINALLY MANAGED TO GET SOME FLUID INSIDE ME BY SUCKING ON A DAMP SPONGE.
"THE WATER COULDN'T GET AWAY IN TIME, BUT IT KEPT ON TRYING--FLOWING TO THE FAR END, SO I HAD TO KEEP TURNING IT OVER.
"SERIOUSLY. THAT'S WHAT IT CAME DOWN TO."

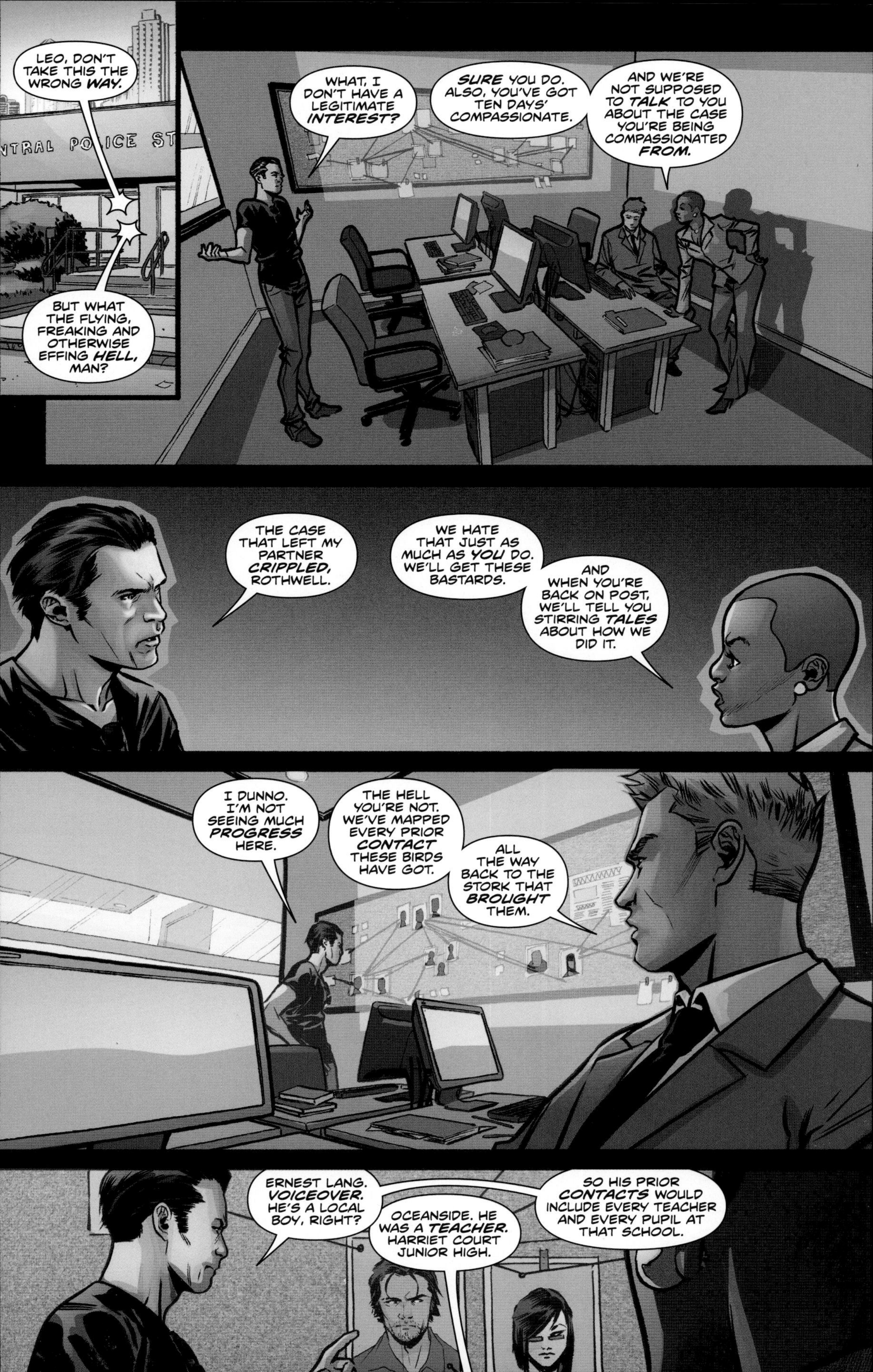

NTRAL POLICE ST
LEO, DON'T TAKE THIS THE WRONG WAY.
BUT WHAT THE FLYING, FREAKING AND OTHERWISE EFFING HELL, MAN?
WHAT, I DON'T HAVE A LEGITIMATE INTEREST?
SURE YOU DO. ALSO, YOU'VE GOT TEN DAYS' COMPASSIONATE.
AND WE'RE NOT SUPPOSED TO TALK TO YOU ABOUT THE CASE YOU'RE BEING COMPASSIONATED FROM.
THE CASE THAT LEFT MY PARTNER CRIPPLED, ROTHWELL.
WE HATE THAT JUST AS MUCH AS YOU DO. WE'LL GET THESE BASTARDS.
AND WHEN YOU'RE BACK ON POST, WE'LL TELL YOU STIRRING TALES ABOUT HOW WE DID IT.
I DUNNO. I'M NOT SEEING MUCH PROGRESS HERE.
THE HELL YOU'RE NOT. WE'VE MAPPED EVERY PRIOR CONTACT THESE BIRDS HAVE GOT.
ALL THE WAY BACK TO THE STORK THAT BROUGHT THEM.
ERNEST LANG. VOICEOVER. HE'S A LOCAL BOY, RIGHT?
OCEANSIDE. HE WAS A TEACHER. HARRIET COURT JUNIOR HIGH.
SO HIS PRIOR CONTACTS WOULD INCLUDE EVERY TEACHER AND EVERY PUPIL AT THAT SCHOOL.

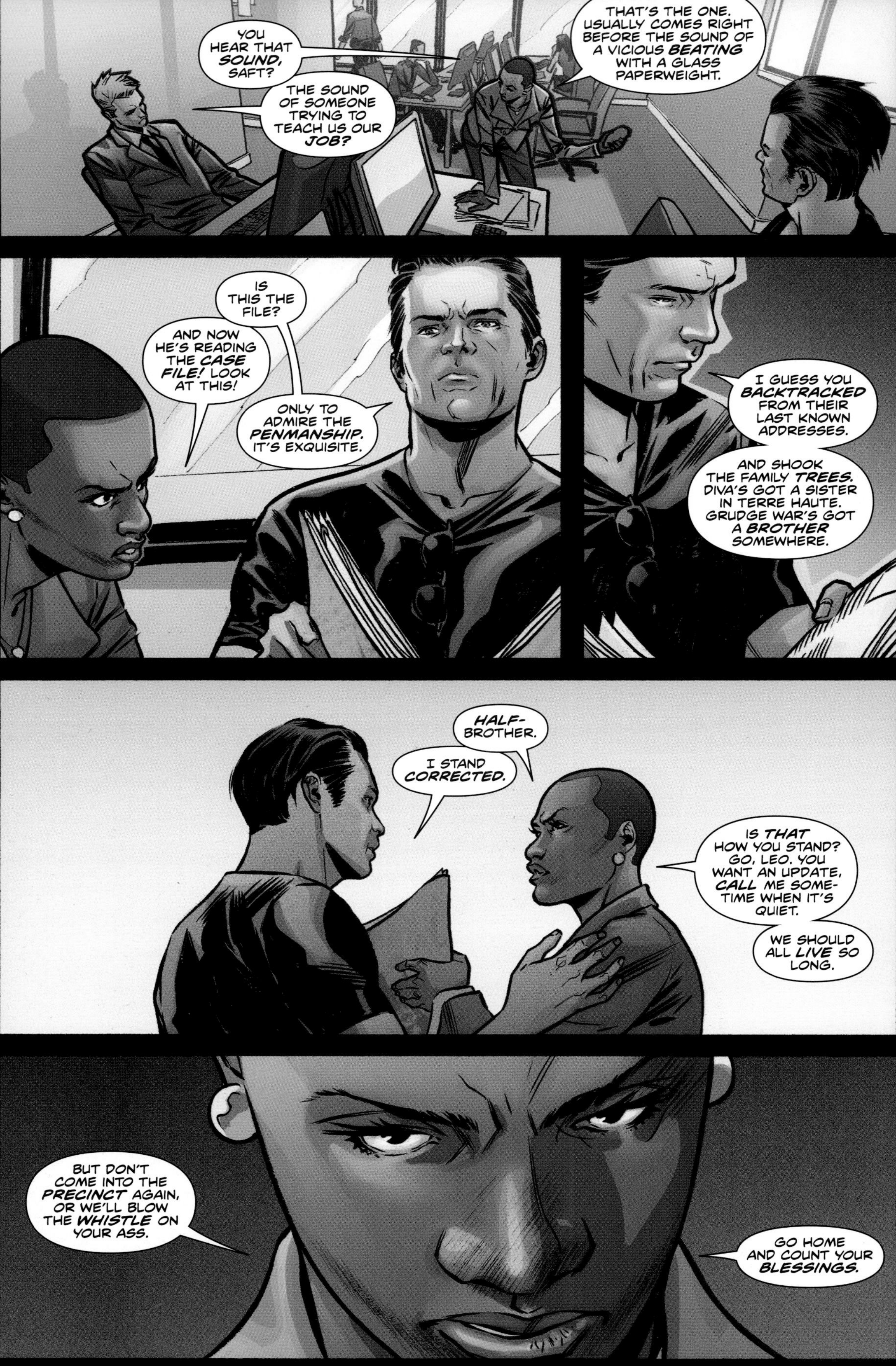
YOU HEAR THAT SOUND, SAFT?
THE SOUND OF SOMEONE TRYING TO TEACH US OUR JOB?
THAT'S THE ONE. USUALLY COMES RIGHT BEFORE THE SOUND OF A VICIOUS BEATING WITH A GLASS PAPERWEIGHT.
IS THIS THE FILE?
AND NOW HE'S READING THE CASE FILE! LOOK AT THIS!
ONLY TO ADMIRE THE PENMANSHIP. IT'S EXQUISITE.
I GUESS YOU BACKTRACKED FROM THEIR LAST KNOWN ADDRESSES.
AND SHOOK THE FAMILY TREES. DIVA'S GOT A SISTER IN TERRE HAUTE. GRUDGE WAR'S GOT A BROTHER SOMEWHERE.
HALF-BROTHER.
I STAND CORRECTED.
IS THAT HOW YOU STAND? GO, LEO. YOU WANT AN UPDATE, CALL ME SOMETIME WHEN IT'S QUIET.
WE SHOULD ALL LIVE SO LONG.
BUT DON'T COME INTO THE PRECINCT AGAIN, OR WE'LL BLOW THE WHISTLE ON YOUR ASS.
GO HOME AND COUNT YOUR BLESSINGS.

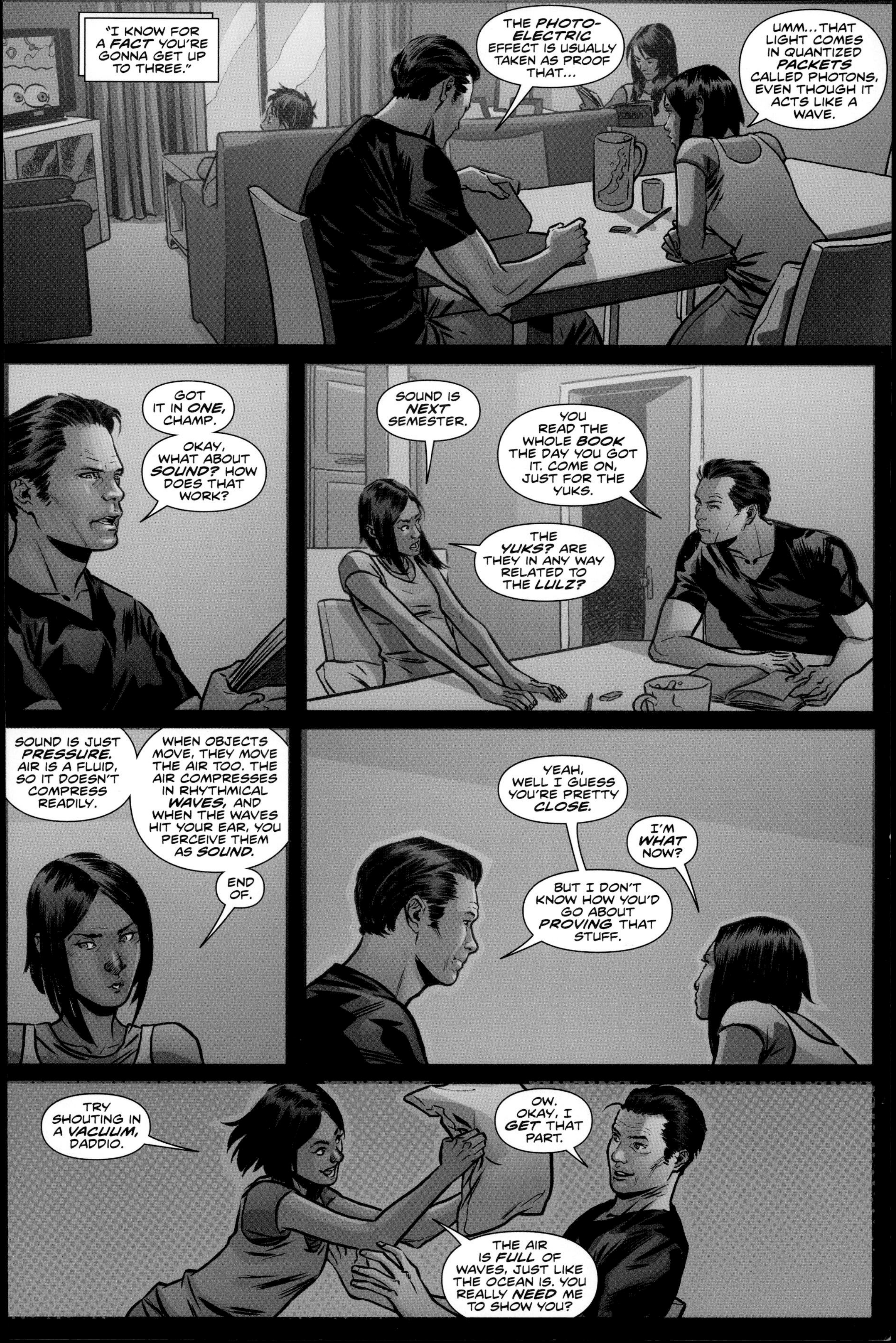
"I KNOW FOR A *FACT* YOU'RE GONNA GET UP TO THREE."
THE *PHOTO-ELECTRIC* EFFECT IS USUALLY TAKEN AS PROOF THAT...
UMM...THAT LIGHT COMES IN QUANTIZED *PACKETS* CALLED PHOTONS, EVEN THOUGH IT ACTS LIKE A WAVE.
GOT IT IN *ONE,* CHAMP.
OKAY, WHAT ABOUT *SOUND?* HOW DOES THAT WORK?
SOUND IS *NEXT* SEMESTER.
YOU READ THE WHOLE *BOOK* THE DAY YOU GOT IT. COME ON, JUST FOR THE YUKS.
THE *YUKS?* ARE THEY IN ANY WAY RELATED TO THE *LULZ?*
SOUND IS JUST *PRESSURE.* AIR IS A FLUID, SO IT DOESN'T COMPRESS READILY.
WHEN OBJECTS MOVE, THEY MOVE THE AIR TOO. THE AIR COMPRESSES IN RHYTHMICAL *WAVES,* AND WHEN THE WAVES HIT YOUR EAR, YOU PERCEIVE THEM AS *SOUND.*
END OF.
YEAH, WELL I GUESS YOU'RE PRETTY *CLOSE.*
I'M *WHAT* NOW?
BUT I DON'T KNOW HOW YOU'D GO ABOUT *PROVING* THAT STUFF.
TRY SHOUTING IN A *VACUUM,* DADDIO.
OW. OKAY, I *GET* THAT PART.
THE AIR IS *FULL* OF WAVES, JUST LIKE THE OCEAN IS. YOU REALLY *NEED* ME TO SHOW YOU?

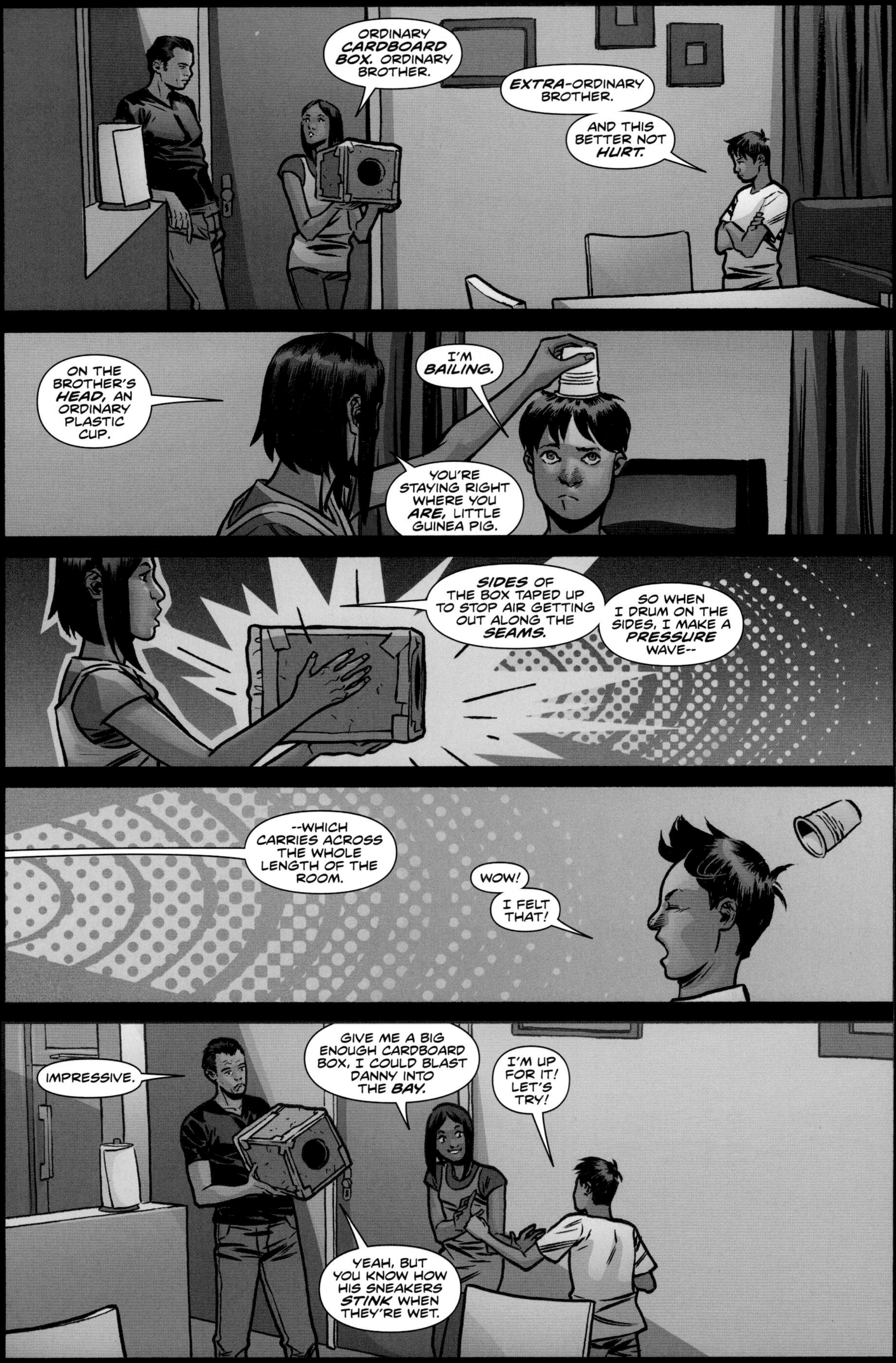
ORDINARY CARDBOARD BOX. ORDINARY BROTHER.
EXTRA-ORDINARY BROTHER.
AND THIS BETTER NOT HURT.
ON THE BROTHER'S HEAD, AN ORDINARY PLASTIC CUP.
I'M BAILING.
YOU'RE STAYING RIGHT WHERE YOU ARE, LITTLE GUINEA PIG.
SIDES OF THE BOX TAPED UP TO STOP AIR GETTING OUT ALONG THE SEAMS.
SO WHEN I DRUM ON THE SIDES, I MAKE A PRESSURE WAVE--
--WHICH CARRIES ACROSS THE WHOLE LENGTH OF THE ROOM.
WOW!
I FELT THAT!
IMPRESSIVE.
GIVE ME A BIG ENOUGH CARDBOARD BOX, I COULD BLAST DANNY INTO THE BAY.
I'M UP FOR IT! LET'S TRY!
YEAH, BUT YOU KNOW HOW HIS SNEAKERS STINK WHEN THEY'RE WET.

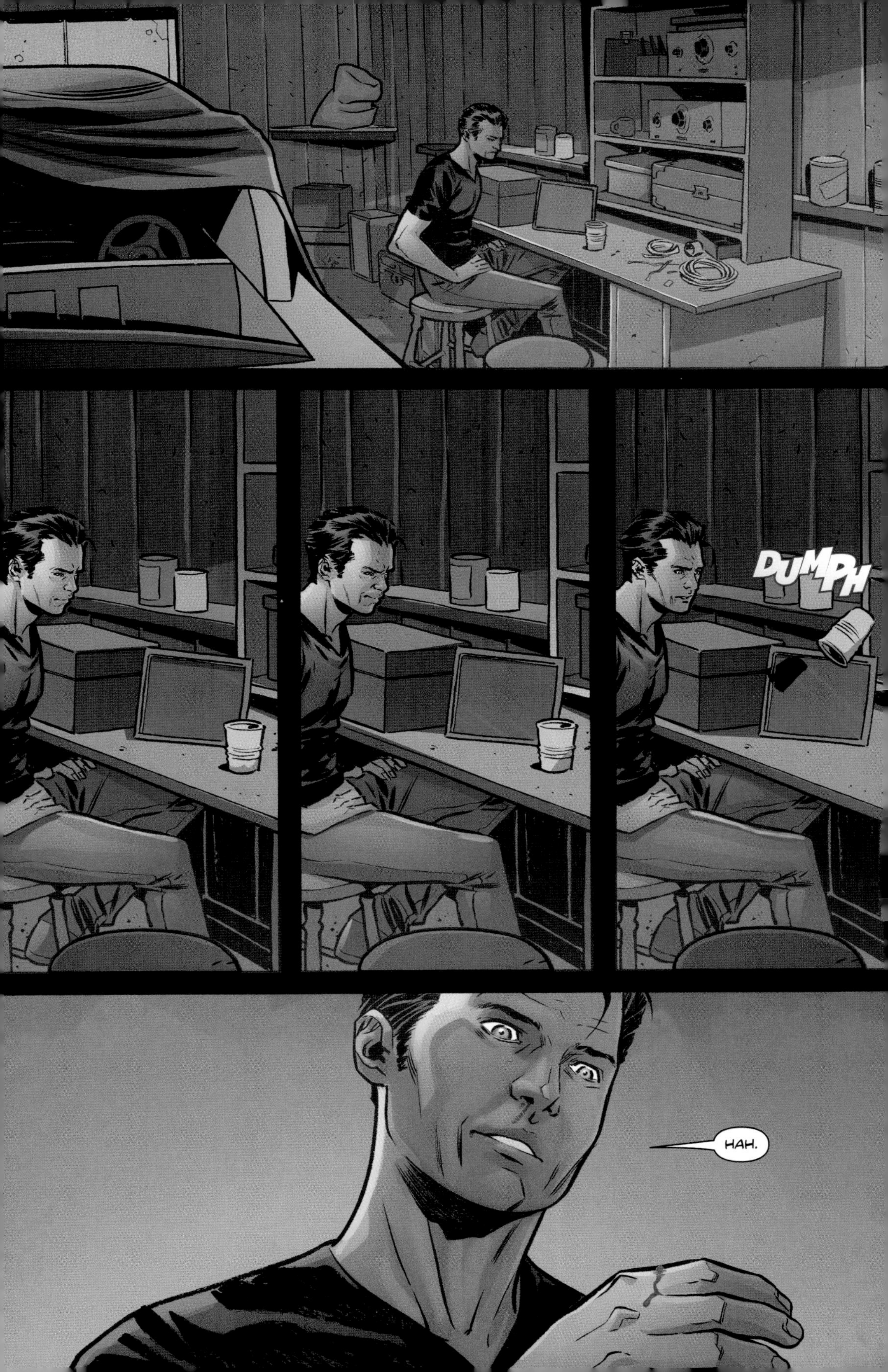
DUMPH
HAH.

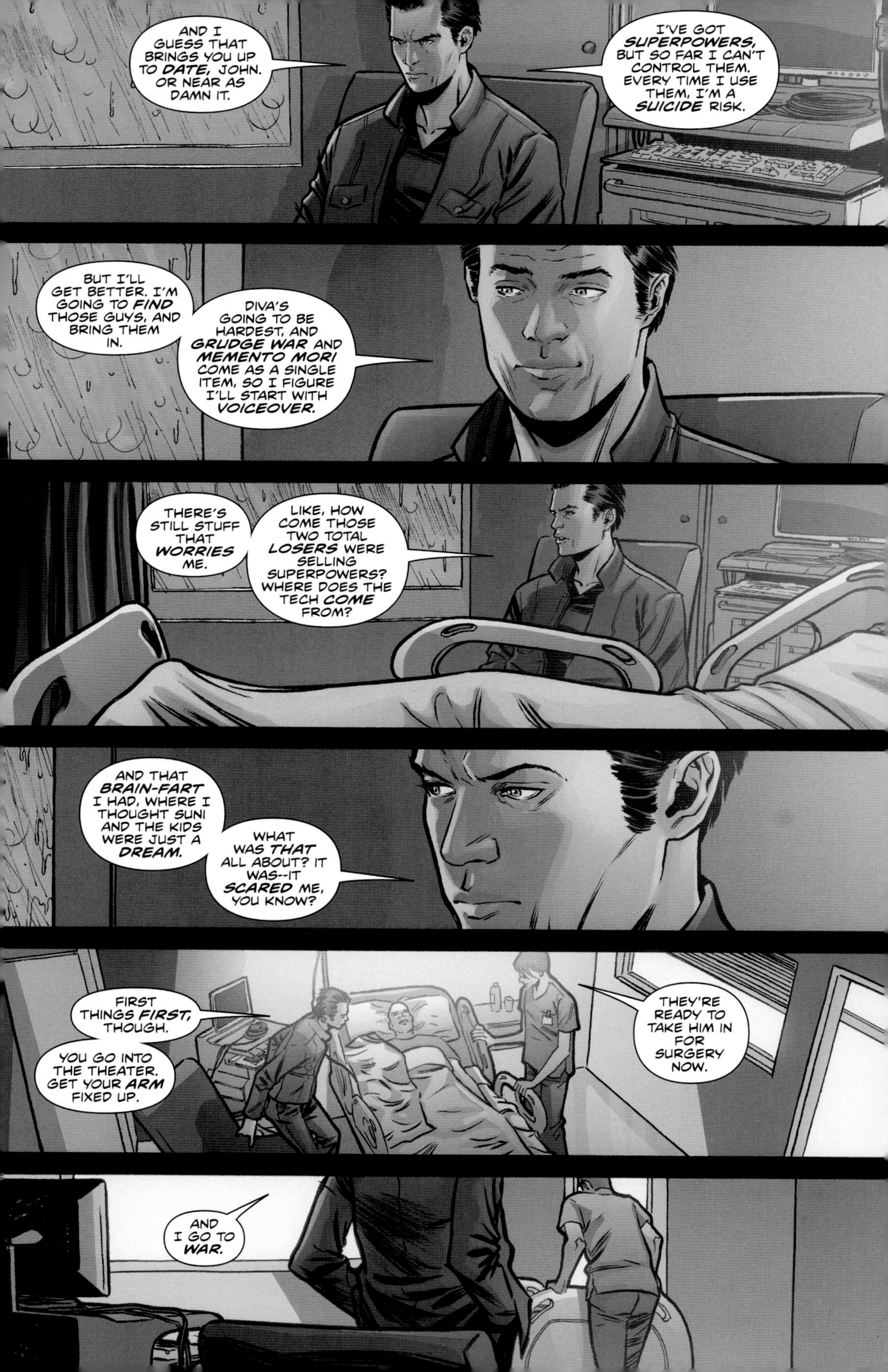
AND I GUESS THAT BRINGS YOU UP TO DATE, JOHN. OR NEAR AS DAMN IT.
I'VE GOT SUPERPOWERS, BUT SO FAR I CAN'T CONTROL THEM. EVERY TIME I USE THEM, I'M A SUICIDE RISK.
BUT I'LL GET BETTER. I'M GOING TO FIND THOSE GUYS, AND BRING THEM IN.
DIVA'S GOING TO BE HARDEST, AND GRUDGE WAR AND MEMENTO MORI COME AS A SINGLE ITEM, SO I FIGURE I'LL START WITH VOICEOVER.
THERE'S STILL STUFF THAT WORRIES ME.
LIKE, HOW COME THOSE TWO TOTAL LOSERS WERE SELLING SUPERPOWERS? WHERE DOES THE TECH COME FROM?
AND THAT BRAIN-FART I HAD, WHERE I THOUGHT SUNI AND THE KIDS WERE JUST A DREAM.
WHAT WAS THAT ALL ABOUT? IT WAS--IT SCARED ME, YOU KNOW?
FIRST THINGS FIRST, THOUGH.
YOU GO INTO THE THEATER. GET YOUR ARM FIXED UP.
THEY'RE READY TO TAKE HIM IN FOR SURGERY NOW.
AND I GO TO WAR.

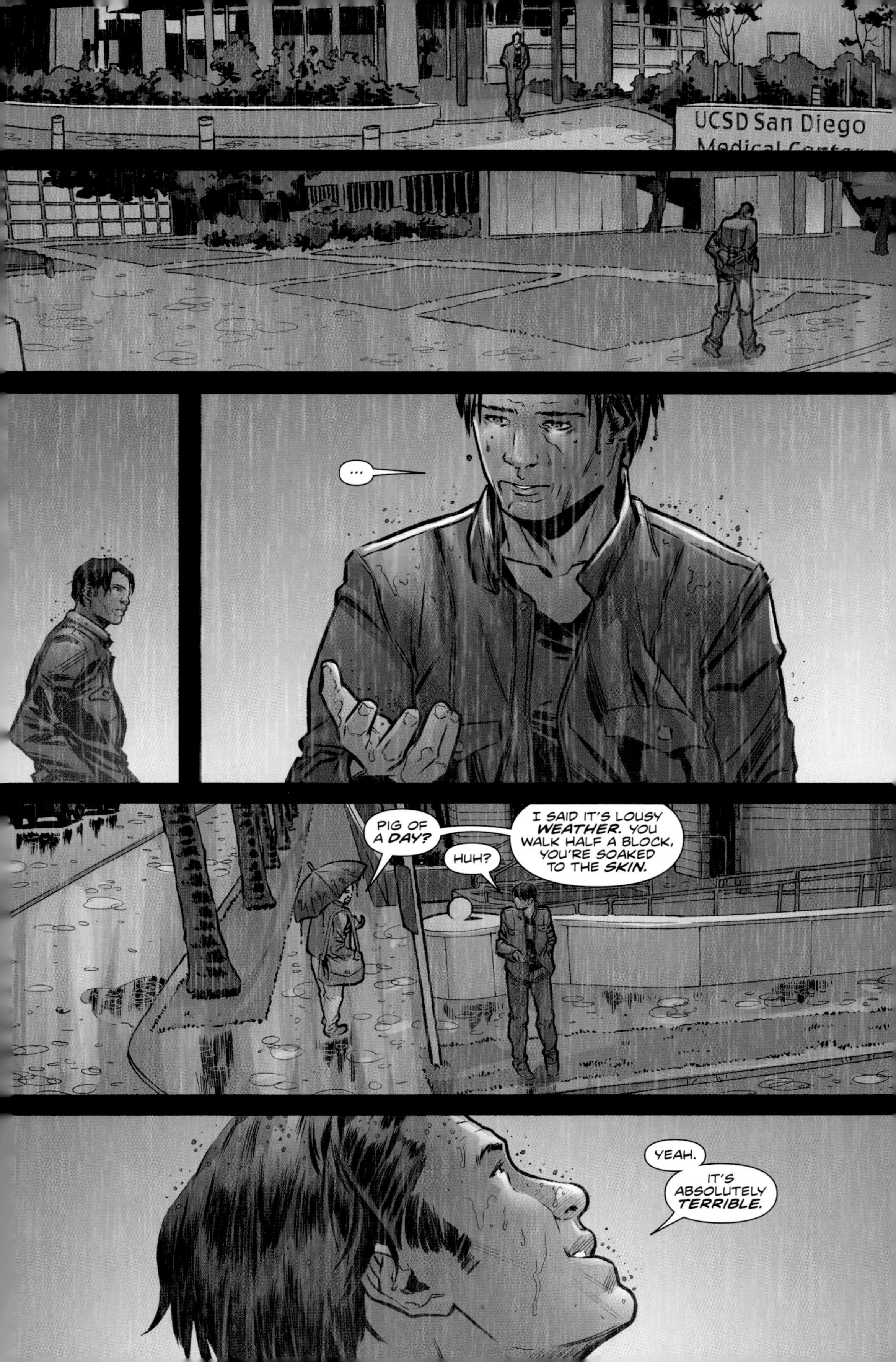
UCSD San Diego
...
PIG OF A DAY?
HUH?
I SAID IT'S LOUSY WEATHER. YOU WALK HALF A BLOCK, YOU'RE SOAKED TO THE SKIN.
YEAH.
IT'S ABSOLUTELY TERRIBLE.

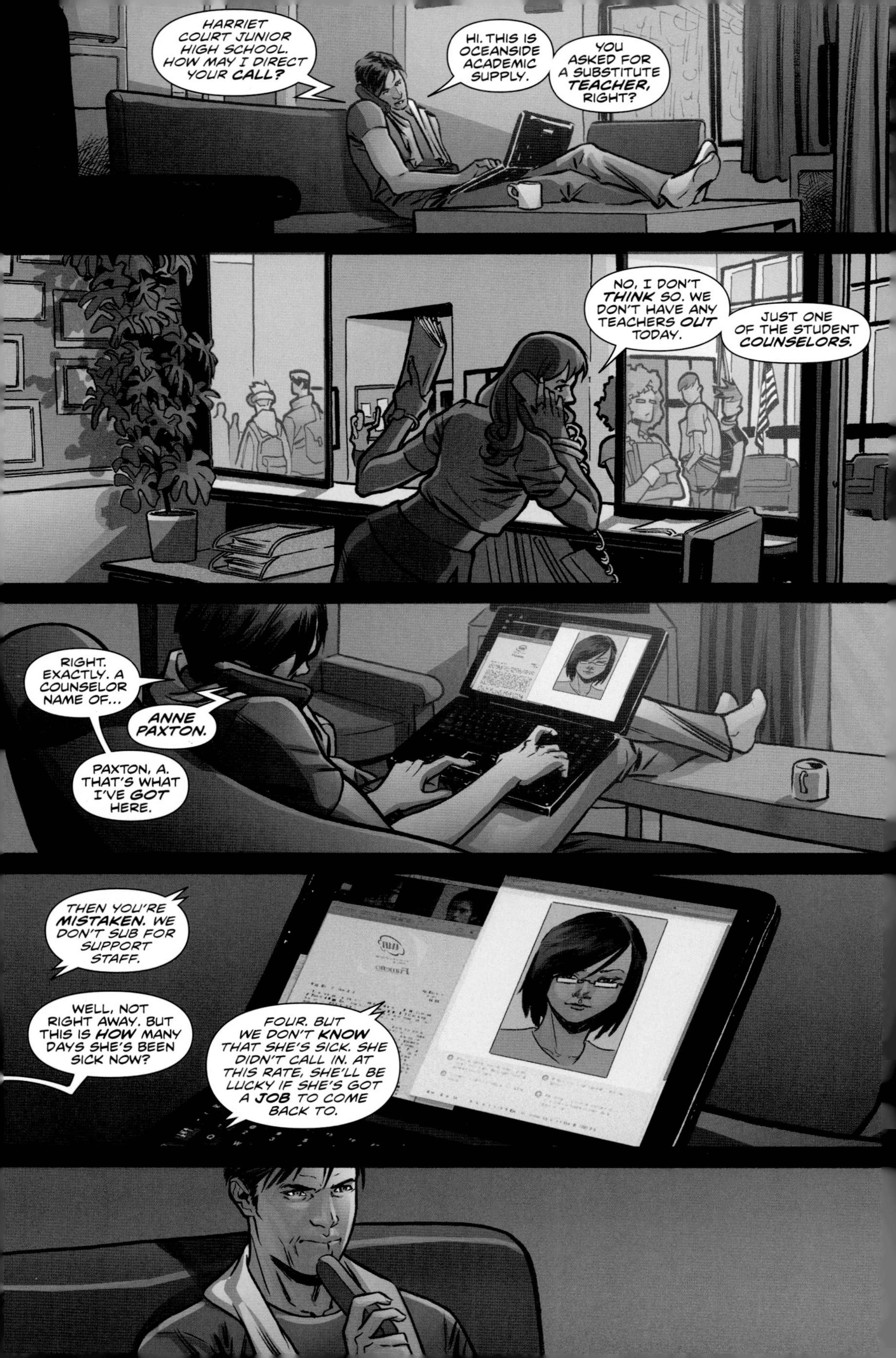
HARRIET COURT JUNIOR HIGH SCHOOL. HOW MAY I DIRECT YOUR CALL?
HI. THIS IS OCEANSIDE ACADEMIC SUPPLY.
YOU ASKED FOR A SUBSTITUTE TEACHER, RIGHT?
NO, I DON'T THINK SO. WE DON'T HAVE ANY TEACHERS OUT TODAY.
JUST ONE OF THE STUDENT COUNSELORS.
RIGHT. EXACTLY. A COUNSELOR NAME OF...
ANNE PAXTON.
PAXTON, A. THAT'S WHAT I'VE GOT HERE.
THEN YOU'RE MISTAKEN. WE DON'T SUB FOR SUPPORT STAFF.
WELL, NOT RIGHT AWAY. BUT THIS IS HOW MANY DAYS SHE'S BEEN SICK NOW?
FOUR. BUT WE DON'T KNOW THAT SHE'S SICK. SHE DIDN'T CALL IN. AT THIS RATE, SHE'LL BE LUCKY IF SHE'S GOT A JOB TO COME BACK TO.

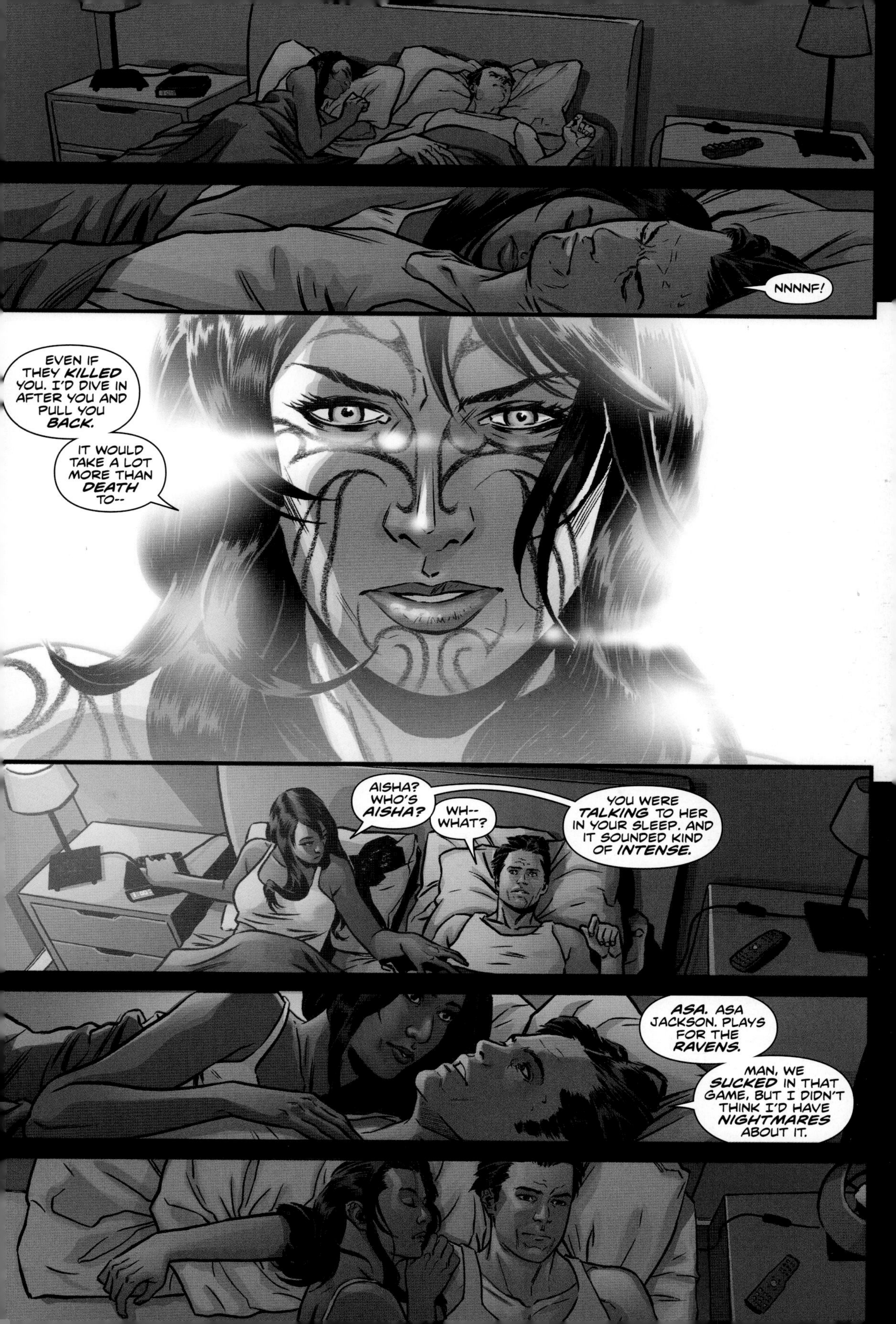
NNNNF!
EVEN IF THEY KILLED YOU. I'D DIVE IN AFTER YOU AND PULL YOU BACK.
IT WOULD TAKE A LOT MORE THAN DEATH TO--
AISHA? WHO'S AISHA?
WH-- WHAT?
YOU WERE TALKING TO HER IN YOUR SLEEP. AND IT SOUNDED KIND OF INTENSE.
ASA. ASA JACKSON. PLAYS FOR THE RAVENS.
MAN, WE SUCKED IN THAT GAME, BUT I DIDN'T THINK I'D HAVE NIGHTMARES ABOUT IT.

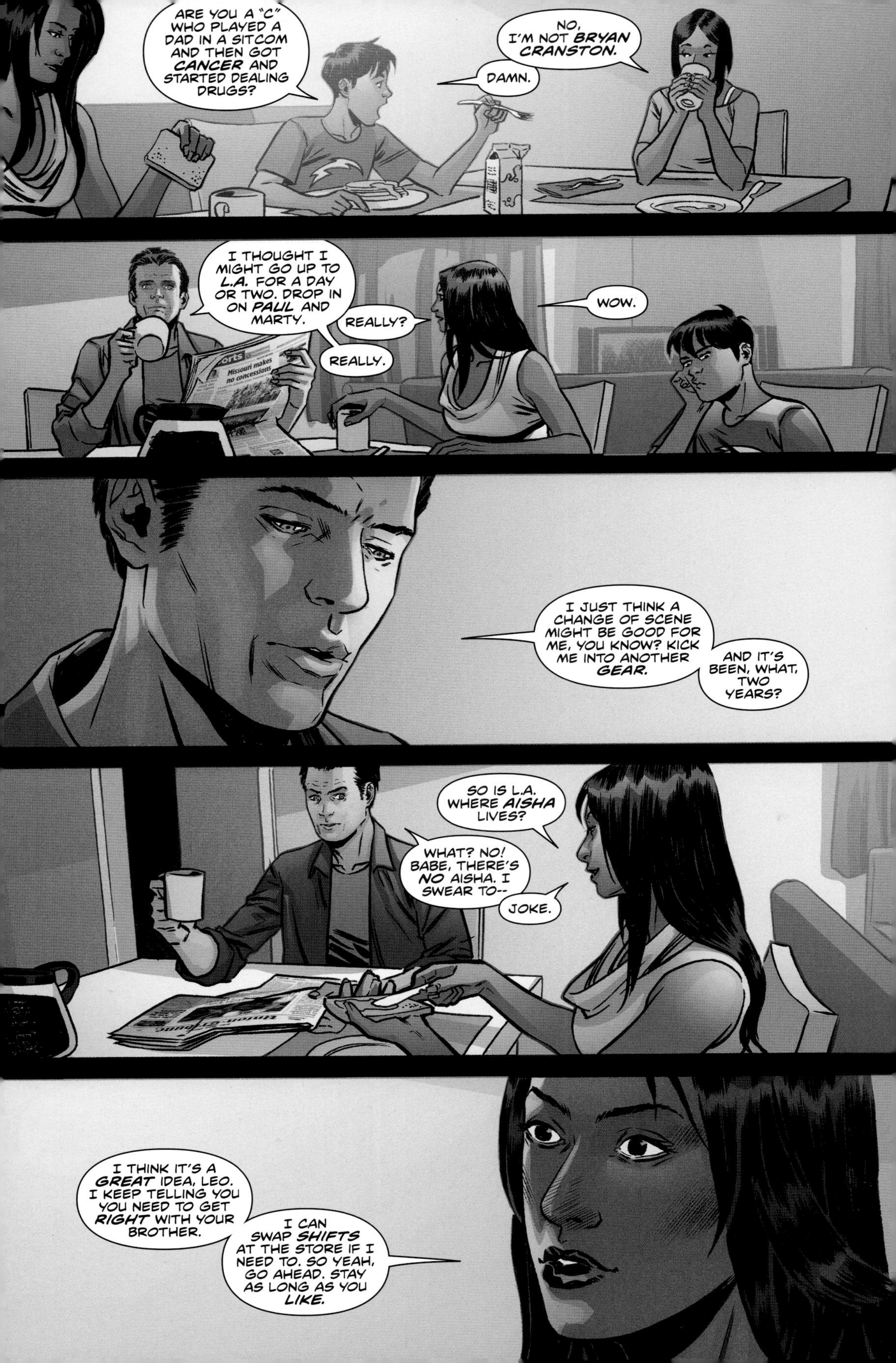

ARE YOU A "C" WHO PLAYED A DAD IN A SITCOM AND THEN GOT CANCER AND STARTED DEALING DRUGS?
NO, I'M NOT BRYAN CRANSTON.
DAMN.
I THOUGHT I MIGHT GO UP TO L.A. FOR A DAY OR TWO. DROP IN ON PAUL AND MARTY.
REALLY?
REALLY.
WOW.
Missouri makes no concessions
I JUST THINK A CHANGE OF SCENE MIGHT BE GOOD FOR ME, YOU KNOW? KICK ME INTO ANOTHER GEAR.
AND IT'S BEEN, WHAT, TWO YEARS?
SO IS L.A. WHERE AISHA LIVES?
WHAT? NO! BABE, THERE'S NO AISHA. I SWEAR TO--
JOKE.
I THINK IT'S A GREAT IDEA, LEO. I KEEP TELLING YOU YOU NEED TO GET RIGHT WITH YOUR BROTHER.
I CAN SWAP SHIFTS AT THE STORE IF I NEED TO. SO YEAH, GO AHEAD. STAY AS LONG AS YOU LIKE.

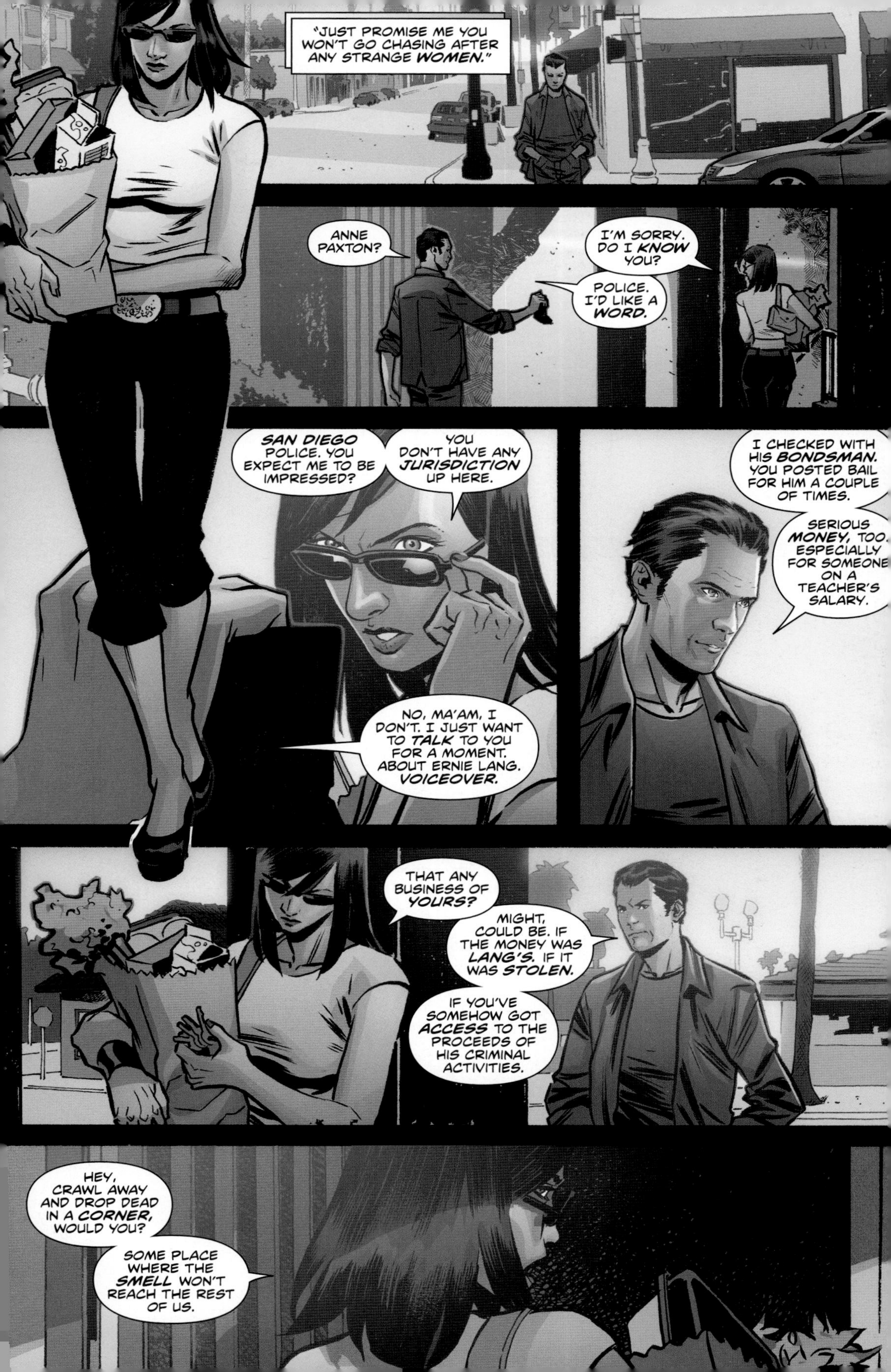

"JUST PROMISE ME YOU WON'T GO CHASING AFTER ANY STRANGE WOMEN."
ANNE PAXTON?
I'M SORRY. DO I KNOW YOU?
POLICE. I'D LIKE A WORD.
SAN DIEGO POLICE. YOU EXPECT ME TO BE IMPRESSED?
YOU DON'T HAVE ANY JURISDICTION UP HERE.
NO, MA'AM, I DON'T. I JUST WANT TO TALK TO YOU FOR A MOMENT. ABOUT ERNIE LANG. VOICEOVER.
I CHECKED WITH HIS BONDSMAN. YOU POSTED BAIL FOR HIM A COUPLE OF TIMES.
SERIOUS MONEY, TOO. ESPECIALLY FOR SOMEONE ON A TEACHER'S SALARY.
THAT ANY BUSINESS OF YOURS?
MIGHT, COULD BE. IF THE MONEY WAS LANG'S. IF IT WAS STOLEN.
IF YOU'VE SOMEHOW GOT ACCESS TO THE PROCEEDS OF HIS CRIMINAL ACTIVITIES.
HEY, CRAWL AWAY AND DROP DEAD IN A CORNER, WOULD YOU?
SOME PLACE WHERE THE SMELL WON'T REACH THE REST OF US.

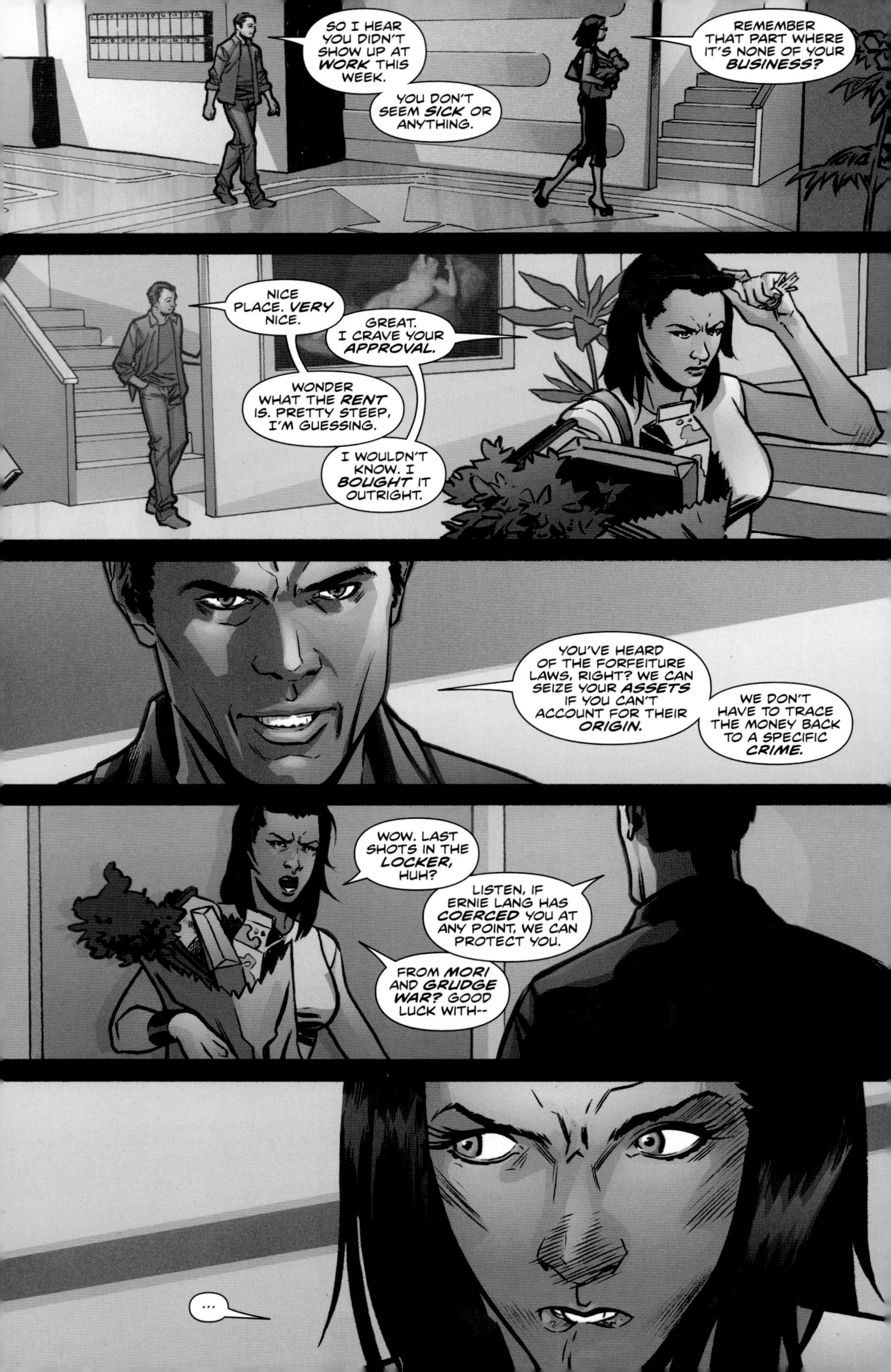
SO I HEAR YOU DIDN'T SHOW UP AT WORK THIS WEEK.
YOU DON'T SEEM SICK OR ANYTHING.
REMEMBER THAT PART WHERE IT'S NONE OF YOUR BUSINESS?
NICE PLACE. VERY NICE.
GREAT. I CRAVE YOUR APPROVAL.
WONDER WHAT THE RENT IS. PRETTY STEEP, I'M GUESSING.
I WOULDN'T KNOW. I BOUGHT IT OUTRIGHT.
YOU'VE HEARD OF THE FORFEITURE LAWS, RIGHT? WE CAN SEIZE YOUR ASSETS IF YOU CAN'T ACCOUNT FOR THEIR ORIGIN.
WE DON'T HAVE TO TRACE THE MONEY BACK TO A SPECIFIC CRIME.
WOW. LAST SHOTS IN THE LOCKER, HUH?
LISTEN, IF ERNIE LANG HAS COERCED YOU AT ANY POINT, WE CAN PROTECT YOU.
FROM MORI AND GRUDGE WAR? GOOD LUCK WITH--
...

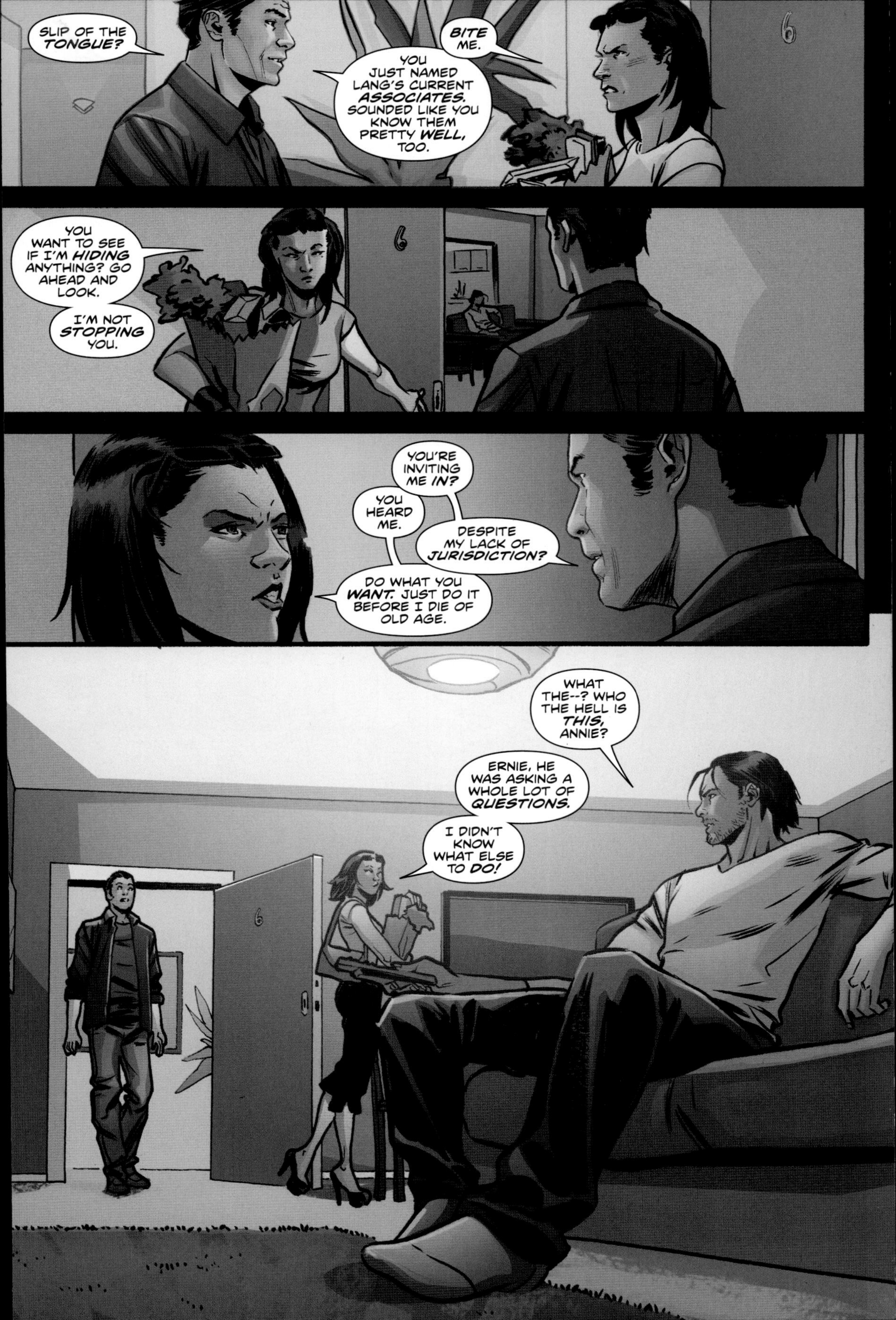
SLIP OF THE TONGUE?
BITE ME.
YOU JUST NAMED LANG'S CURRENT ASSOCIATES. SOUNDED LIKE YOU KNOW THEM PRETTY WELL, TOO.
YOU WANT TO SEE IF I'M HIDING ANYTHING? GO AHEAD AND LOOK.
I'M NOT STOPPING YOU.
YOU'RE INVITING ME IN?
YOU HEARD ME.
DESPITE MY LACK OF JURISDICTION?
DO WHAT YOU WANT. JUST DO IT BEFORE I DIE OF OLD AGE.
WHAT THE--? WHO THE HELL IS THIS, ANNIE?
ERNIE, HE WAS ASKING A WHOLE LOT OF QUESTIONS.
I DIDN'T KNOW WHAT ELSE TO DO!

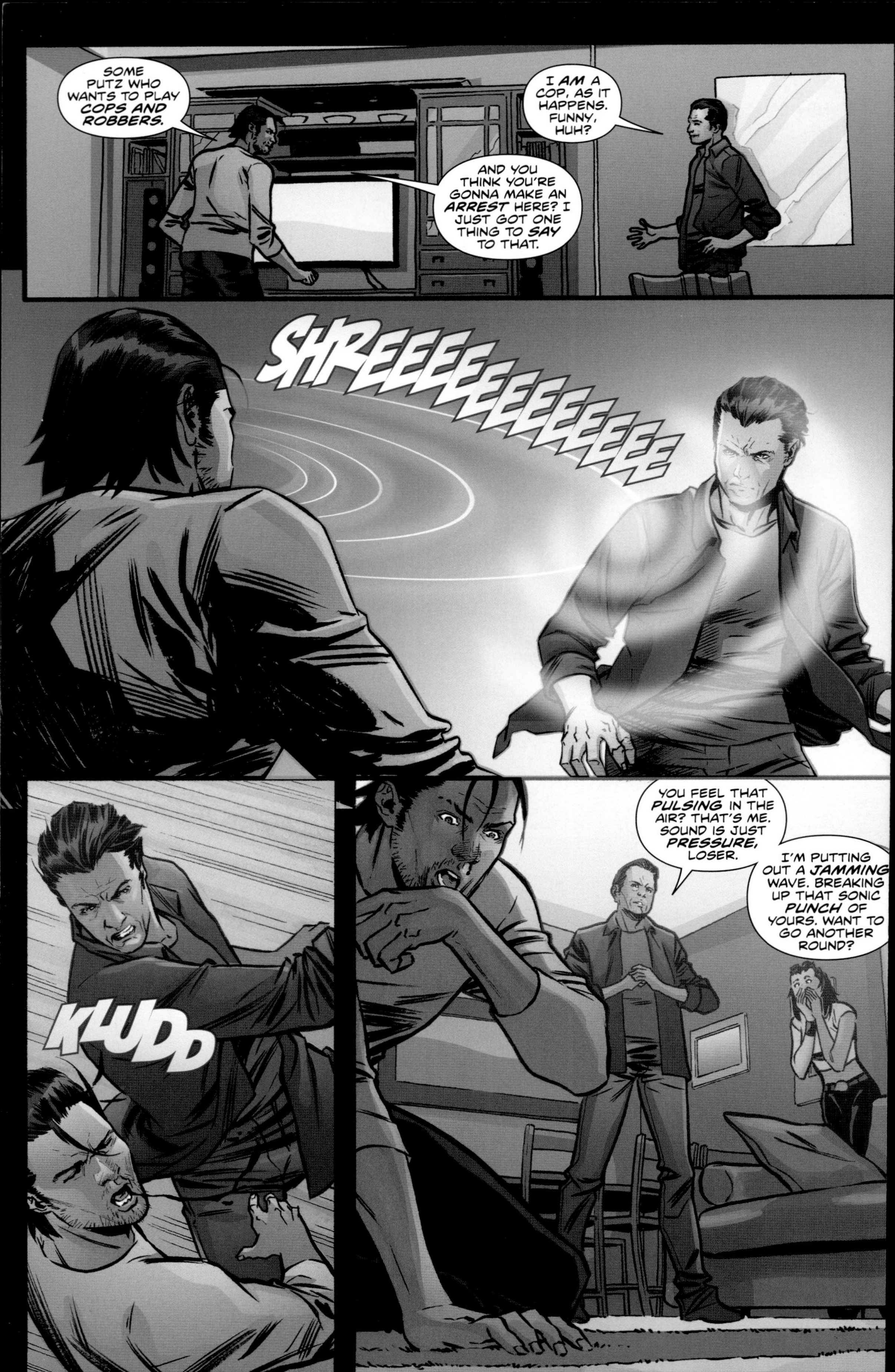

SOME PUTZ WHO WANTS TO PLAY *COPS AND ROBBERS.*
I *AM* A COP, AS IT HAPPENS. FUNNY, HUH?
AND YOU THINK YOU'RE GONNA MAKE AN *ARREST* HERE? I JUST GOT ONE THING TO *SAY* TO THAT.
SHREEEEEEEEEEEEEE
KLUDD
YOU FEEL THAT *PULSING* IN THE AIR? THAT'S ME. SOUND IS JUST *PRESSURE,* LOSER.
I'M PUTTING OUT A *JAMMING* WAVE. BREAKING UP THAT SONIC *PUNCH* OF YOURS. WANT TO GO ANOTHER ROUND?

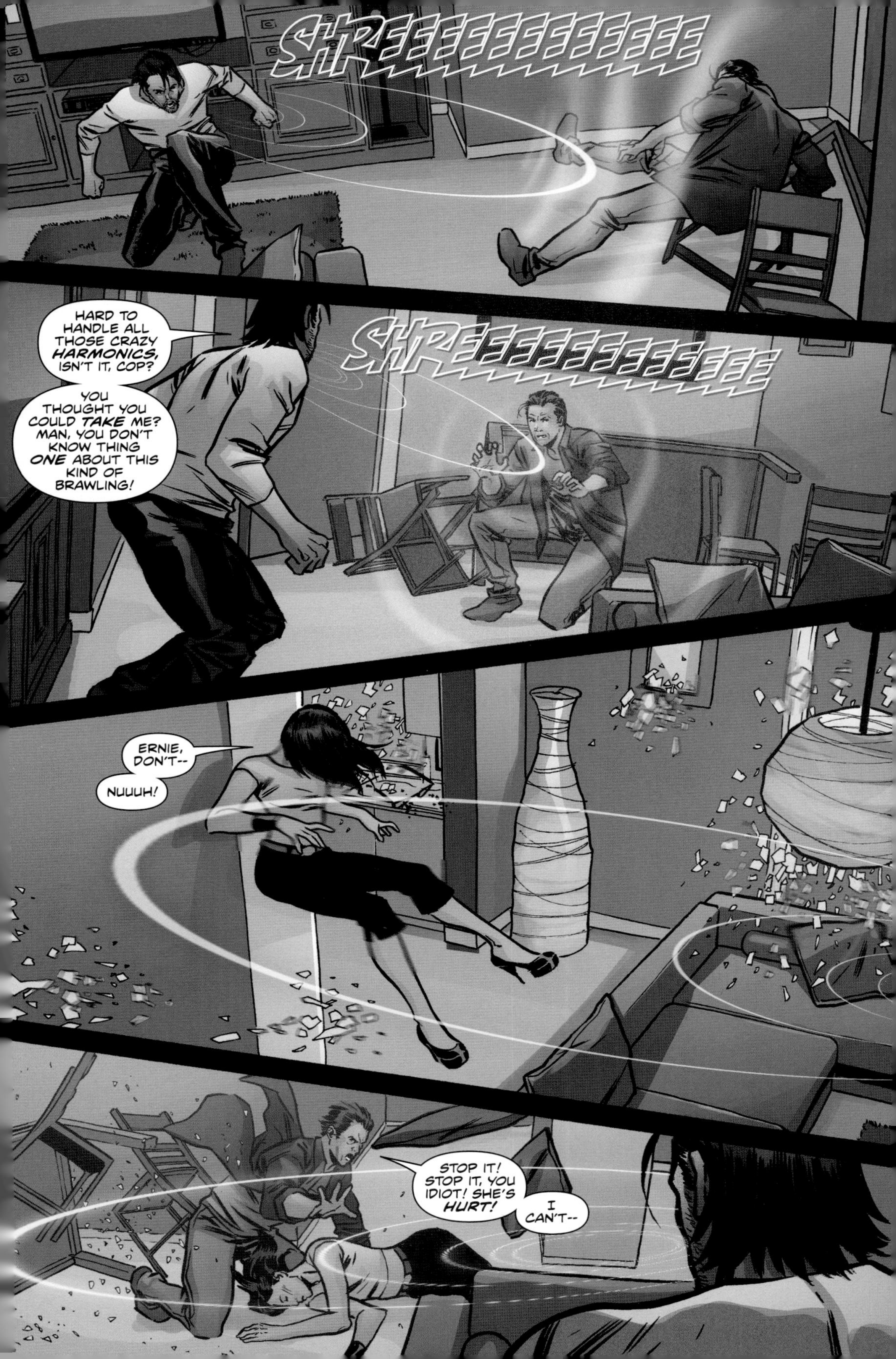
SHREEEEEEEEEEE
HARD TO HANDLE ALL THOSE CRAZY HARMONICS, ISN'T IT, COP?
YOU THOUGHT YOU COULD TAKE ME? MAN, YOU DON'T KNOW THING ONE ABOUT THIS KIND OF BRAWLING!
SHREEEEEEEEEEEEE
ERNIE, DON'T--
NUUUH!
STOP IT! STOP IT, YOU IDIOT! SHE'S HURT!
I CAN'T--

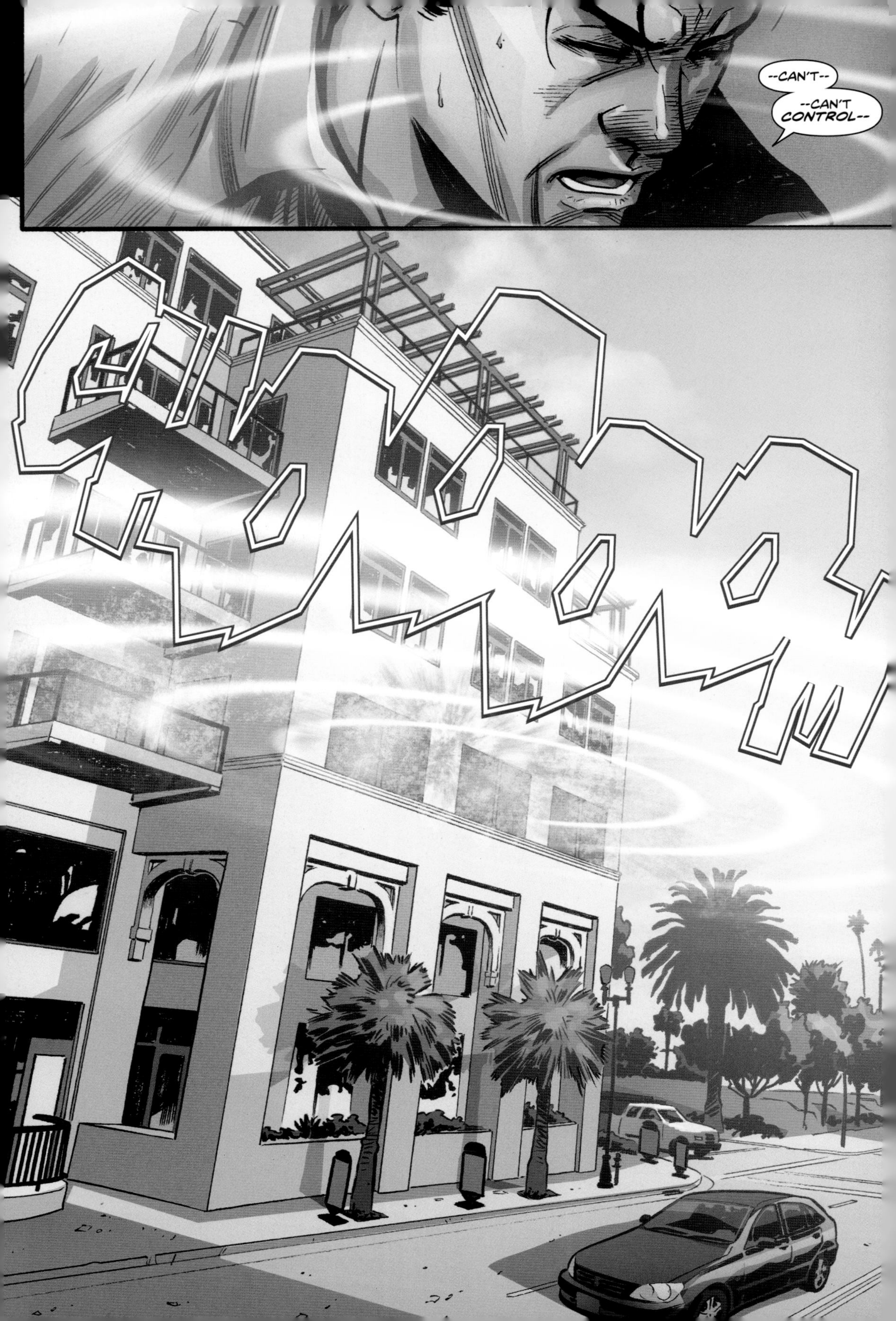
--CAN'T--
--CAN'T CONTROL--

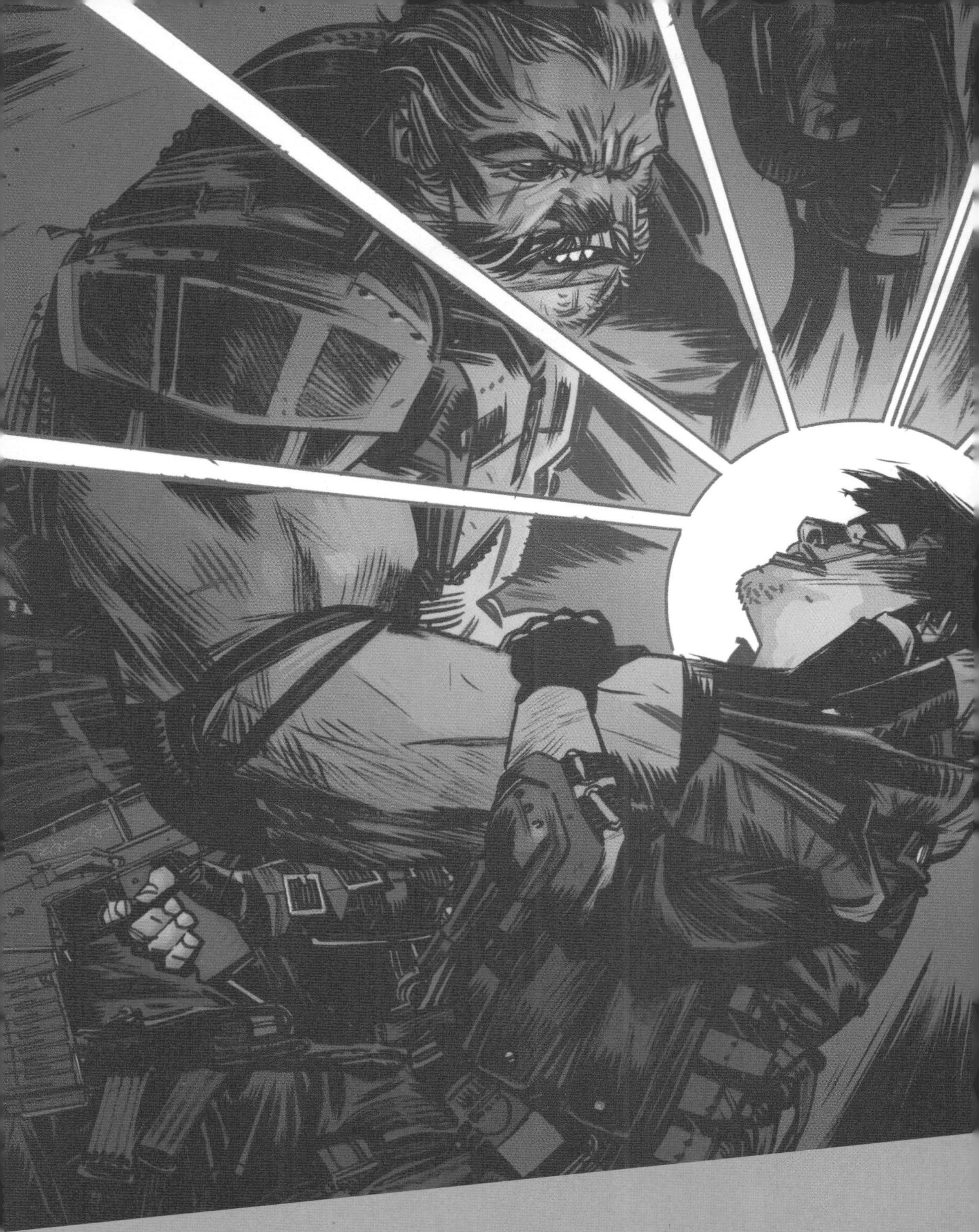

"THE BUSINESS THAT WAS BETWEEN US WAS NEVER CONCLUDED...YOU CAN'T DIE UNTIL YOUR **DEBT** IS PAID."

Chapter 3

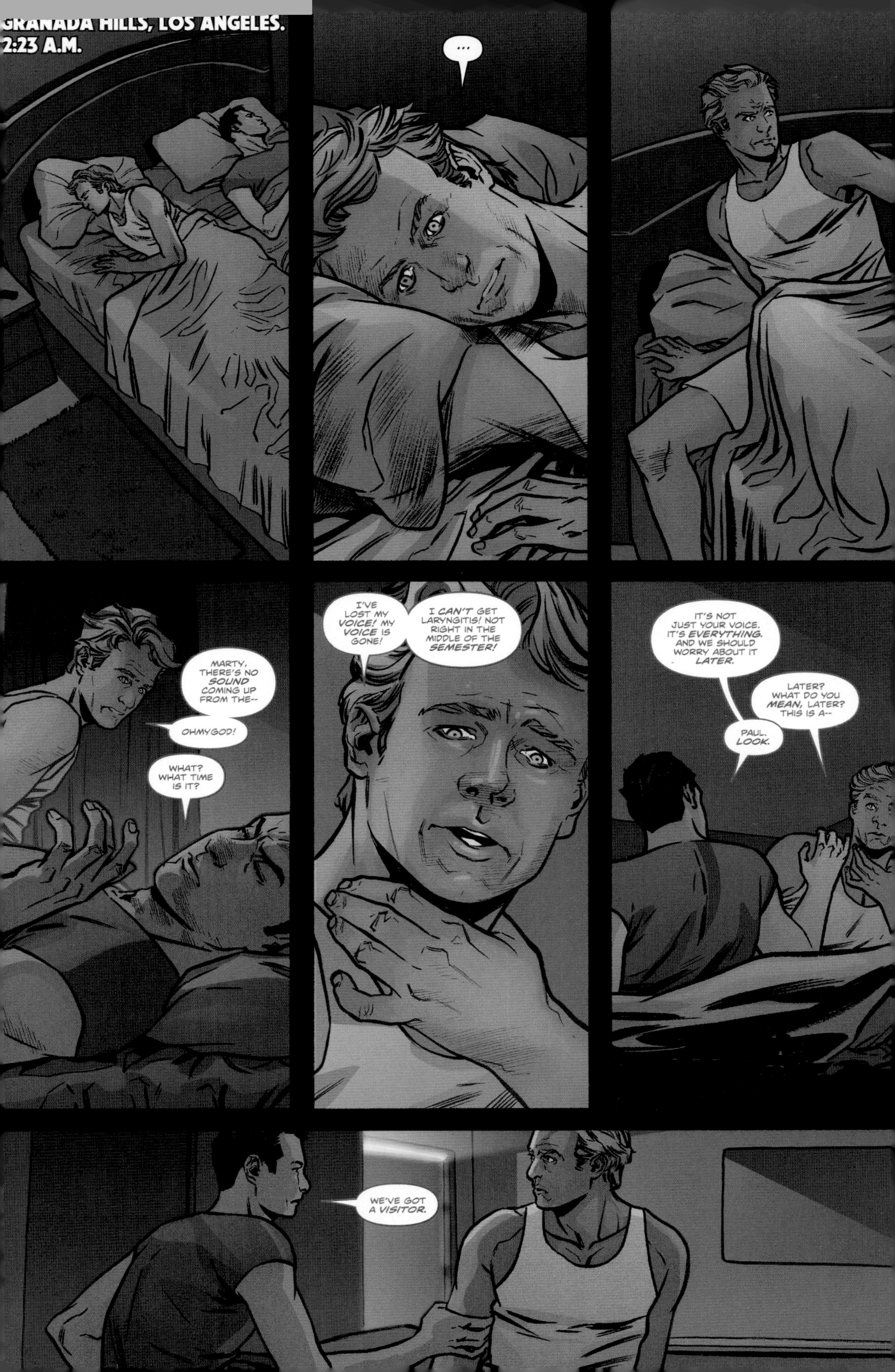
GRANADA HILLS, LOS ANGELES. 2:23 A.M.
...
MARTY, THERE'S NO SOUND COMING UP FROM THE--
OHMYGOD!
WHAT? WHAT TIME IS IT?
I'VE LOST MY VOICE! MY VOICE IS GONE!
I CAN'T GET LARYNGITIS! NOT RIGHT IN THE MIDDLE OF THE SEMESTER!
IT'S NOT JUST YOUR VOICE. IT'S EVERYTHING. AND WE SHOULD WORRY ABOUT IT LATER.
LATER? WHAT DO YOU MEAN, LATER? THIS IS A--
PAUL. LOOK.
WE'VE GOT A VISITOR.

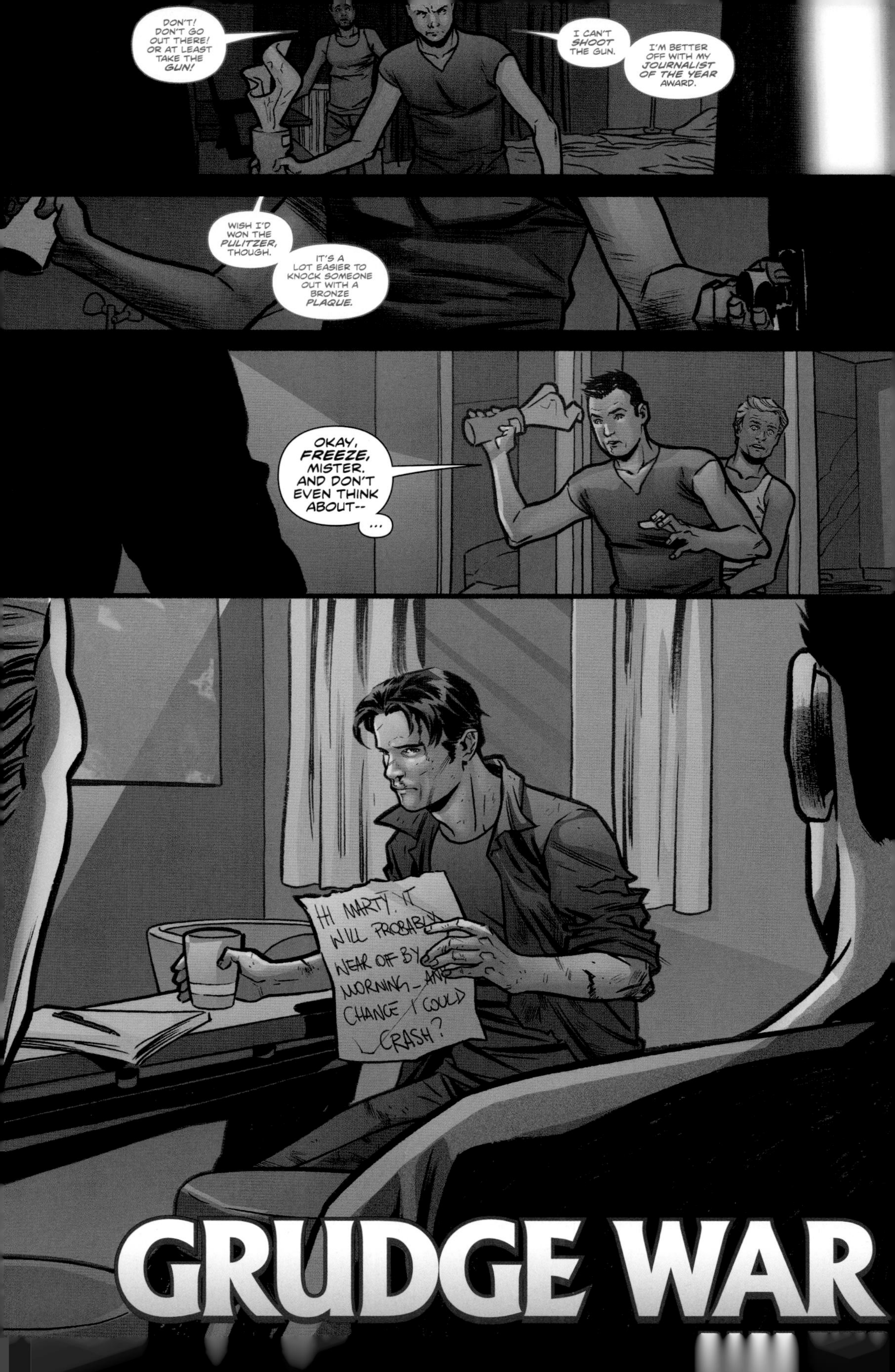
DON'T! DON'T GO OUT THERE! OR AT LEAST TAKE THE GUN!
I CAN'T SHOOT THE GUN.
I'M BETTER OFF WITH MY JOURNALIST OF THE YEAR AWARD.
WISH I'D WON THE PULITZER, THOUGH.
IT'S A LOT EASIER TO KNOCK SOMEONE OUT WITH A BRONZE PLAQUE.
OKAY, FREEZE, MISTER. AND DON'T EVEN THINK ABOUT--
...
HI MARTY. IT WILL PROBABLY WEAR OFF BY MORNING. ANY CHANCE I COULD CRASH?
GRUDGE WAR

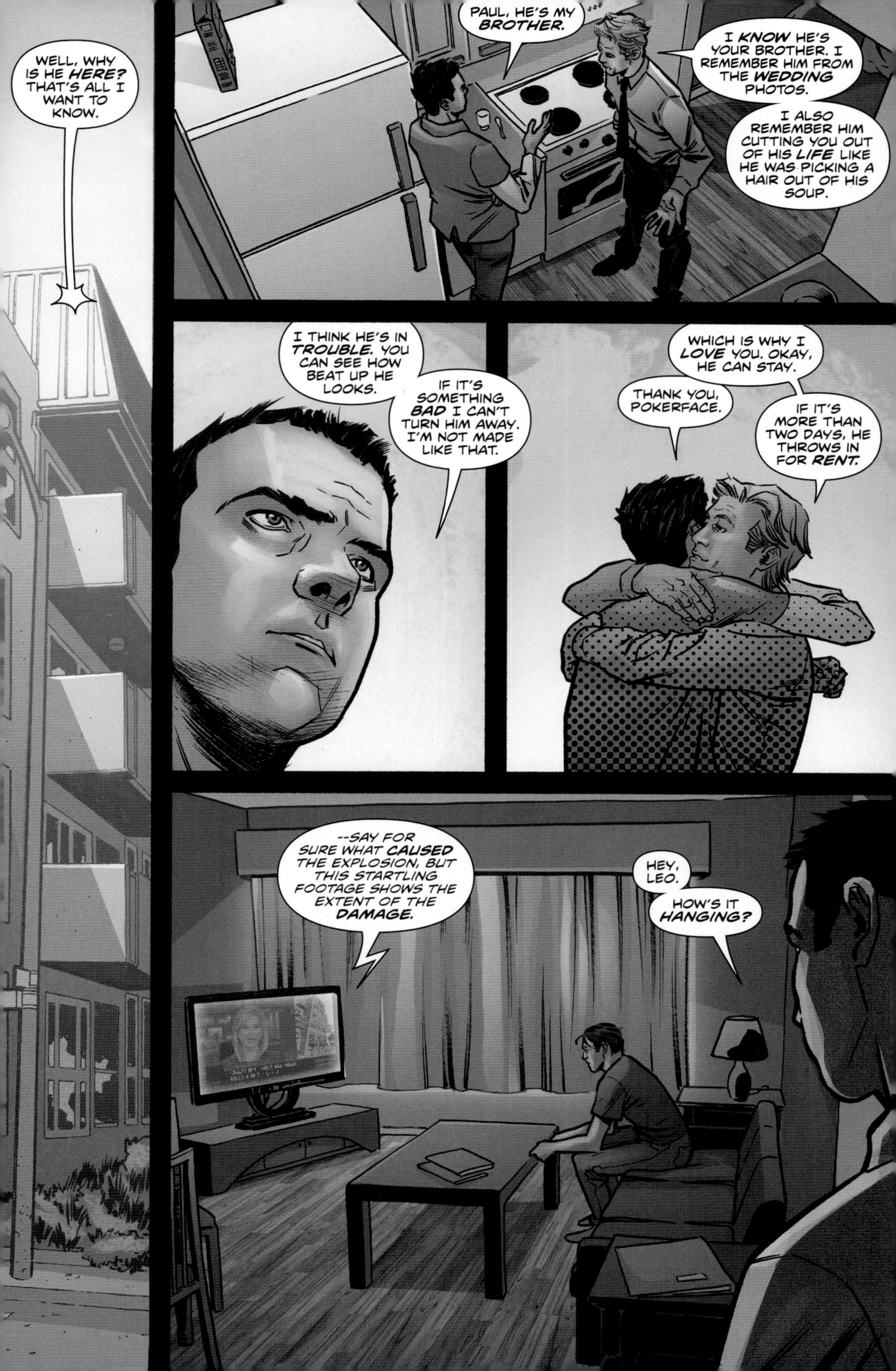
WELL, WHY IS HE HERE? THAT'S ALL I WANT TO KNOW.
PAUL, HE'S MY BROTHER.
I KNOW HE'S YOUR BROTHER. I REMEMBER HIM FROM THE WEDDING PHOTOS.
I ALSO REMEMBER HIM CUTTING YOU OUT OF HIS LIFE LIKE HE WAS PICKING A HAIR OUT OF HIS SOUP.
I THINK HE'S IN TROUBLE. YOU CAN SEE HOW BEAT UP HE LOOKS.
IF IT'S SOMETHING BAD I CAN'T TURN HIM AWAY. I'M NOT MADE LIKE THAT.
WHICH IS WHY I LOVE YOU. OKAY, HE CAN STAY.
THANK YOU, POKERFACE.
IF IT'S MORE THAN TWO DAYS, HE THROWS IN FOR RENT.
--SAY FOR SURE WHAT CAUSED THE EXPLOSION, BUT THIS STARTLING FOOTAGE SHOWS THE EXTENT OF THE DAMAGE.
HEY, LEO.
HOW'S IT HANGING?

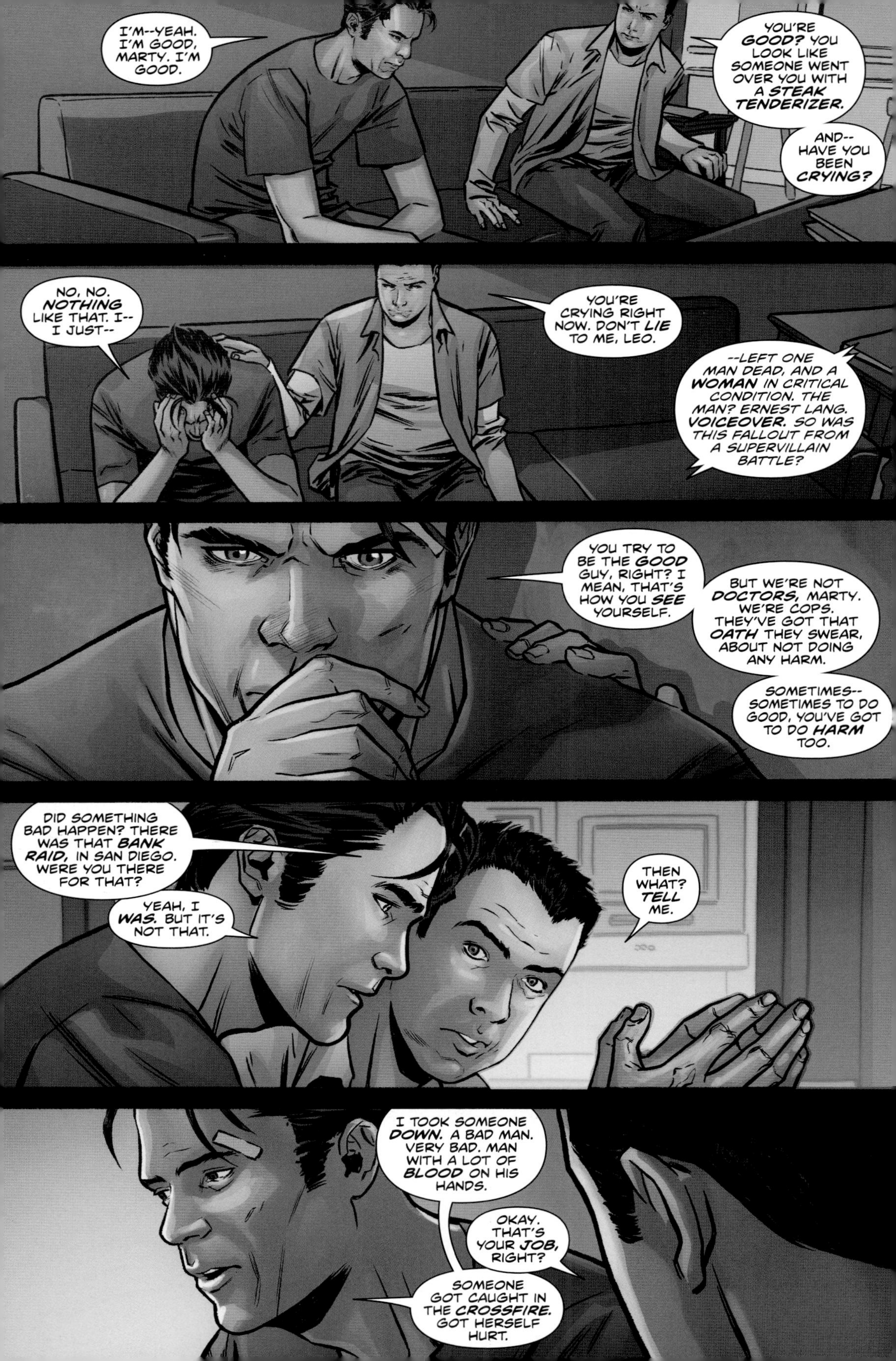

I'M--YEAH. I'M GOOD, MARTY. I'M GOOD.
YOU'RE GOOD? YOU LOOK LIKE SOMEONE WENT OVER YOU WITH A STEAK TENDERIZER.
AND-- HAVE YOU BEEN CRYING?
NO, NO. NOTHING LIKE THAT. I-- I JUST--
YOU'RE CRYING RIGHT NOW. DON'T LIE TO ME, LEO.
--LEFT ONE MAN DEAD, AND A WOMAN IN CRITICAL CONDITION. THE MAN? ERNEST LANG. VOICEOVER. SO WAS THIS FALLOUT FROM A SUPERVILLAIN BATTLE?
YOU TRY TO BE THE GOOD GUY, RIGHT? I MEAN, THAT'S HOW YOU SEE YOURSELF.
BUT WE'RE NOT DOCTORS, MARTY. WE'RE COPS. THEY'VE GOT THAT OATH THEY SWEAR, ABOUT NOT DOING ANY HARM.
SOMETIMES-- SOMETIMES TO DO GOOD, YOU'VE GOT TO DO HARM TOO.
DID SOMETHING BAD HAPPEN? THERE WAS THAT BANK RAID, IN SAN DIEGO. WERE YOU THERE FOR THAT?
YEAH, I WAS. BUT IT'S NOT THAT.
THEN WHAT? TELL ME.
I TOOK SOMEONE DOWN. A BAD MAN. VERY BAD. MAN WITH A LOT OF BLOOD ON HIS HANDS.
OKAY. THAT'S YOUR JOB, RIGHT?
SOMEONE GOT CAUGHT IN THE CROSSFIRE. GOT HERSELF HURT.

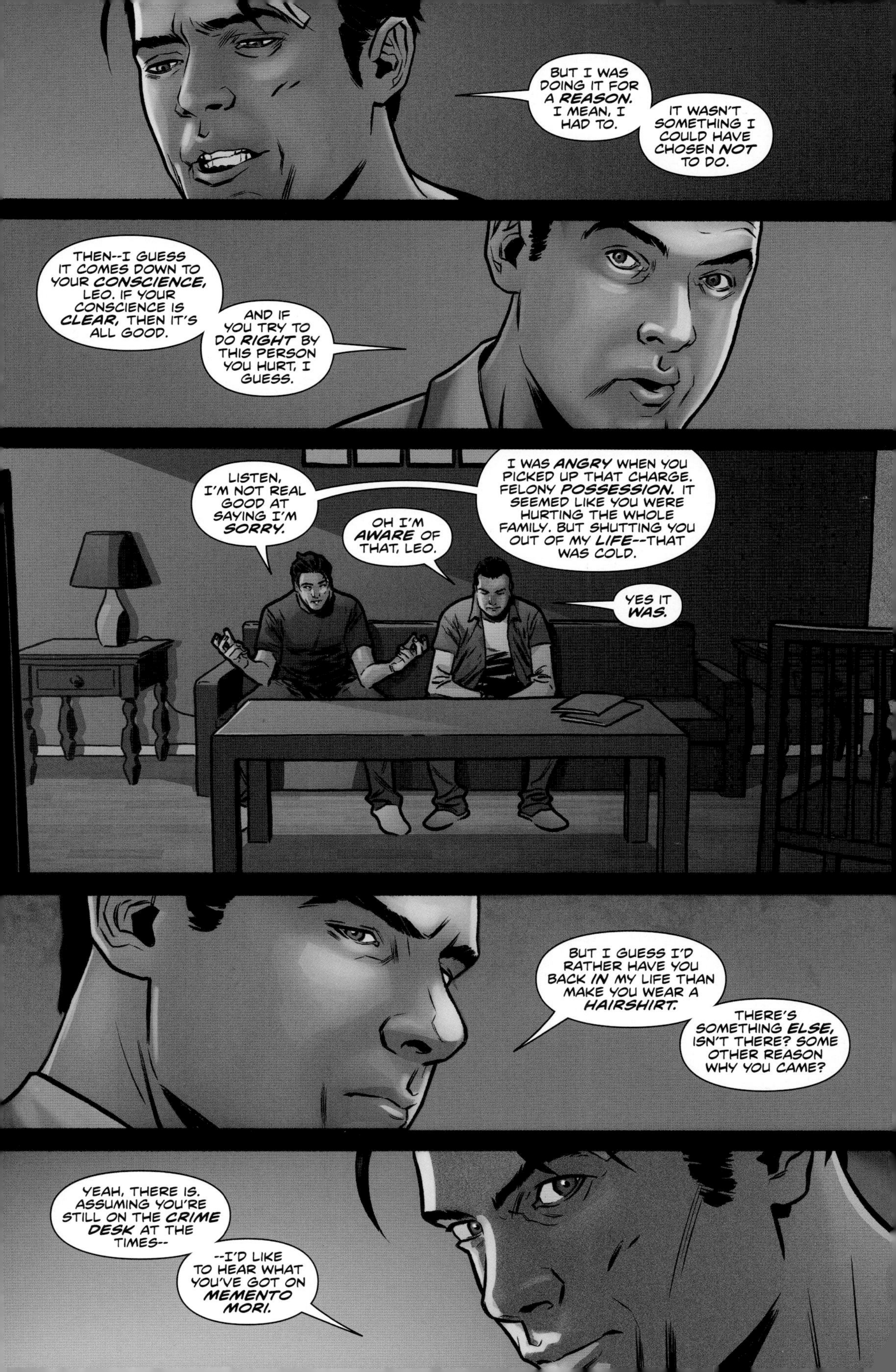
BUT I WAS DOING IT FOR A REASON. I MEAN, I HAD TO.
IT WASN'T SOMETHING I COULD HAVE CHOSEN NOT TO DO.
THEN--I GUESS IT COMES DOWN TO YOUR CONSCIENCE, LEO. IF YOUR CONSCIENCE IS CLEAR, THEN IT'S ALL GOOD.
AND IF YOU TRY TO DO RIGHT BY THIS PERSON YOU HURT, I GUESS.
LISTEN, I'M NOT REAL GOOD AT SAYING I'M SORRY.
OH I'M AWARE OF THAT, LEO.
I WAS ANGRY WHEN YOU PICKED UP THAT CHARGE. FELONY POSSESSION. IT SEEMED LIKE YOU WERE HURTING THE WHOLE FAMILY. BUT SHUTTING YOU OUT OF MY LIFE--THAT WAS COLD.
YES IT WAS.
BUT I GUESS I'D RATHER HAVE YOU BACK IN MY LIFE THAN MAKE YOU WEAR A HAIRSHIRT.
THERE'S SOMETHING ELSE, ISN'T THERE? SOME OTHER REASON WHY YOU CAME?
YEAH, THERE IS. ASSUMING YOU'RE STILL ON THE CRIME DESK AT THE TIMES--
--I'D LIKE TO HEAR WHAT YOU'VE GOT ON MEMENTO MORI.

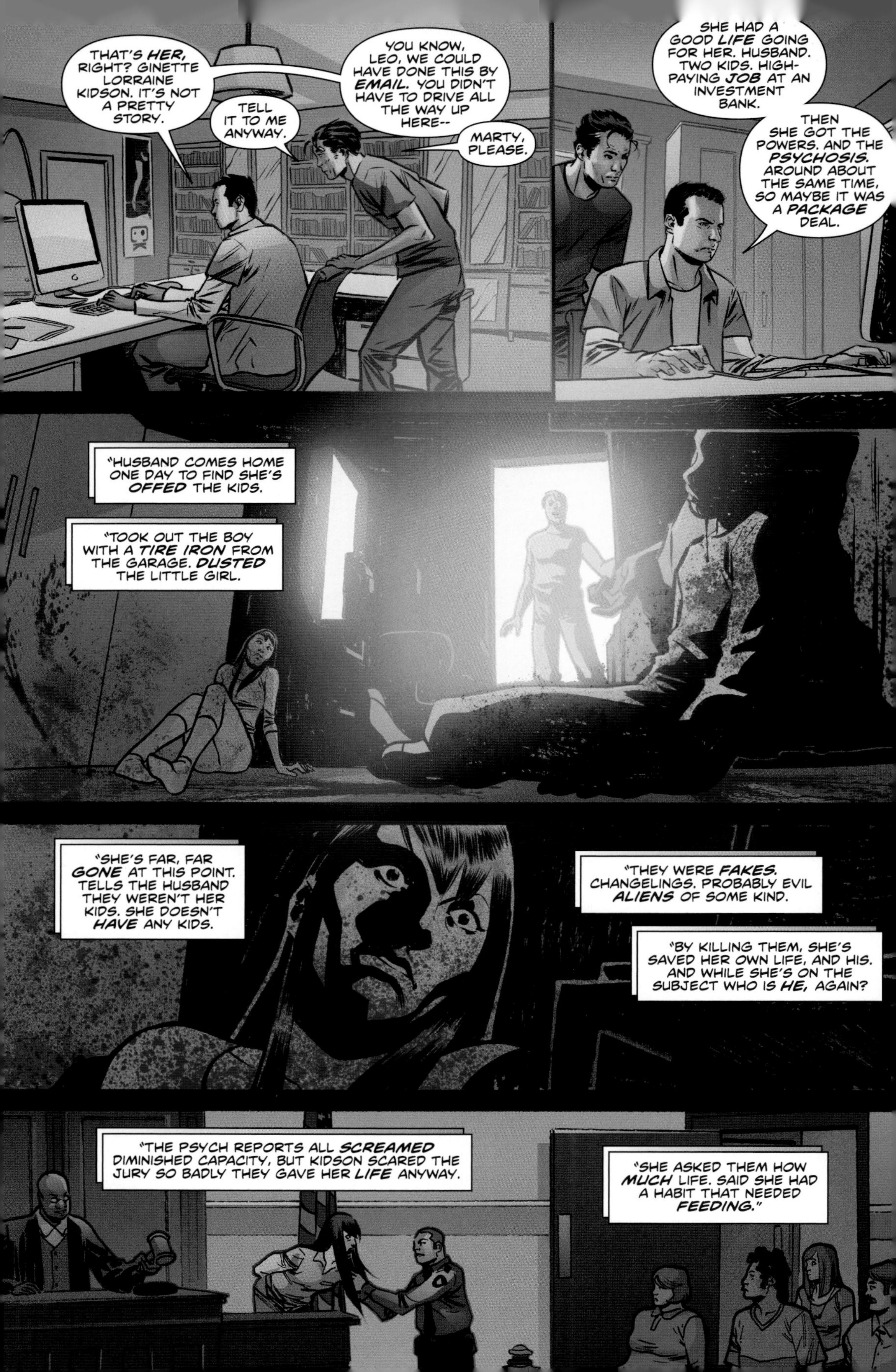
THAT'S HER, RIGHT? GINETTE LORRAINE KIDSON. IT'S NOT A PRETTY STORY.
YOU KNOW, LEO, WE COULD HAVE DONE THIS BY EMAIL. YOU DIDN'T HAVE TO DRIVE ALL THE WAY UP HERE--
TELL IT TO ME ANYWAY.
MARTY, PLEASE.
SHE HAD A GOOD LIFE GOING FOR HER. HUSBAND. TWO KIDS. HIGH-PAYING JOB AT AN INVESTMENT BANK.
THEN SHE GOT THE POWERS. AND THE PSYCHOSIS. AROUND ABOUT THE SAME TIME, SO MAYBE IT WAS A PACKAGE DEAL.
"HUSBAND COMES HOME ONE DAY TO FIND SHE'S OFFED THE KIDS.
"TOOK OUT THE BOY WITH A TIRE IRON FROM THE GARAGE. DUSTED THE LITTLE GIRL.
"SHE'S FAR, FAR GONE AT THIS POINT. TELLS THE HUSBAND THEY WEREN'T HER KIDS. SHE DOESN'T HAVE ANY KIDS.
"THEY WERE FAKES. CHANGELINGS. PROBABLY EVIL ALIENS OF SOME KIND.
"BY KILLING THEM, SHE'S SAVED HER OWN LIFE, AND HIS. AND WHILE SHE'S ON THE SUBJECT WHO IS HE, AGAIN?
"THE PSYCH REPORTS ALL SCREAMED DIMINISHED CAPACITY, BUT KIDSON SCARED THE JURY SO BADLY THEY GAVE HER LIFE ANYWAY.
"SHE ASKED THEM HOW MUCH LIFE. SAID SHE HAD A HABIT THAT NEEDED FEEDING."

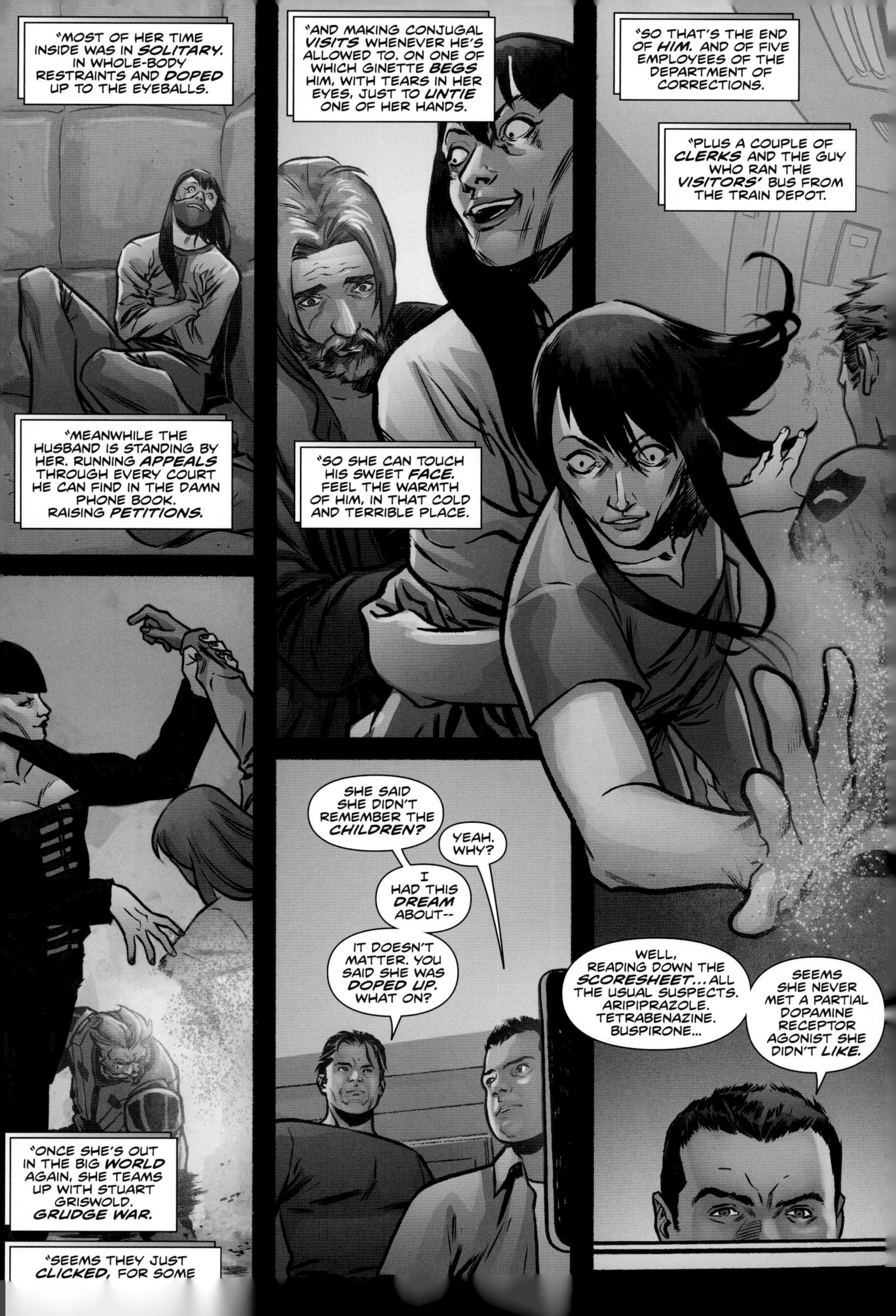
"MOST OF HER TIME INSIDE WAS IN *SOLITARY.* IN WHOLE-BODY RESTRAINTS AND *DOPED* UP TO THE EYEBALLS.
"MEANWHILE THE HUSBAND IS STANDING BY HER. RUNNING *APPEALS* THROUGH EVERY COURT HE CAN FIND IN THE DAMN PHONE BOOK. RAISING *PETITIONS.*
"AND MAKING CONJUGAL *VISITS* WHENEVER HE'S ALLOWED TO. ON ONE OF WHICH GINETTE *BEGS* HIM, WITH TEARS IN HER EYES, JUST TO *UNTIE* ONE OF HER HANDS.
"SO SHE CAN TOUCH HIS SWEET *FACE.* FEEL THE WARMTH OF HIM, IN THAT COLD AND TERRIBLE PLACE.
"SO THAT'S THE END OF *HIM.* AND OF FIVE EMPLOYEES OF THE DEPARTMENT OF CORRECTIONS.
"PLUS A COUPLE OF *CLERKS* AND THE GUY WHO RAN THE *VISITORS'* BUS FROM THE TRAIN DEPOT.
"ONCE SHE'S OUT IN THE BIG *WORLD* AGAIN, SHE TEAMS UP WITH STUART GRISWOLD. *GRUDGE WAR.*
"SEEMS THEY JUST *CLICKED,* FOR SOME
SHE SAID SHE DIDN'T REMEMBER THE *CHILDREN?*
YEAH. WHY?
I HAD THIS *DREAM* ABOUT--
IT DOESN'T MATTER. YOU SAID SHE WAS *DOPED UP.* WHAT ON?
WELL, READING DOWN THE *SCORESHEET...* ALL THE USUAL SUSPECTS. ARIPIPRAZOLE. TETRABENAZINE. BUSPIRONE...
SEEMS SHE NEVER MET A PARTIAL DOPAMINE RECEPTOR AGONIST SHE DIDN'T *LIKE.*

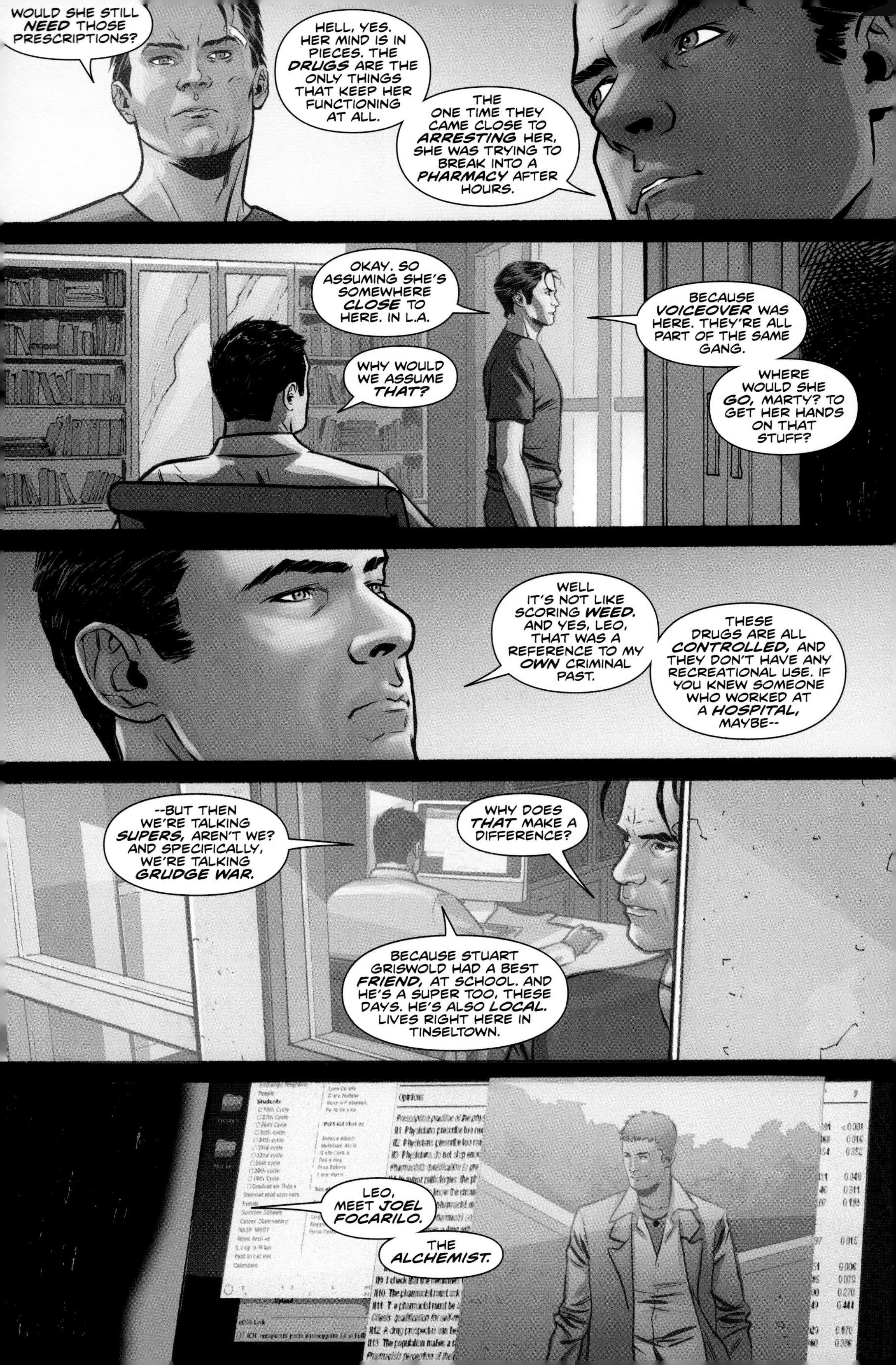
WOULD SHE STILL NEED THOSE PRESCRIPTIONS?
HELL, YES. HER MIND IS IN PIECES. THE DRUGS ARE THE ONLY THINGS THAT KEEP HER FUNCTIONING AT ALL.
THE ONE TIME THEY CAME CLOSE TO ARRESTING HER, SHE WAS TRYING TO BREAK INTO A PHARMACY AFTER HOURS.
OKAY. SO ASSUMING SHE'S SOMEWHERE CLOSE TO HERE. IN L.A.
WHY WOULD WE ASSUME THAT?
BECAUSE VOICEOVER WAS HERE. THEY'RE ALL PART OF THE SAME GANG.
WHERE WOULD SHE GO, MARTY? TO GET HER HANDS ON THAT STUFF?
WELL IT'S NOT LIKE SCORING WEED. AND YES, LEO, THAT WAS A REFERENCE TO MY OWN CRIMINAL PAST.
THESE DRUGS ARE ALL CONTROLLED, AND THEY DON'T HAVE ANY RECREATIONAL USE. IF YOU KNEW SOMEONE WHO WORKED AT A HOSPITAL, MAYBE--
--BUT THEN WE'RE TALKING SUPERS, AREN'T WE? AND SPECIFICALLY, WE'RE TALKING GRUDGE WAR.
WHY DOES THAT MAKE A DIFFERENCE?
BECAUSE STUART GRISWOLD HAD A BEST FRIEND, AT SCHOOL. AND HE'S A SUPER TOO, THESE DAYS. HE'S ALSO LOCAL. LIVES RIGHT HERE IN TINSELTOWN.
LEO, MEET JOEL FOCARILO.
THE ALCHEMIST.

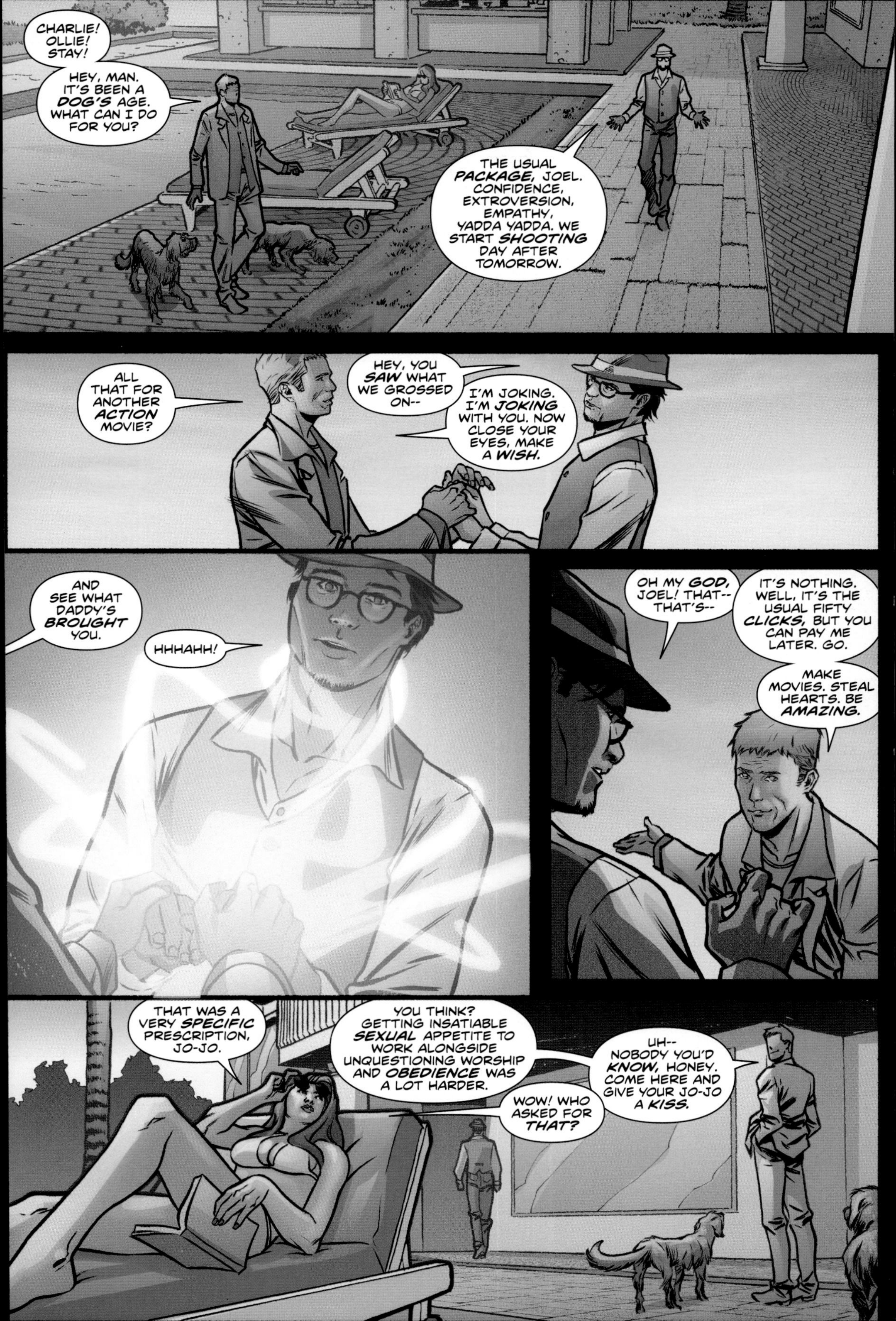
CHARLIE! OLLIE! STAY!
HEY, MAN. IT'S BEEN A DOG'S AGE. WHAT CAN I DO FOR YOU?
THE USUAL PACKAGE, JOEL. CONFIDENCE, EXTROVERSION, EMPATHY, YADDA YADDA. WE START SHOOTING DAY AFTER TOMORROW.
ALL THAT FOR ANOTHER ACTION MOVIE?
HEY, YOU SAW WHAT WE GROSSED ON--
I'M JOKING. I'M JOKING WITH YOU. NOW CLOSE YOUR EYES, MAKE A WISH.
AND SEE WHAT DADDY'S BROUGHT YOU.
HHHAHH!
OH MY GOD, JOEL! THAT-- THAT'S--
IT'S NOTHING. WELL, IT'S THE USUAL FIFTY CLICKS, BUT YOU CAN PAY ME LATER. GO.
MAKE MOVIES. STEAL HEARTS. BE AMAZING.
THAT WAS A VERY SPECIFIC PRESCRIPTION, JO-JO.
YOU THINK? GETTING INSATIABLE SEXUAL APPETITE TO WORK ALONGSIDE UNQUESTIONING WORSHIP AND OBEDIENCE WAS A LOT HARDER.
WOW! WHO ASKED FOR THAT?
UH-- NOBODY YOU'D KNOW, HONEY. COME HERE AND GIVE YOUR JO-JO A KISS.

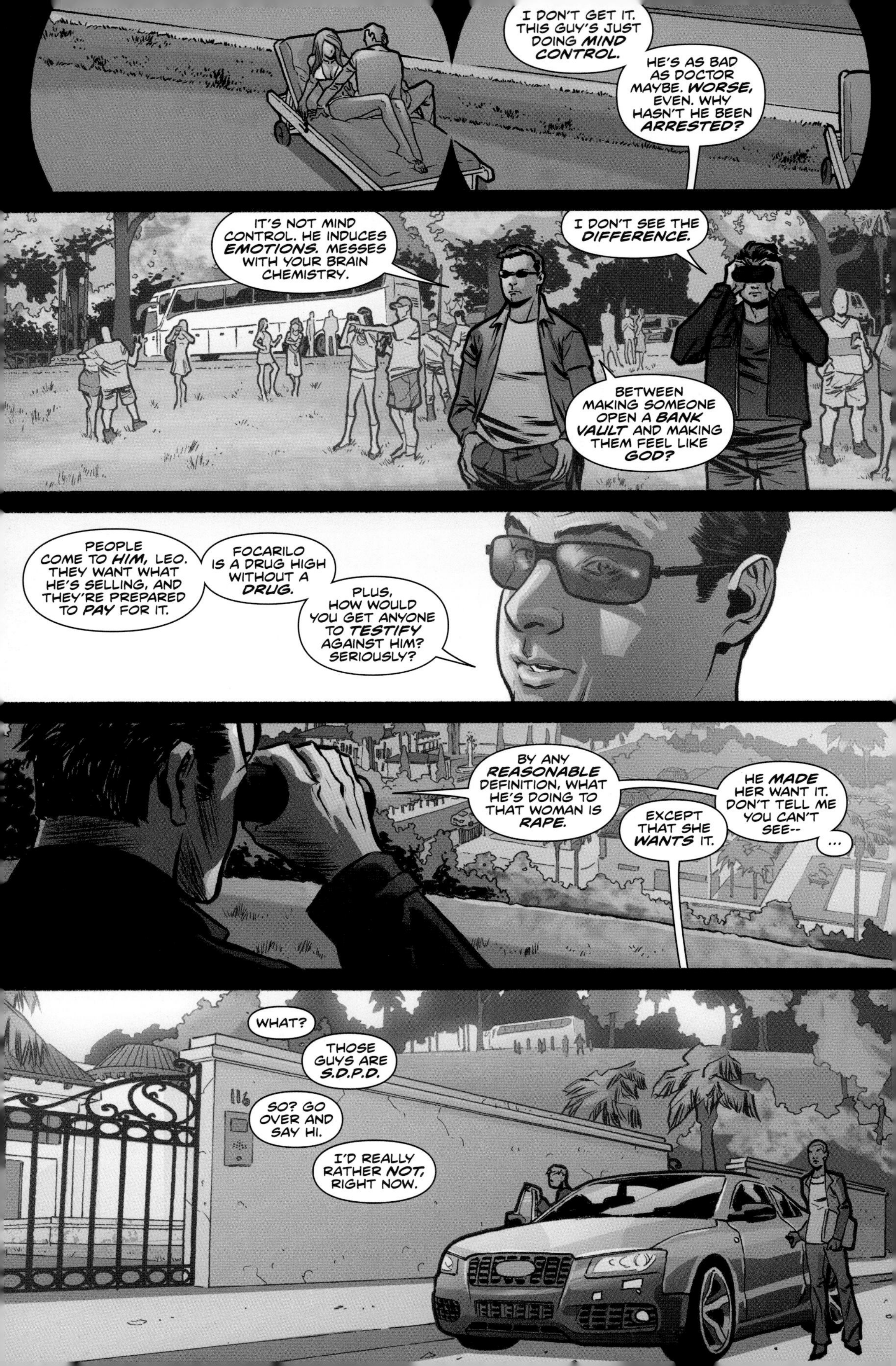
I DON'T GET IT. THIS GUY'S JUST DOING MIND CONTROL.
HE'S AS BAD AS DOCTOR MAYBE. WORSE, EVEN. WHY HASN'T HE BEEN ARRESTED?
IT'S NOT MIND CONTROL. HE INDUCES EMOTIONS. MESSES WITH YOUR BRAIN CHEMISTRY.
I DON'T SEE THE DIFFERENCE.
BETWEEN MAKING SOMEONE OPEN A BANK VAULT AND MAKING THEM FEEL LIKE GOD?
PEOPLE COME TO HIM, LEO. THEY WANT WHAT HE'S SELLING, AND THEY'RE PREPARED TO PAY FOR IT.
FOCARILO IS A DRUG HIGH WITHOUT A DRUG.
PLUS, HOW WOULD YOU GET ANYONE TO TESTIFY AGAINST HIM? SERIOUSLY?
BY ANY REASONABLE DEFINITION, WHAT HE'S DOING TO THAT WOMAN IS RAPE.
EXCEPT THAT SHE WANTS IT.
HE MADE HER WANT IT. DON'T TELL ME YOU CAN'T SEE--
...
WHAT?
THOSE GUYS ARE S.D.P.D.
SO? GO OVER AND SAY HI.
I'D REALLY RATHER NOT, RIGHT NOW.
116

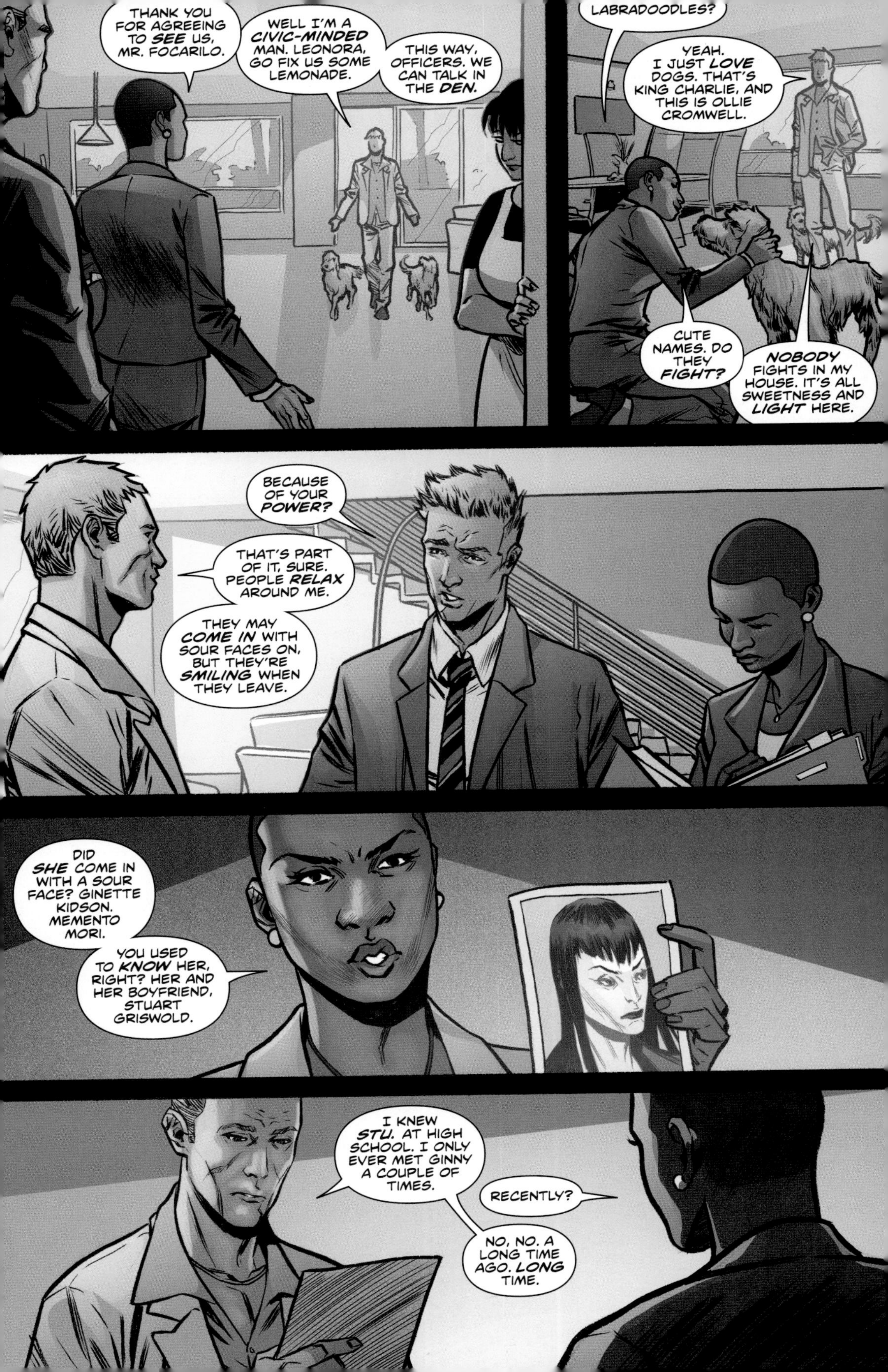
THANK YOU FOR AGREEING TO SEE US, MR. FOCARILO.
WELL I'M A CIVIC-MINDED MAN. LEONORA, GO FIX US SOME LEMONADE.
THIS WAY, OFFICERS. WE CAN TALK IN THE DEN.
LABRADOODLES?
YEAH. I JUST LOVE DOGS. THAT'S KING CHARLIE, AND THIS IS OLLIE CROMWELL.
CUTE NAMES. DO THEY FIGHT?
NOBODY FIGHTS IN MY HOUSE. IT'S ALL SWEETNESS AND LIGHT HERE.
BECAUSE OF YOUR POWER?
THAT'S PART OF IT, SURE. PEOPLE RELAX AROUND ME.
THEY MAY COME IN WITH SOUR FACES ON, BUT THEY'RE SMILING WHEN THEY LEAVE.
DID SHE COME IN WITH A SOUR FACE? GINETTE KIDSON. MEMENTO MORI.
YOU USED TO KNOW HER, RIGHT? HER AND HER BOYFRIEND, STUART GRISWOLD.
I KNEW STU. AT HIGH SCHOOL. I ONLY EVER MET GINNY A COUPLE OF TIMES.
RECENTLY?
NO, NO. A LONG TIME AGO. LONG TIME.

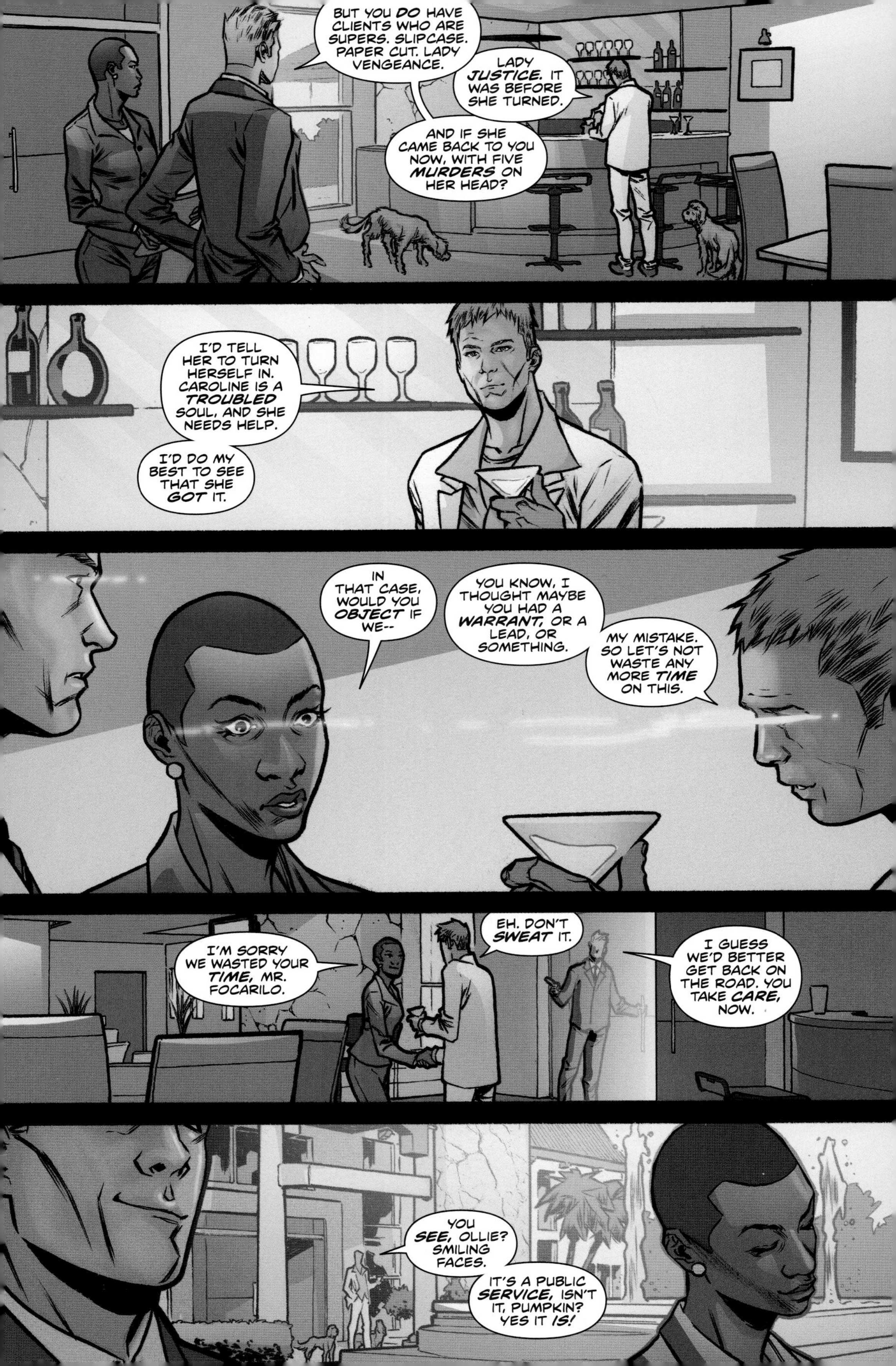
BUT YOU DO HAVE CLIENTS WHO ARE SUPERS. SLIPCASE. PAPER CUT. LADY VENGEANCE.
LADY JUSTICE. IT WAS BEFORE SHE TURNED.
AND IF SHE CAME BACK TO YOU NOW, WITH FIVE MURDERS ON HER HEAD?
I'D TELL HER TO TURN HERSELF IN. CAROLINE IS A TROUBLED SOUL, AND SHE NEEDS HELP.
I'D DO MY BEST TO SEE THAT SHE GOT IT.
IN THAT CASE, WOULD YOU OBJECT IF WE--
YOU KNOW, I THOUGHT MAYBE YOU HAD A WARRANT, OR A LEAD, OR SOMETHING.
MY MISTAKE. SO LET'S NOT WASTE ANY MORE TIME ON THIS.
I'M SORRY WE WASTED YOUR TIME, MR. FOCARILO.
EH. DON'T SWEAT IT.
I GUESS WE'D BETTER GET BACK ON THE ROAD. YOU TAKE CARE, NOW.
YOU SEE, OLLIE? SMILING FACES.
IT'S A PUBLIC SERVICE, ISN'T IT, PUMPKIN? YES IT IS!

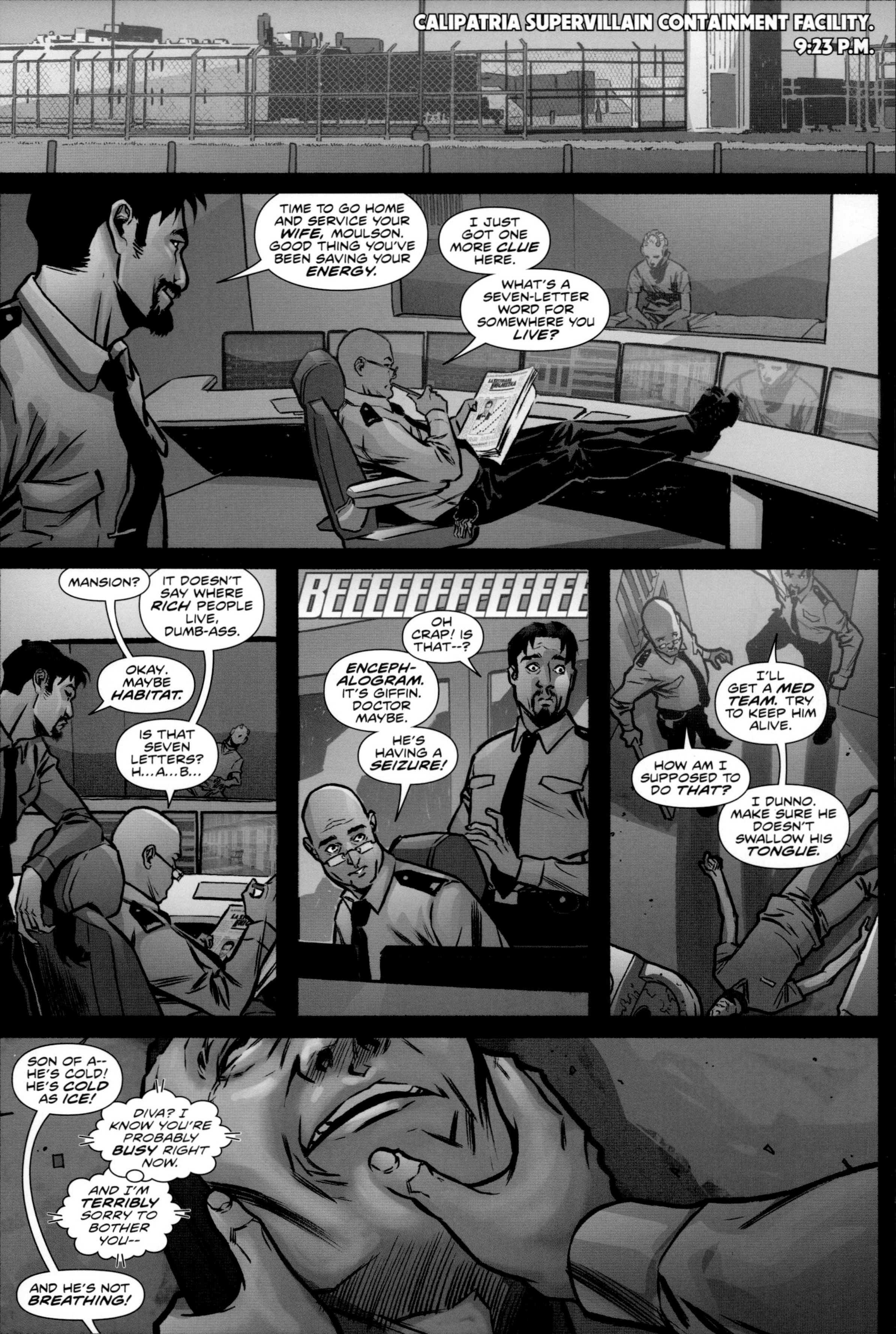
CALIPATRIA SUPERVILLAIN CONTAINMENT FACILITY. 9:23 P.M.
TIME TO GO HOME AND SERVICE YOUR WIFE, MOULSON. GOOD THING YOU'VE BEEN SAVING YOUR ENERGY.
I JUST GOT ONE MORE CLUE HERE.
WHAT'S A SEVEN-LETTER WORD FOR SOMEWHERE YOU LIVE?
MANSION?
IT DOESN'T SAY WHERE RICH PEOPLE LIVE, DUMB-ASS.
OKAY. MAYBE HABITAT.
IS THAT SEVEN LETTERS? H...A...B...
BEEEEEEEEEEEEE
OH CRAP! IS THAT--?
ENCEPH-ALOGRAM. IT'S GIFFIN. DOCTOR MAYBE.
HE'S HAVING A SEIZURE!
I'LL GET A MED TEAM. TRY TO KEEP HIM ALIVE.
HOW AM I SUPPOSED TO DO THAT?
I DUNNO. MAKE SURE HE DOESN'T SWALLOW HIS TONGUE.
SON OF A-- HE'S COLD! HE'S COLD AS ICE!
DIVA? I KNOW YOU'RE PROBABLY BUSY RIGHT NOW.
AND I'M TERRIBLY SORRY TO BOTHER YOU--
AND HE'S NOT BREATHING!

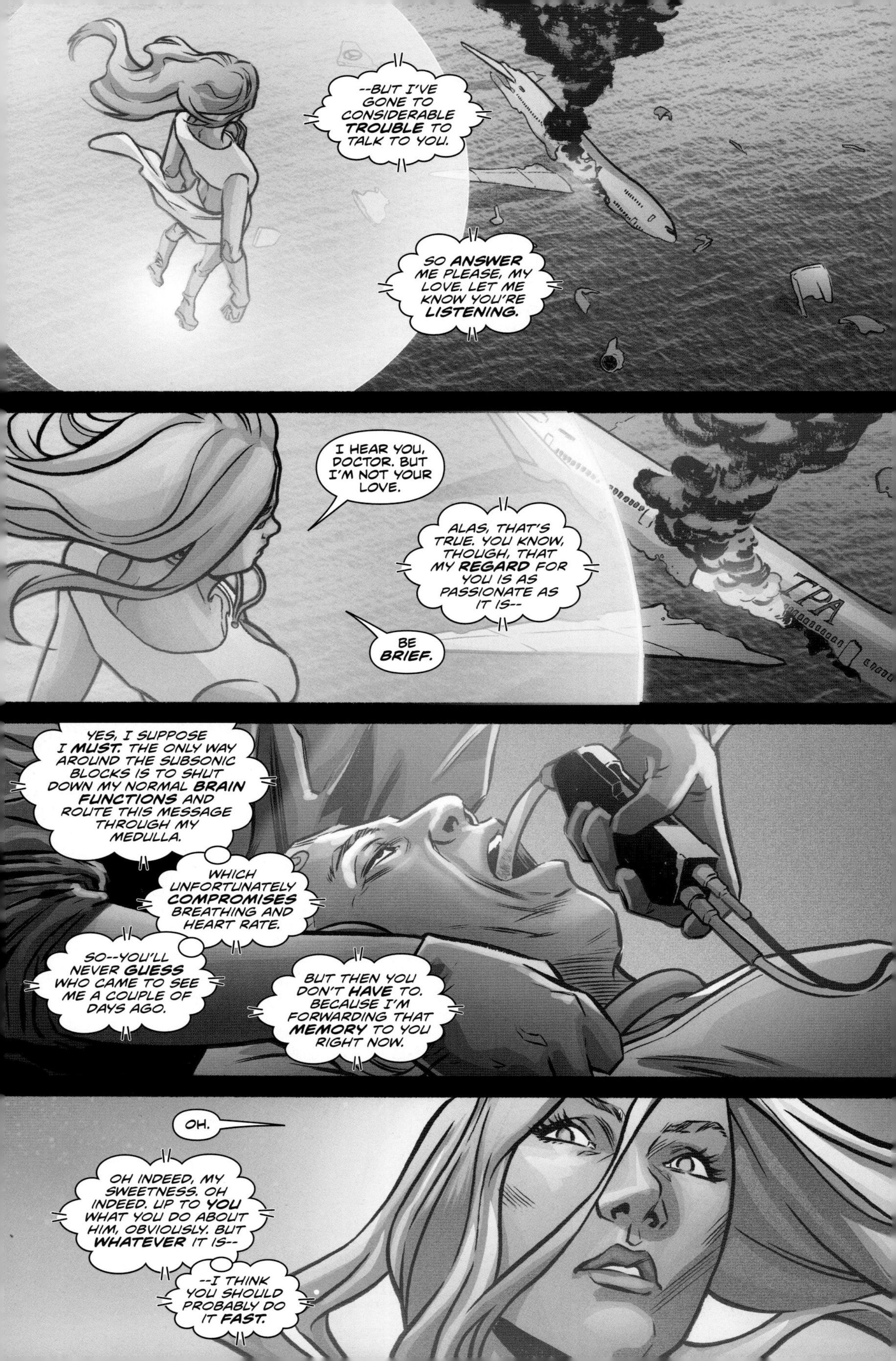

--BUT I'VE GONE TO CONSIDERABLE TROUBLE TO TALK TO YOU.
SO ANSWER ME PLEASE, MY LOVE. LET ME KNOW YOU'RE LISTENING.
I HEAR YOU, DOCTOR. BUT I'M NOT YOUR LOVE.
ALAS, THAT'S TRUE. YOU KNOW, THOUGH, THAT MY REGARD FOR YOU IS AS PASSIONATE AS IT IS--
TPA
BE BRIEF.
YES, I SUPPOSE I MUST. THE ONLY WAY AROUND THE SUBSONIC BLOCKS IS TO SHUT DOWN MY NORMAL BRAIN FUNCTIONS AND ROUTE THIS MESSAGE THROUGH MY MEDULLA.
WHICH UNFORTUNATELY COMPROMISES BREATHING AND HEART RATE.
SO--YOU'LL NEVER GUESS WHO CAME TO SEE ME A COUPLE OF DAYS AGO.
BUT THEN YOU DON'T HAVE TO. BECAUSE I'M FORWARDING THAT MEMORY TO YOU RIGHT NOW.
OH.
OH INDEED, MY SWEETNESS. OH INDEED. UP TO YOU WHAT YOU DO ABOUT HIM, OBVIOUSLY. BUT WHATEVER IT IS--
--I THINK YOU SHOULD PROBABLY DO IT FAST.

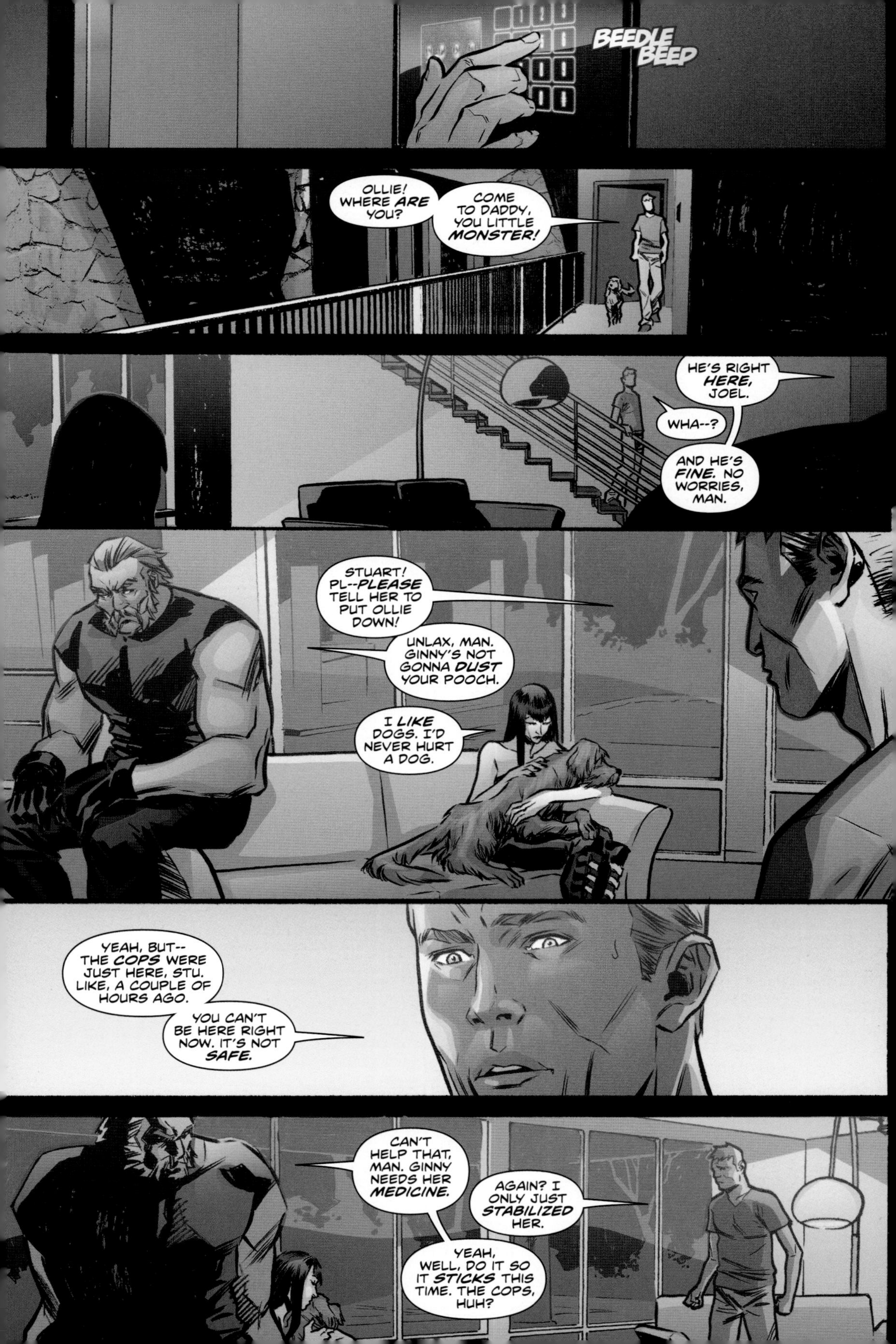
BEEDLE BEEP
OLLIE! WHERE ARE YOU?
COME TO DADDY, YOU LITTLE MONSTER!
HE'S RIGHT HERE, JOEL.
WHA--?
AND HE'S FINE. NO WORRIES, MAN.
STUART! PL--PLEASE TELL HER TO PUT OLLIE DOWN!
UNLAX, MAN. GINNY'S NOT GONNA DUST YOUR POOCH.
I LIKE DOGS. I'D NEVER HURT A DOG.
YEAH, BUT-- THE COPS WERE JUST HERE, STU. LIKE, A COUPLE OF HOURS AGO.
YOU CAN'T BE HERE RIGHT NOW. IT'S NOT SAFE.
CAN'T HELP THAT, MAN. GINNY NEEDS HER MEDICINE.
AGAIN? I ONLY JUST STABILIZED HER.
YEAH, WELL, DO IT SO IT STICKS THIS TIME. THE COPS, HUH?

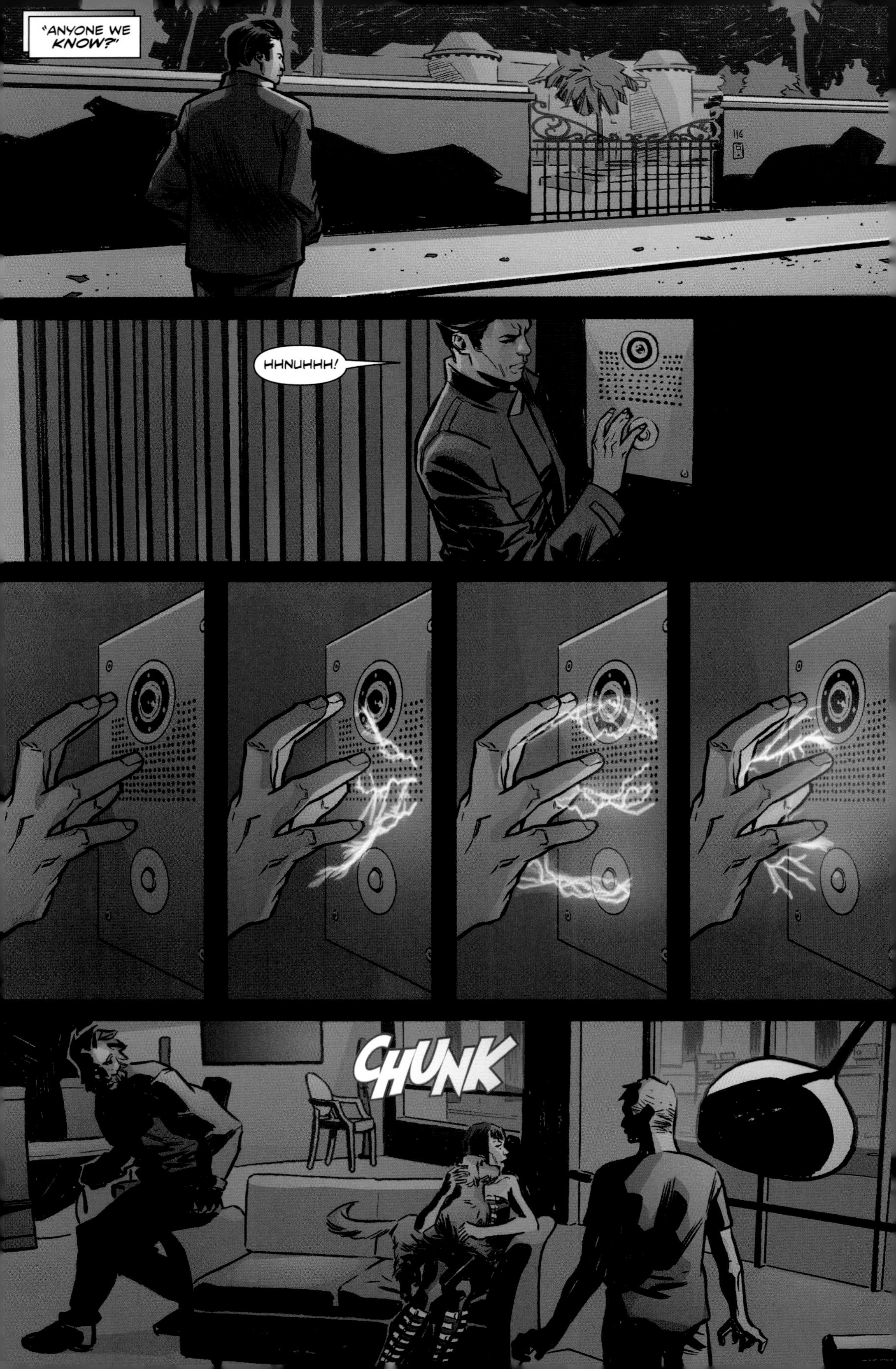
"ANYONE WE KNOW?"
HHNUHHH!
CHUNK

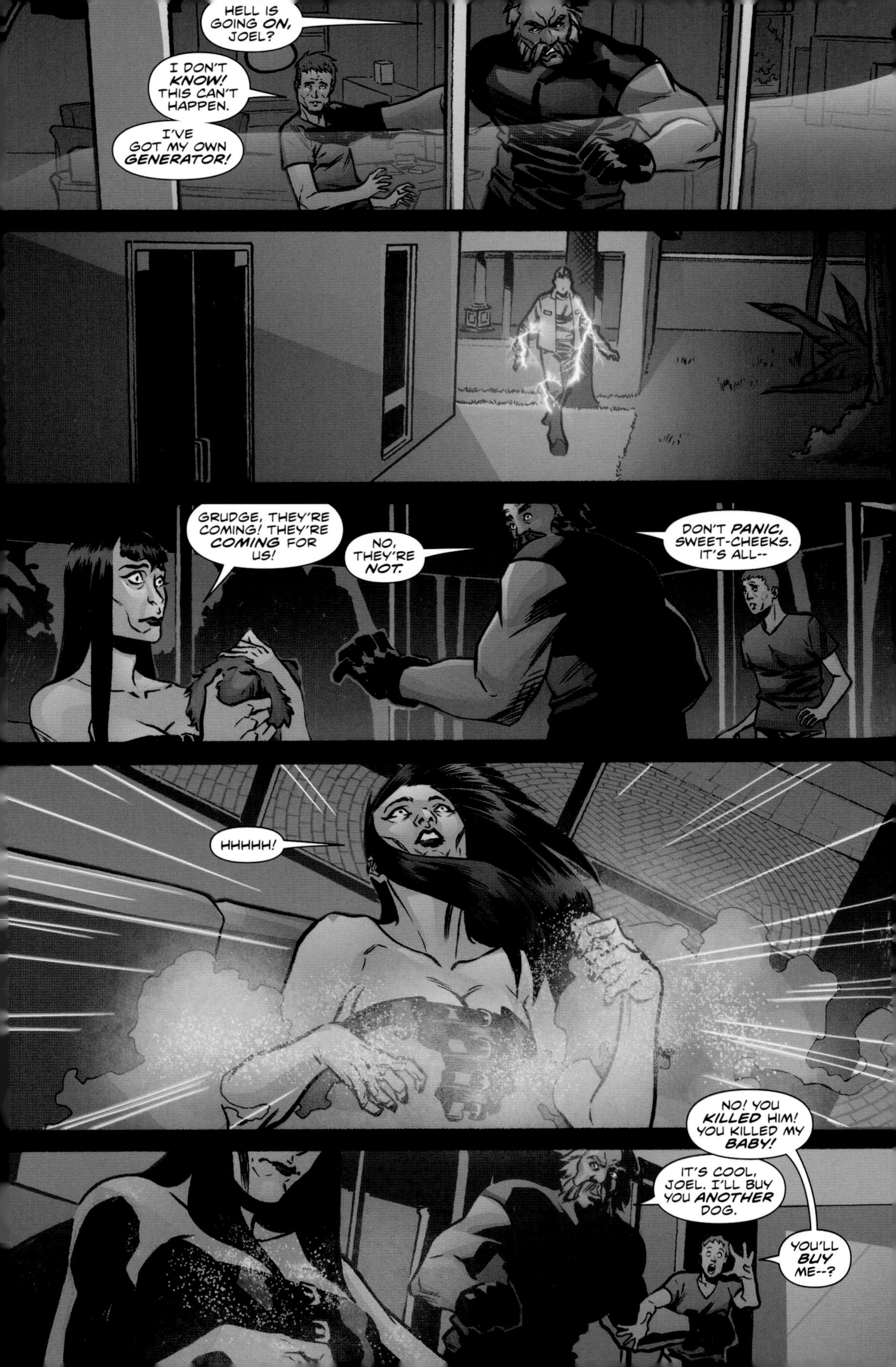
HELL IS GOING ON, JOEL?
I DON'T KNOW! THIS CAN'T HAPPEN.
I'VE GOT MY OWN GENERATOR!
GRUDGE, THEY'RE COMING! THEY'RE COMING FOR US!
NO, THEY'RE NOT.
DON'T PANIC, SWEET-CHEEKS. IT'S ALL--
HHHHH!
NO! YOU KILLED HIM! YOU KILLED MY BABY!
IT'S COOL, JOEL. I'LL BUY YOU ANOTHER DOG.
YOU'LL BUY ME--?

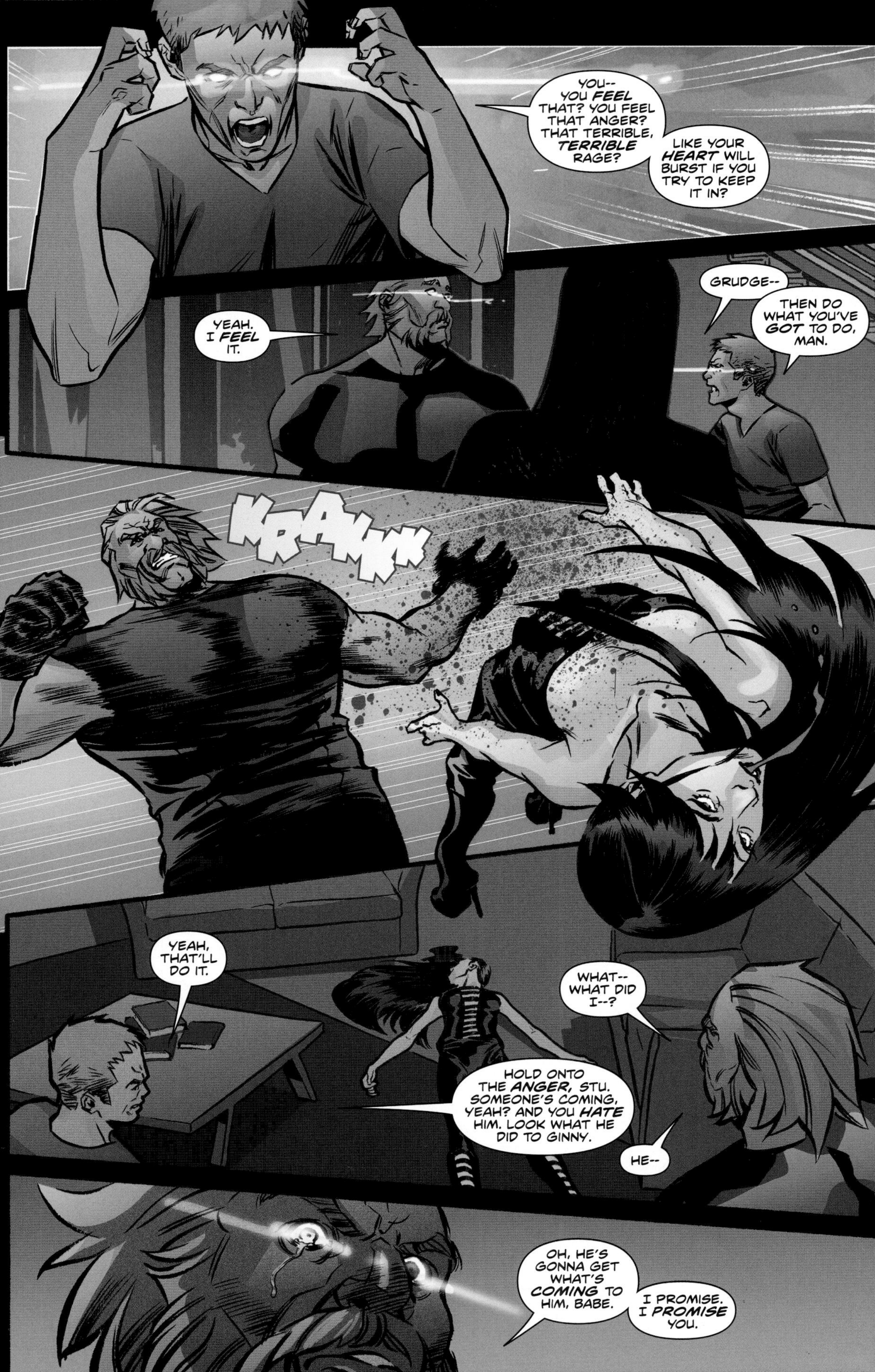
YOU-- YOU FEEL THAT? YOU FEEL THAT ANGER? THAT TERRIBLE, TERRIBLE RAGE?
LIKE YOUR HEART WILL BURST IF YOU TRY TO KEEP IT IN?
YEAH. I FEEL IT.
GRUDGE--
THEN DO WHAT YOU'VE GOT TO DO, MAN.
KRAANKK
YEAH, THAT'LL DO IT.
WHAT-- WHAT DID I--?
HOLD ONTO THE ANGER, STU. SOMEONE'S COMING, YEAH? AND YOU HATE HIM. LOOK WHAT HE DID TO GINNY.
HE--
OH, HE'S GONNA GET WHAT'S COMING TO HIM, BABE.
I PROMISE. I PROMISE YOU.

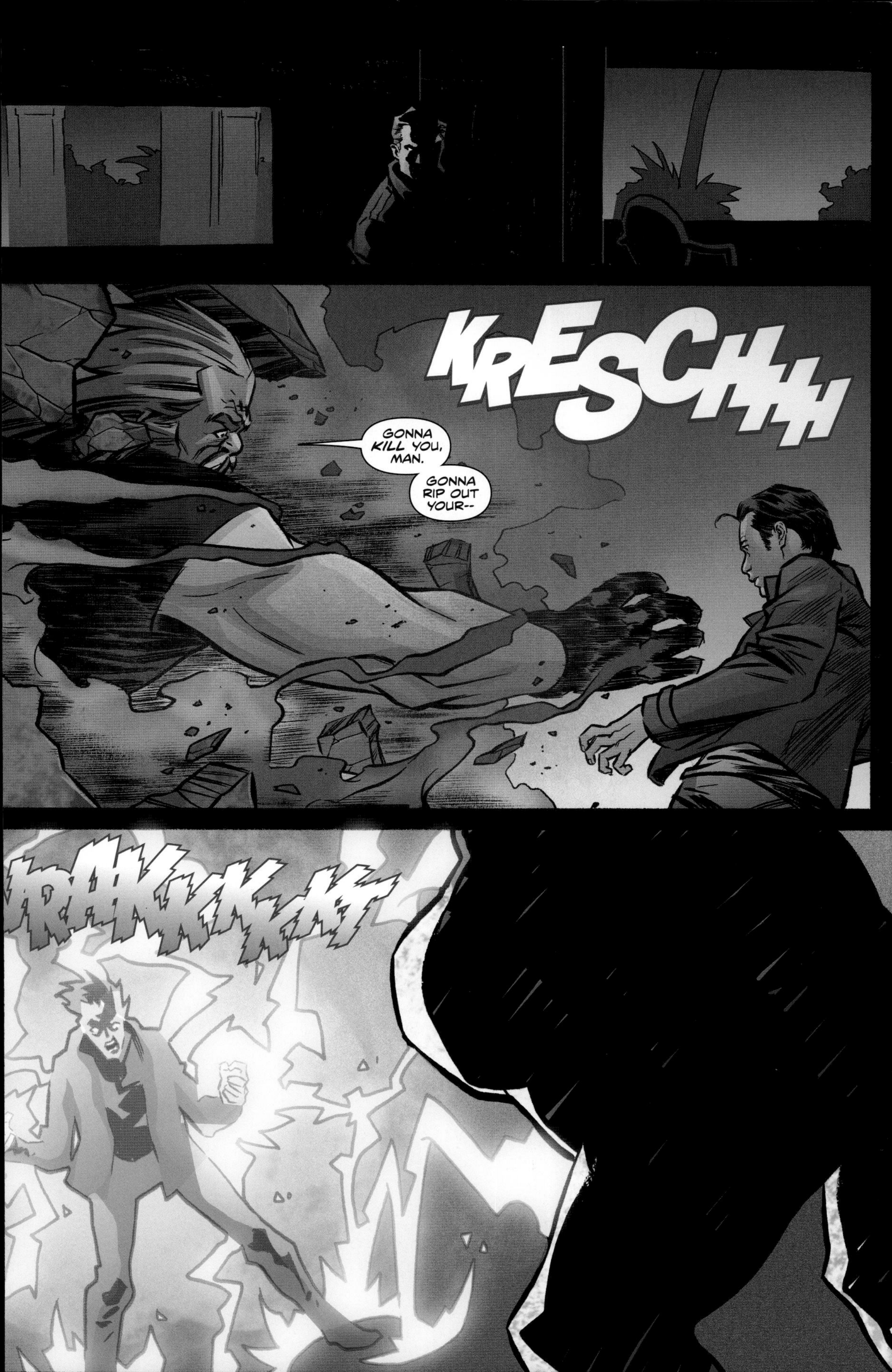
KRESCHHH
GONNA KILL YOU, MAN.
GONNA RIP OUT YOUR--

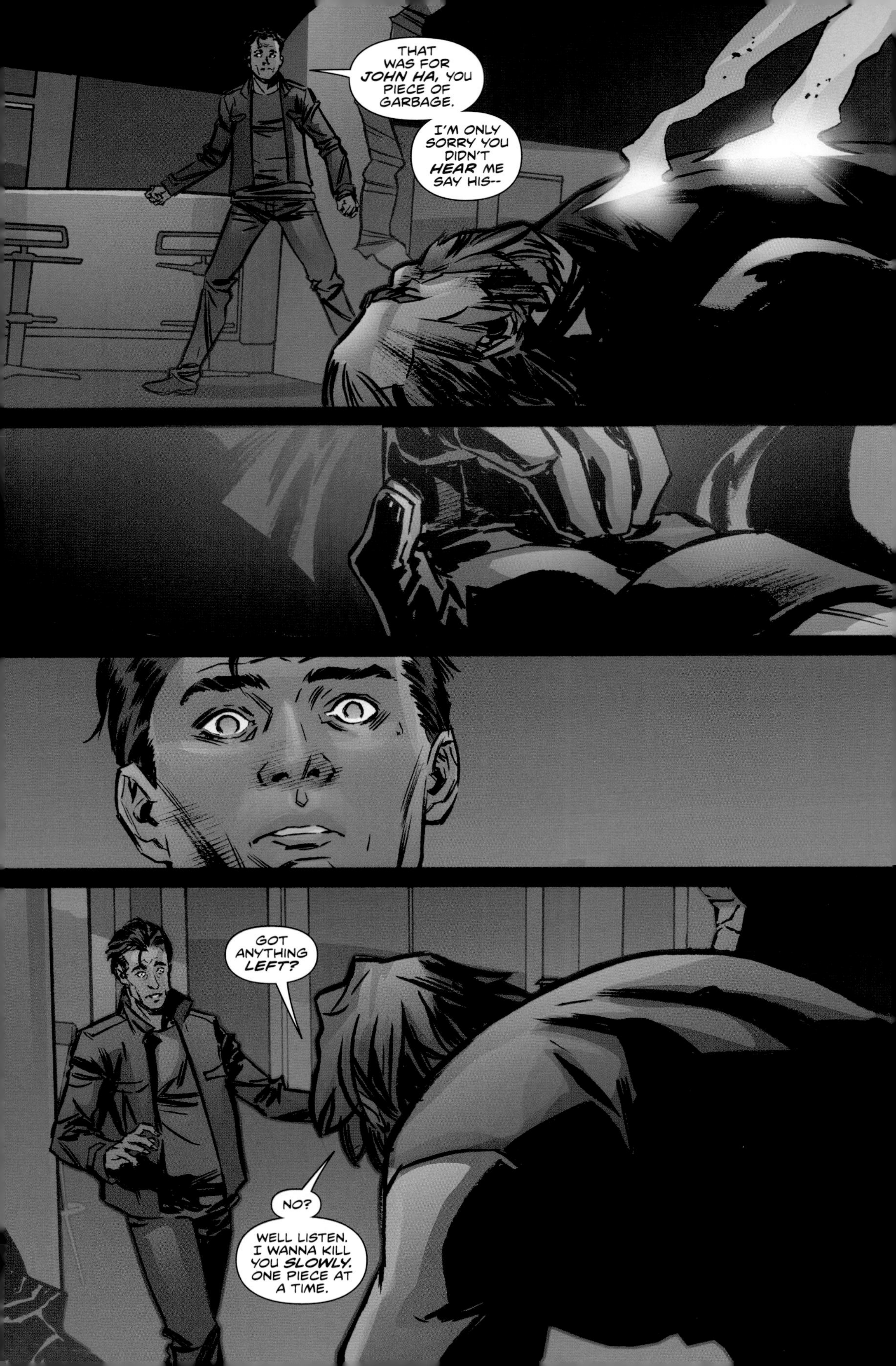
THAT WAS FOR JOHN HA, YOU PIECE OF GARBAGE.
I'M ONLY SORRY YOU DIDN'T HEAR ME SAY HIS--
GOT ANYTHING LEFT?
NO?
WELL LISTEN. I WANNA KILL YOU SLOWLY. ONE PIECE AT A TIME.

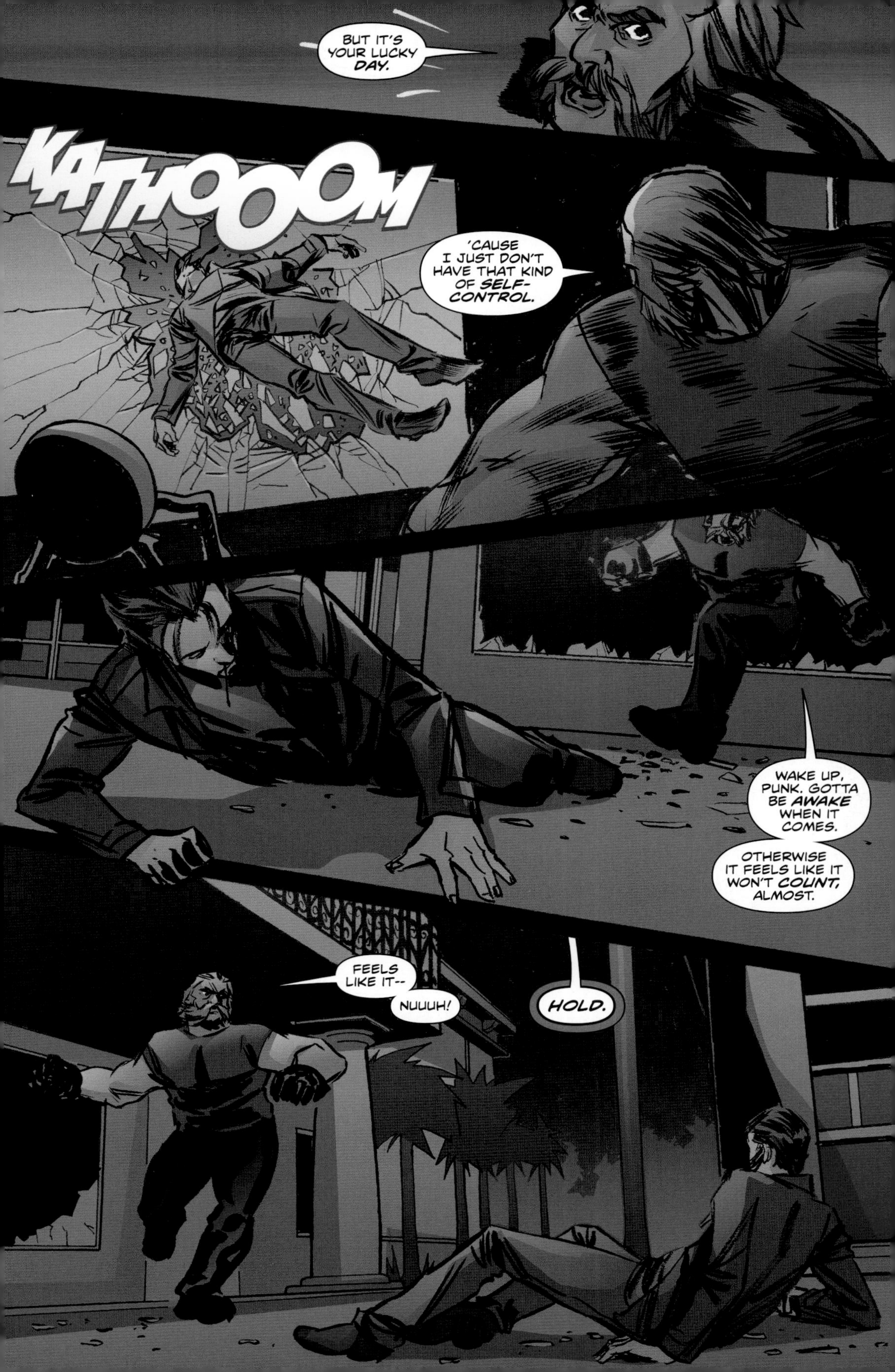

BUT IT'S YOUR LUCKY DAY.
KATHOOOOM
'CAUSE I JUST DON'T HAVE THAT KIND OF SELF-CONTROL.
WAKE UP, PUNK. GOTTA BE AWAKE WHEN IT COMES.
OTHERWISE IT FEELS LIKE IT WON'T COUNT, ALMOST.
FEELS LIKE IT--
NUUUH!
HOLD.

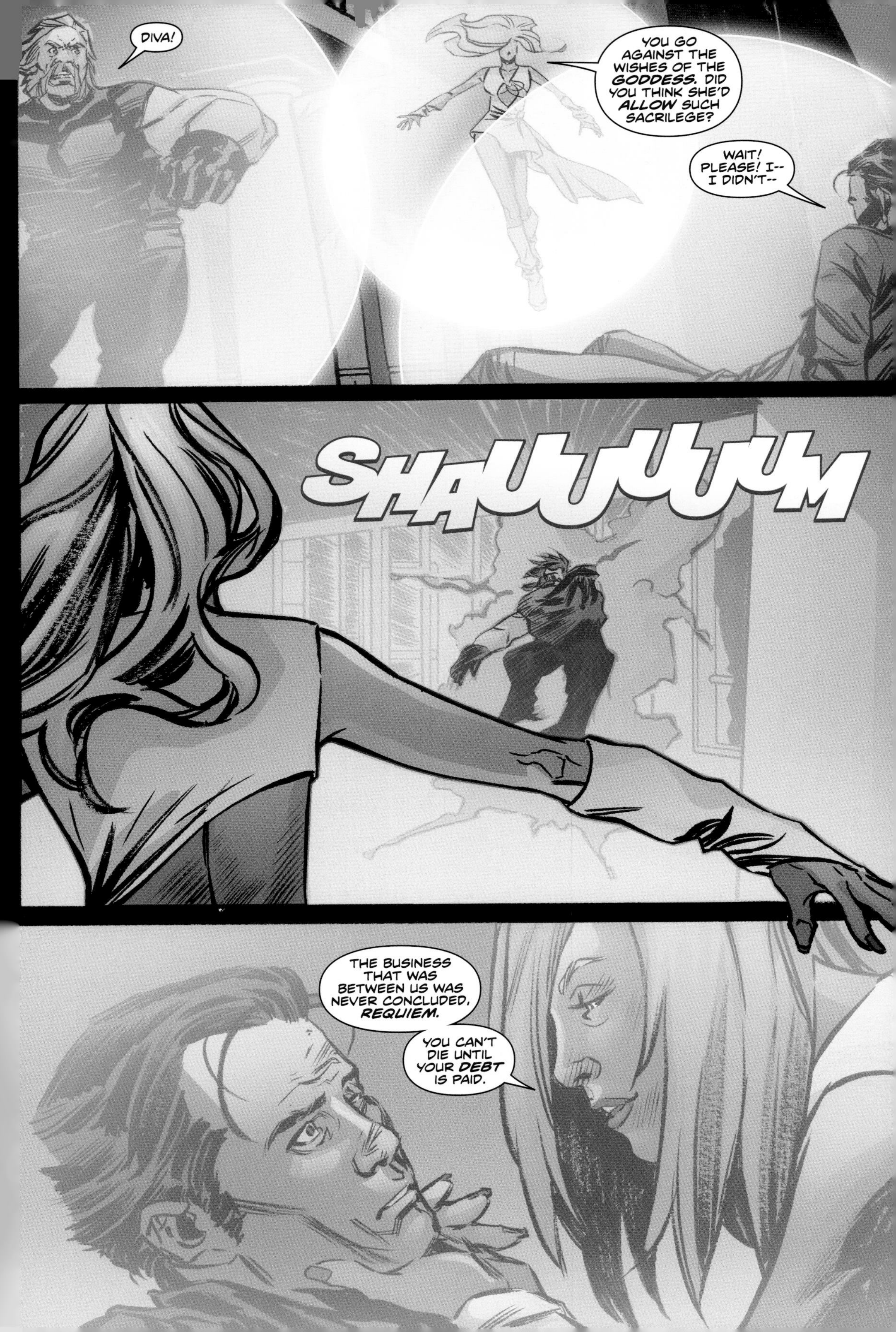
DIVA!
YOU GO AGAINST THE WISHES OF THE GODDESS. DID YOU THINK SHE'D ALLOW SUCH SACRILEGE?
WAIT! PLEASE! I-- I DIDN'T--
SHAUUUUUM
THE BUSINESS THAT WAS BETWEEN US WAS NEVER CONCLUDED, REQUIEM.
YOU CAN'T DIE UNTIL YOUR DEBT IS PAID.

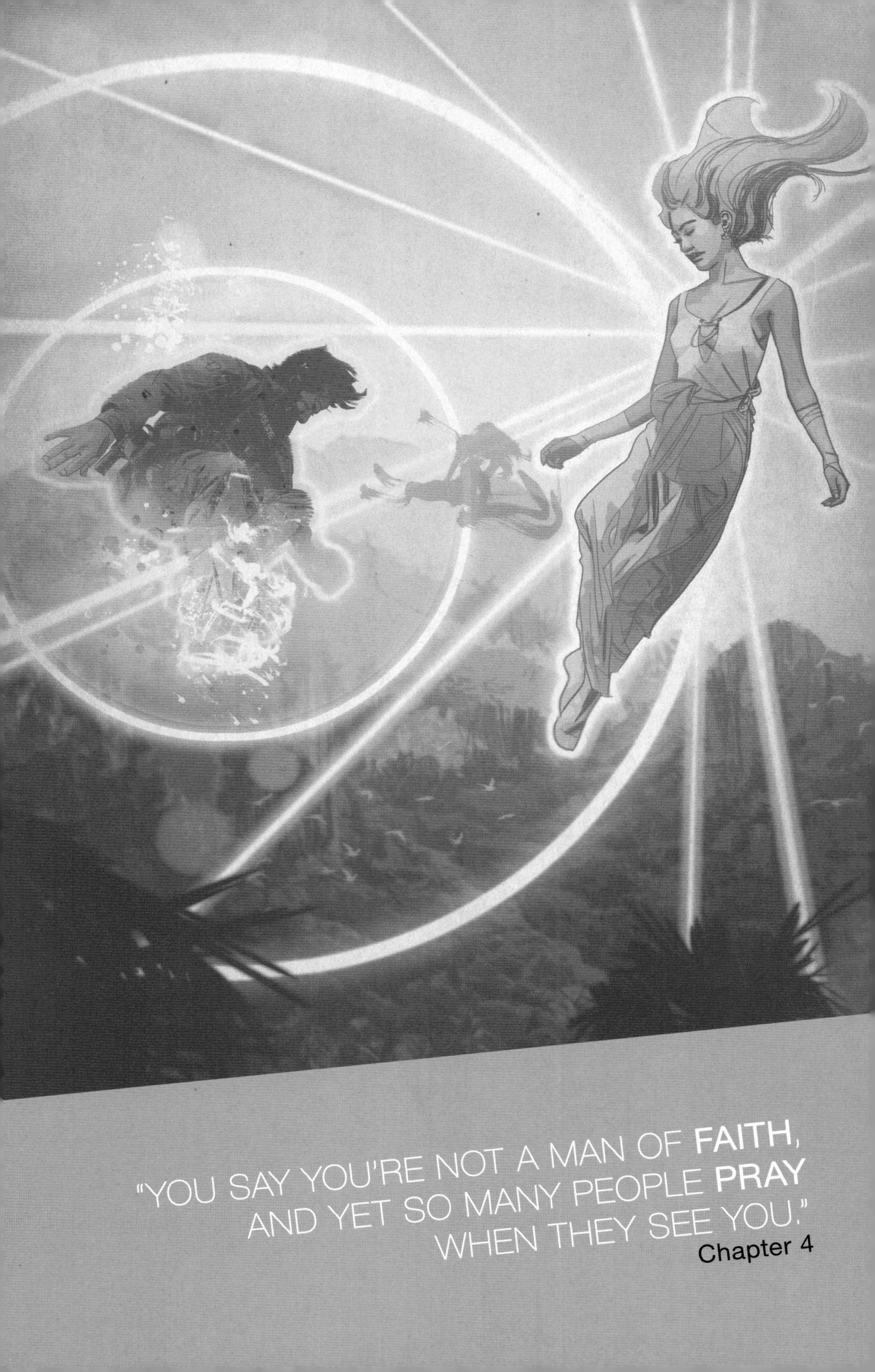

"YOU SAY YOU'RE NOT A MAN OF **FAITH**,
AND YET SO MANY PEOPLE **PRAY**
WHEN THEY SEE YOU."
Chapter 4

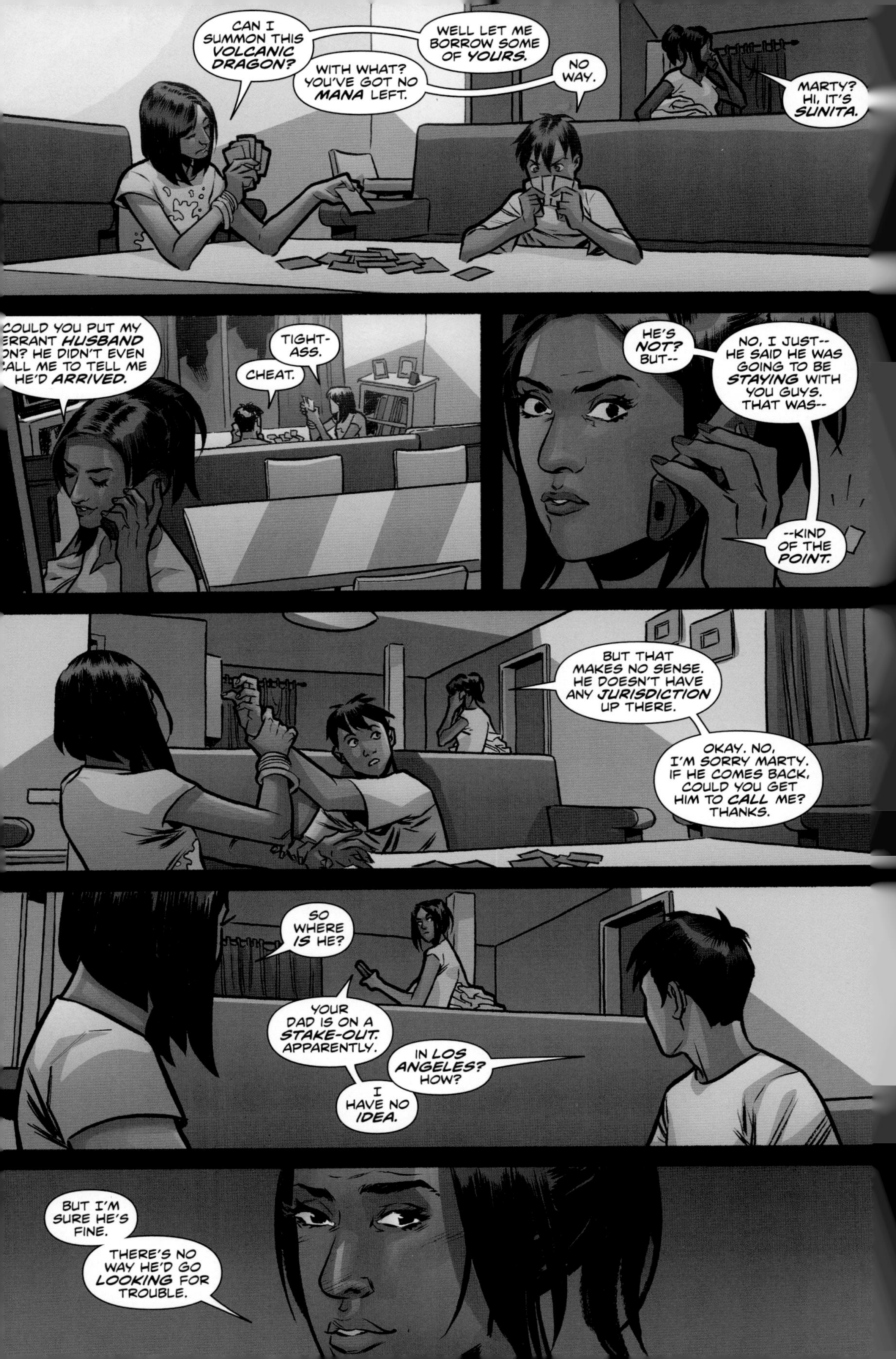
CAN I SUMMON THIS VOLCANIC DRAGON?
WITH WHAT? YOU'VE GOT NO MANA LEFT.
WELL LET ME BORROW SOME OF YOURS.
NO WAY.
MARTY? HI, IT'S SUNITA.
COULD YOU PUT MY ERRANT HUSBAND ON? HE DIDN'T EVEN CALL ME TO TELL ME HE'D ARRIVED.
CHEAT.
TIGHT-ASS.
HE'S NOT? BUT--
NO, I JUST-- HE SAID HE WAS GOING TO BE STAYING WITH YOU GUYS. THAT WAS--
--KIND OF THE POINT.
BUT THAT MAKES NO SENSE. HE DOESN'T HAVE ANY JURISDICTION UP THERE.
OKAY. NO, I'M SORRY MARTY. IF HE COMES BACK, COULD YOU GET HIM TO CALL ME? THANKS.
SO WHERE IS HE?
YOUR DAD IS ON A STAKE-OUT. APPARENTLY.
IN LOS ANGELES? HOW?
I HAVE NO IDEA.
BUT I'M SURE HE'S FINE.
THERE'S NO WAY HE'D GO LOOKING FOR TROUBLE.

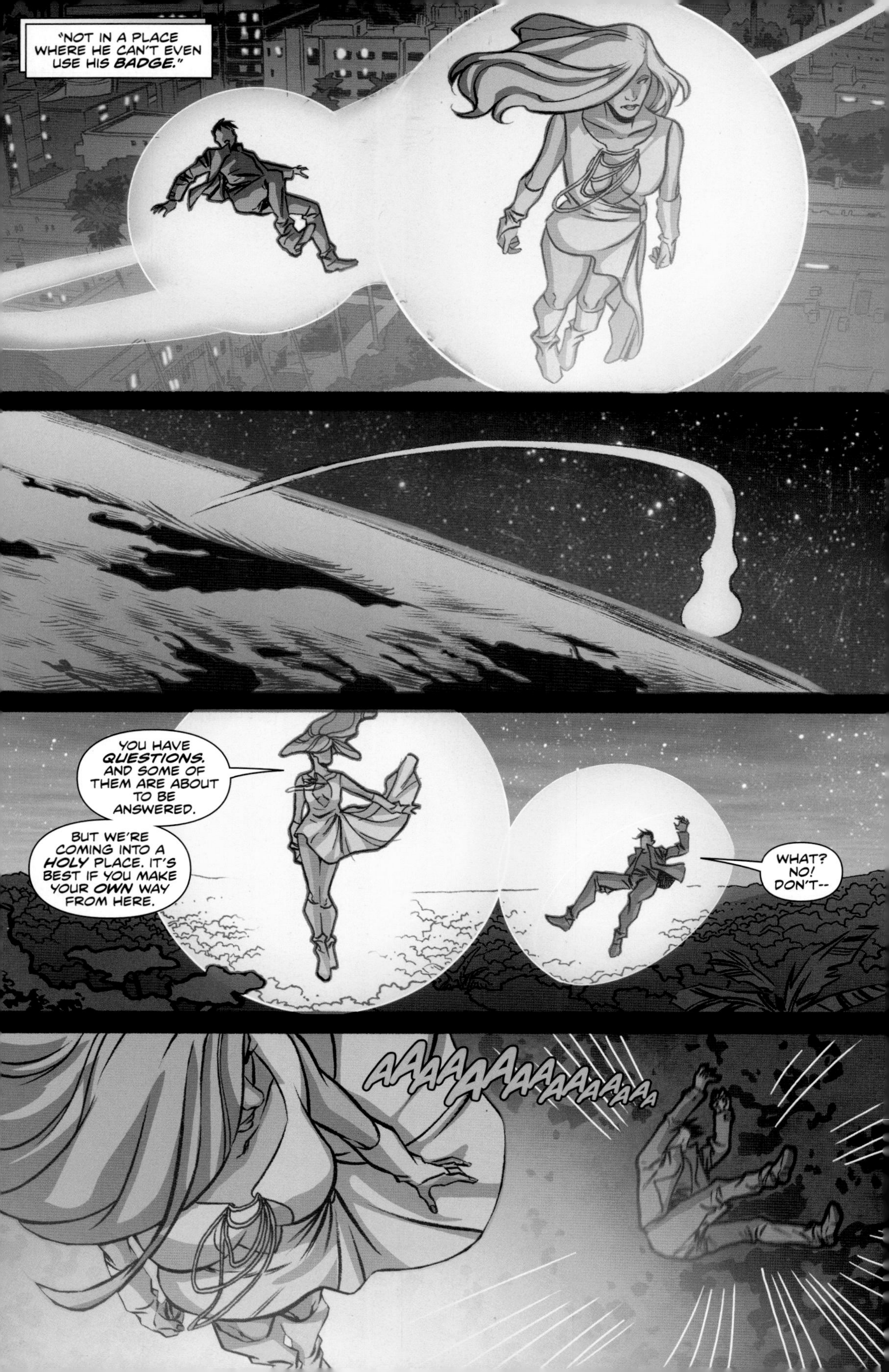
"NOT IN A PLACE WHERE HE CAN'T EVEN USE HIS *BADGE*."
YOU HAVE *QUESTIONS*. AND SOME OF THEM ARE ABOUT TO BE ANSWERED.
BUT WE'RE COMING INTO A *HOLY* PLACE. IT'S BEST IF YOU MAKE YOUR *OWN* WAY FROM HERE.
WHAT? NO! DON'T--
AAAAAAAAAAAAAAAA

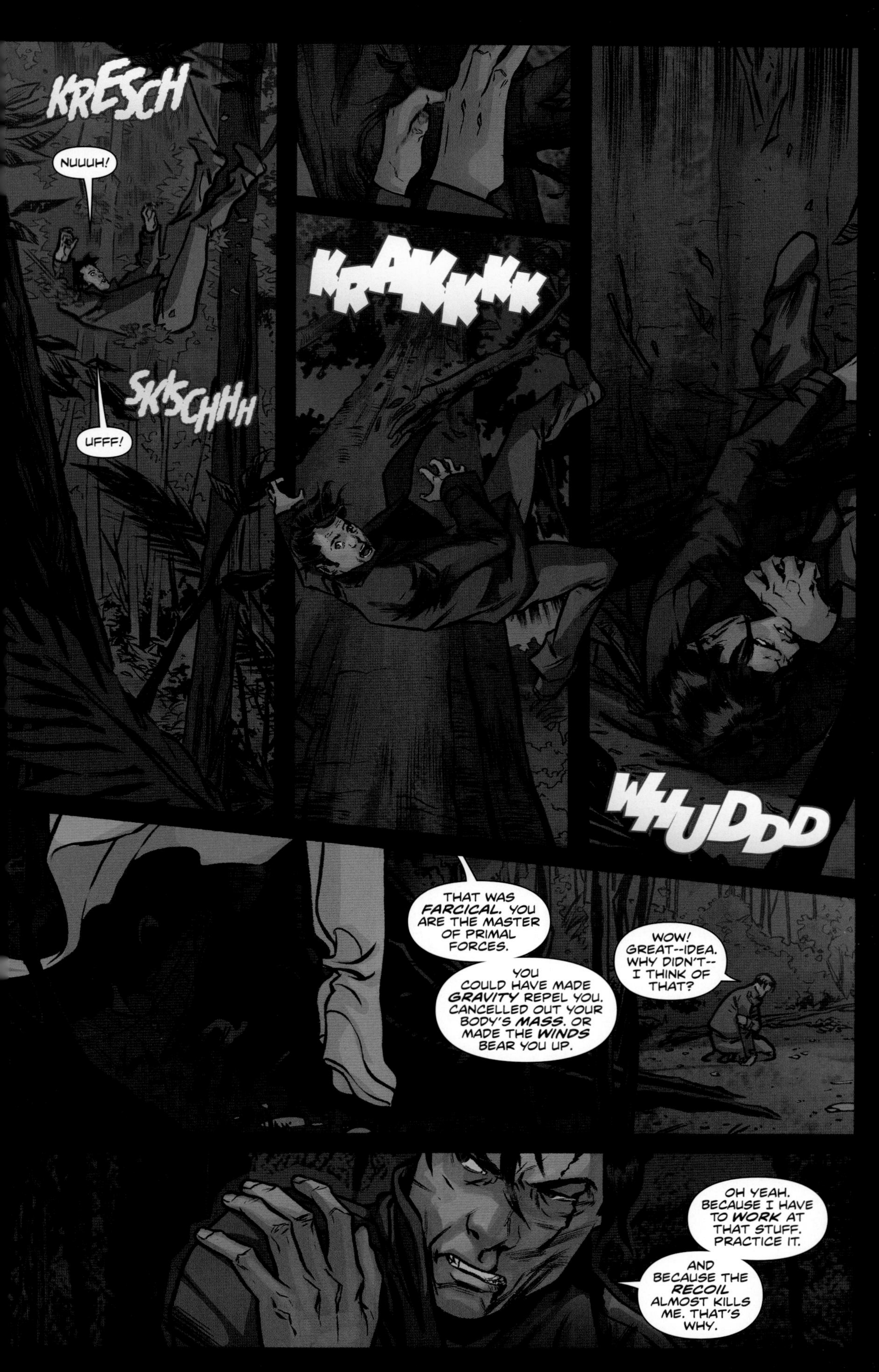
KRESCH
NUUUH!
SKSCHHH
UFFF!
KRAKKKK
WHUDDD
THAT WAS FARCICAL. YOU ARE THE MASTER OF PRIMAL FORCES.
YOU COULD HAVE MADE GRAVITY REPEL YOU. CANCELLED OUT YOUR BODY'S MASS. OR MADE THE WINDS BEAR YOU UP.
WOW! GREAT--IDEA. WHY DIDN'T-- I THINK OF THAT?
OH YEAH. BECAUSE I HAVE TO WORK AT THAT STUFF. PRACTICE IT.
AND BECAUSE THE RECOIL ALMOST KILLS ME. THAT'S WHY.

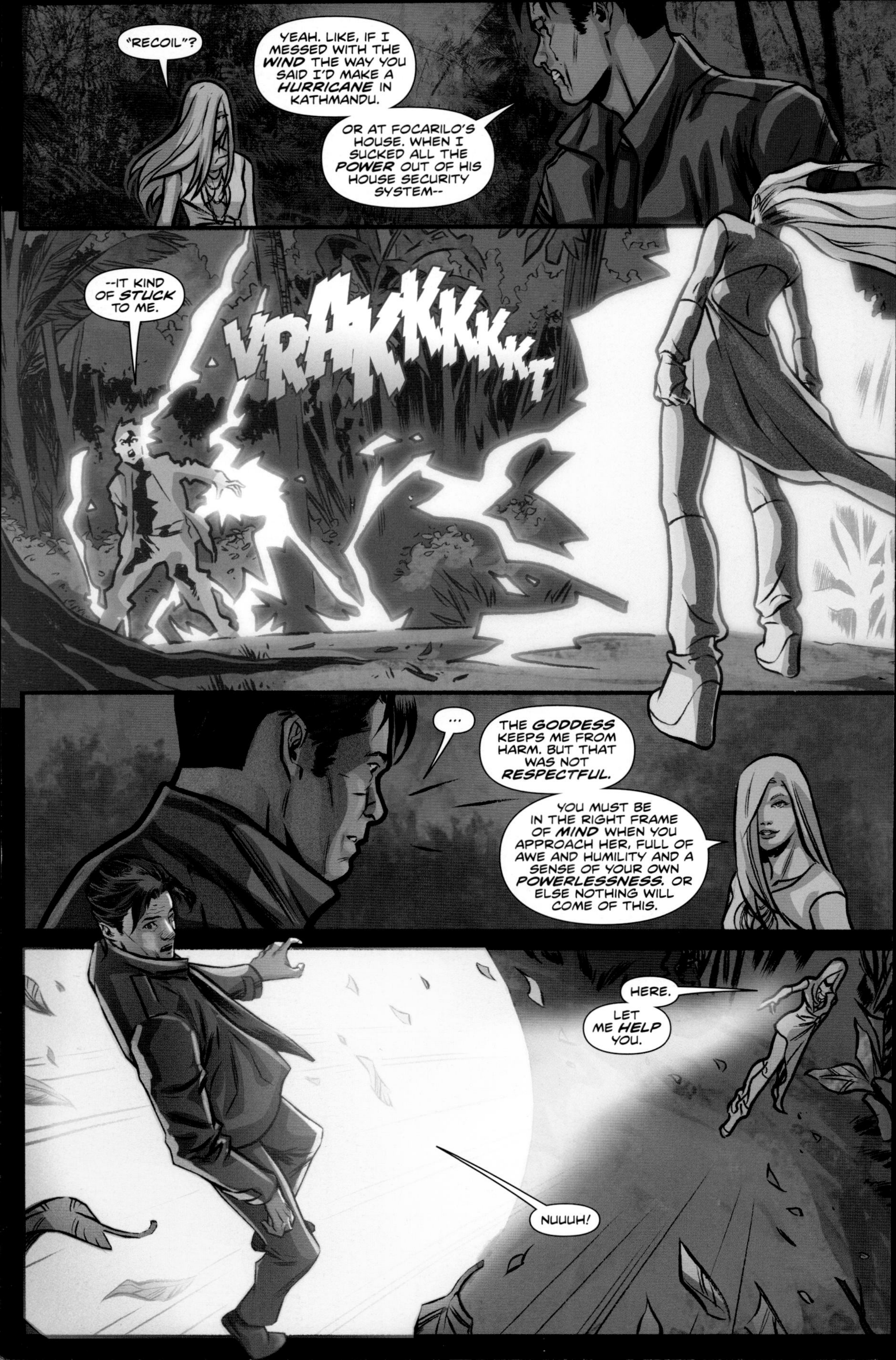
"RECOIL"?
YEAH. LIKE, IF I MESSED WITH THE WIND THE WAY YOU SAID I'D MAKE A HURRICANE IN KATHMANDU.
OR AT FOCARILO'S HOUSE. WHEN I SUCKED ALL THE POWER OUT OF HIS HOUSE SECURITY SYSTEM--
--IT KIND OF STUCK TO ME.
VRAKKKKKKT
...
THE GODDESS KEEPS ME FROM HARM. BUT THAT WAS NOT RESPECTFUL.
YOU MUST BE IN THE RIGHT FRAME OF MIND WHEN YOU APPROACH HER, FULL OF AWE AND HUMILITY AND A SENSE OF YOUR OWN POWERLESSNESS. OR ELSE NOTHING WILL COME OF THIS.
HERE.
LET ME HELP YOU.
NUUUH!

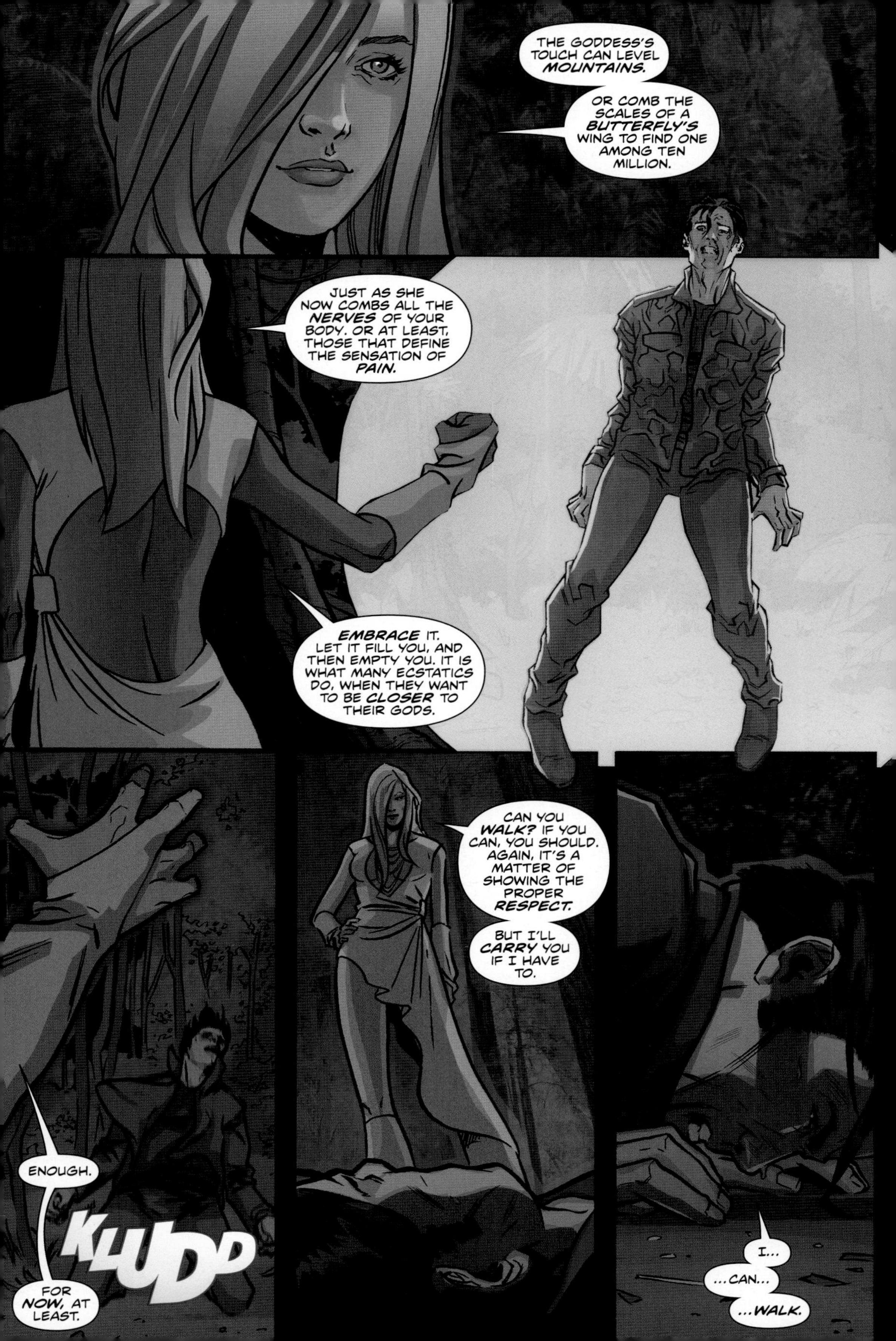
THE GODDESS'S TOUCH CAN LEVEL MOUNTAINS.
OR COMB THE SCALES OF A BUTTERFLY'S WING TO FIND ONE AMONG TEN MILLION.
JUST AS SHE NOW COMBS ALL THE NERVES OF YOUR BODY. OR AT LEAST, THOSE THAT DEFINE THE SENSATION OF PAIN.
EMBRACE IT. LET IT FILL YOU, AND THEN EMPTY YOU. IT IS WHAT MANY ECSTATICS DO, WHEN THEY WANT TO BE CLOSER TO THEIR GODS.
ENOUGH.
KLUDD
FOR NOW, AT LEAST.
CAN YOU WALK? IF YOU CAN, YOU SHOULD. AGAIN, IT'S A MATTER OF SHOWING THE PROPER RESPECT.
BUT I'LL CARRY YOU IF I HAVE TO.
I...
...CAN...
...WALK.

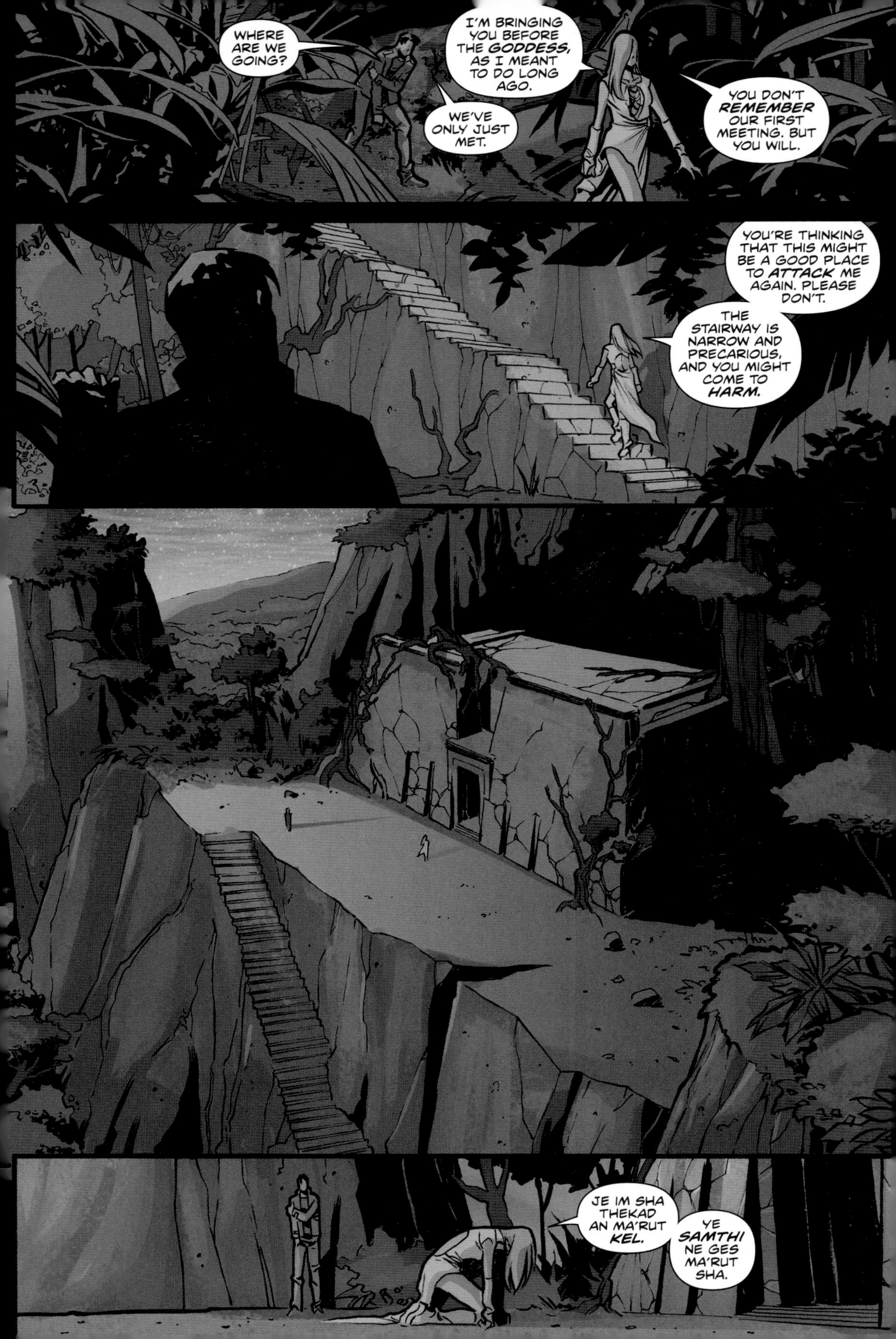
WHERE ARE WE GOING?
I'M BRINGING YOU BEFORE THE GODDESS, AS I MEANT TO DO LONG AGO.
WE'VE ONLY JUST MET.
YOU DON'T REMEMBER OUR FIRST MEETING. BUT YOU WILL.
YOU'RE THINKING THAT THIS MIGHT BE A GOOD PLACE TO ATTACK ME AGAIN. PLEASE DON'T.
THE STAIRWAY IS NARROW AND PRECARIOUS, AND YOU MIGHT COME TO HARM.
JE IM SHA THEKAD AN MA'RUT KEL.
YE SAMTHI NE GES MA'RUT SHA.

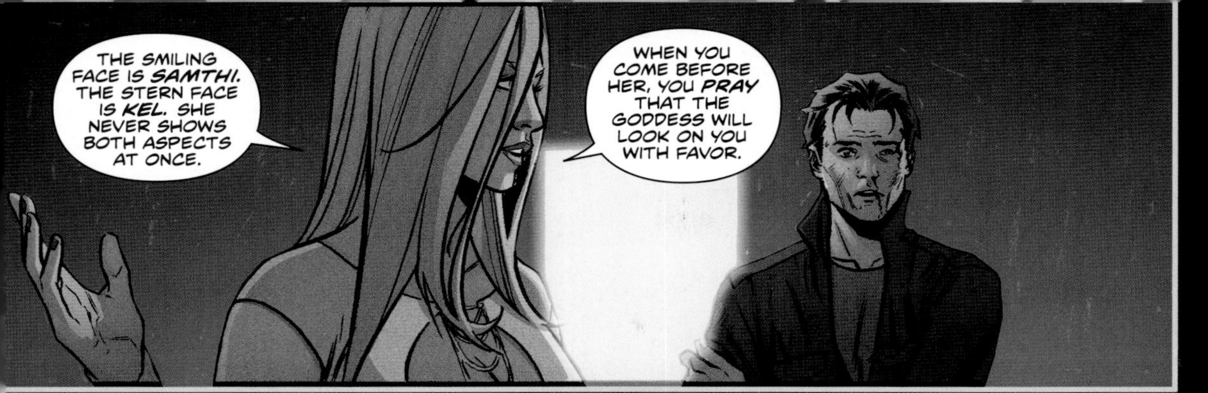
THE SMILING FACE IS SAMTHI. THE STERN FACE IS KEL. SHE NEVER SHOWS BOTH ASPECTS AT ONCE.
WHEN YOU COME BEFORE HER, YOU PRAY THAT THE GODDESS WILL LOOK ON YOU WITH FAVOR.

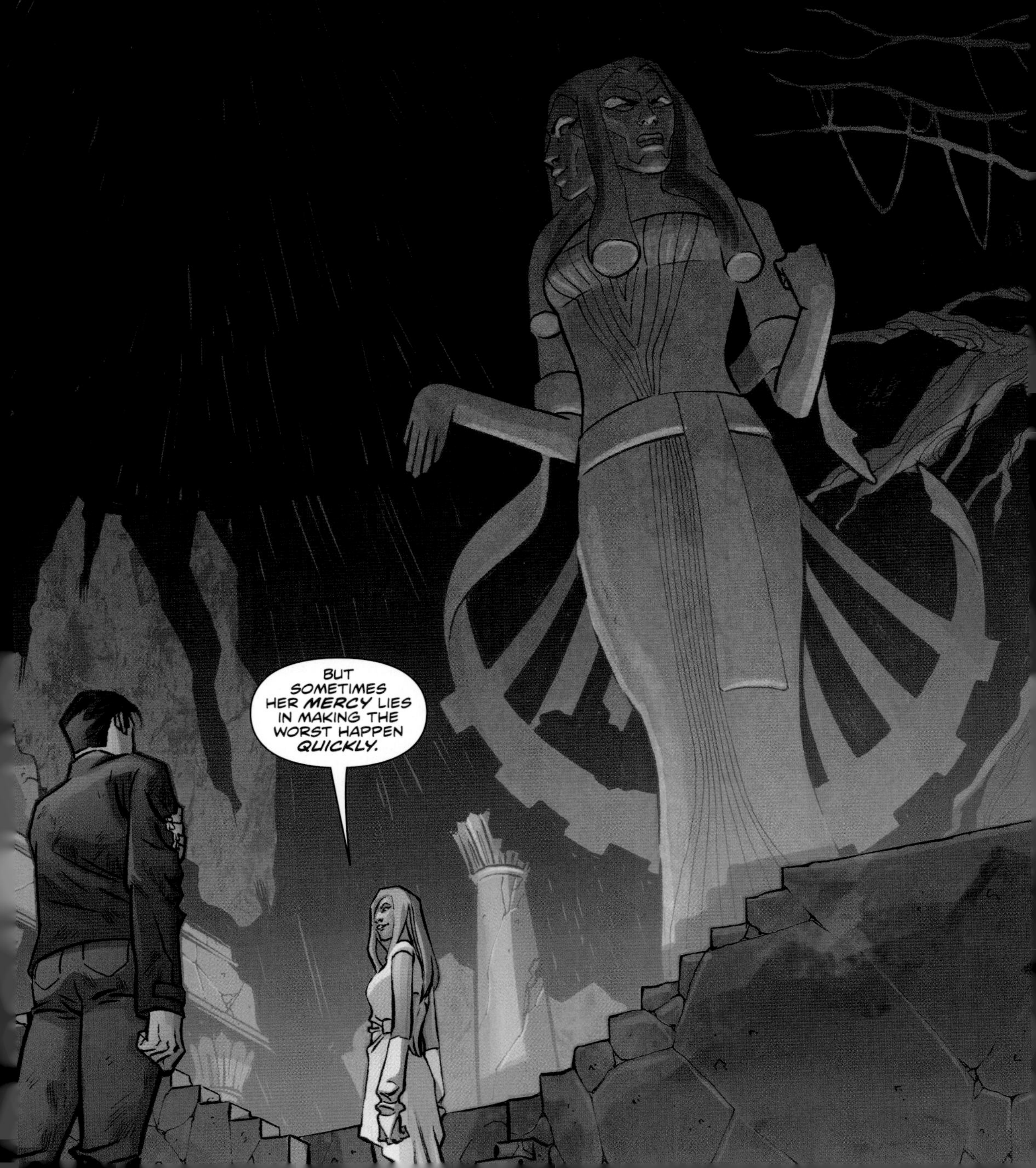
BUT SOMETIMES HER MERCY LIES IN MAKING THE WORST HAPPEN QUICKLY.

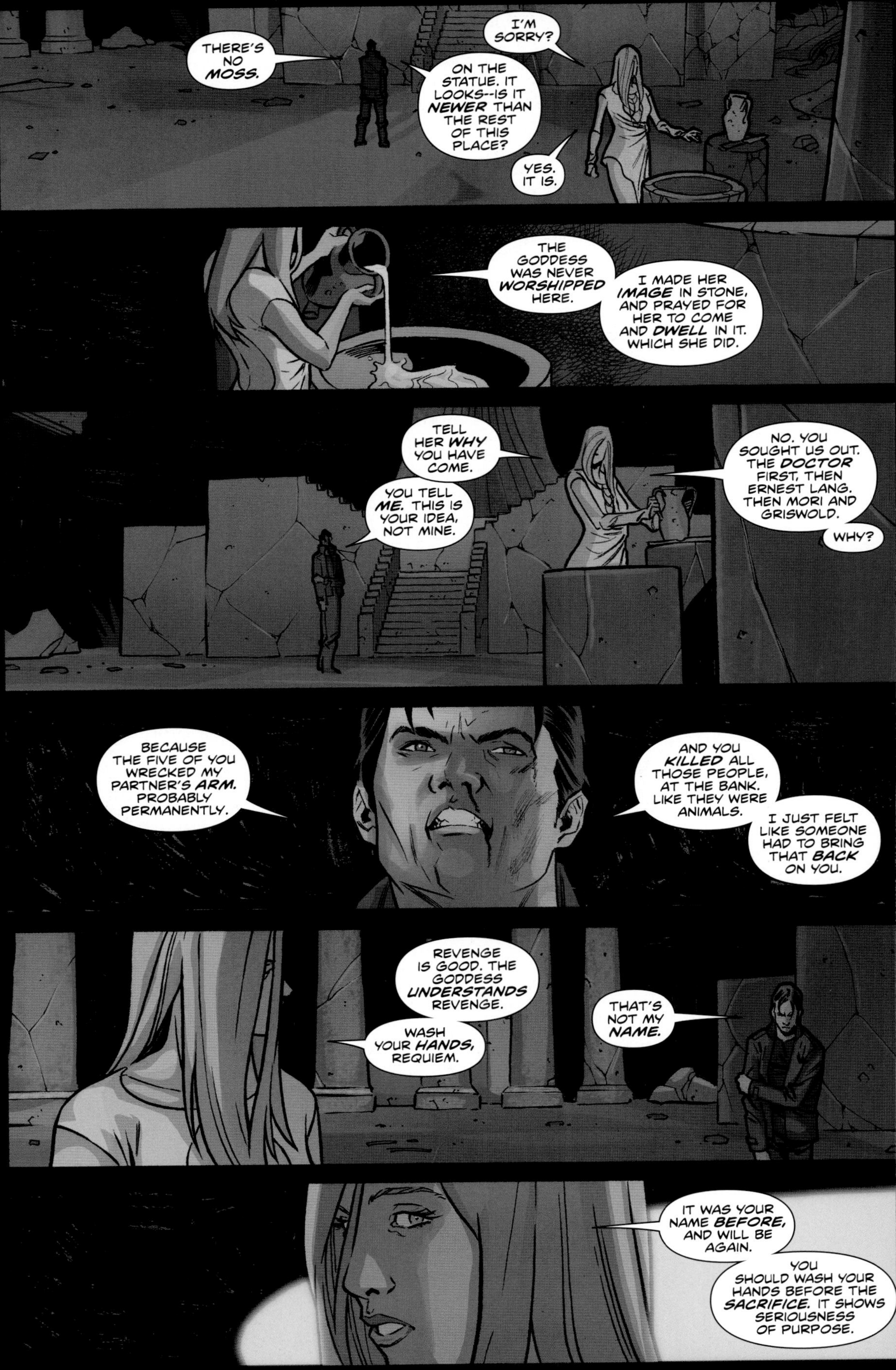
THERE'S NO MOSS.
I'M SORRY?
ON THE STATUE. IT LOOKS--IS IT NEWER THAN THE REST OF THIS PLACE?
YES. IT IS.
THE GODDESS WAS NEVER WORSHIPPED HERE.
I MADE HER IMAGE IN STONE, AND PRAYED FOR HER TO COME AND DWELL IN IT. WHICH SHE DID.
TELL HER WHY YOU HAVE COME.
YOU TELL ME. THIS IS YOUR IDEA, NOT MINE.
NO. YOU SOUGHT US OUT. THE DOCTOR FIRST, THEN ERNEST LANG. THEN MORI AND GRISWOLD.
WHY?
BECAUSE THE FIVE OF YOU WRECKED MY PARTNER'S ARM. PROBABLY PERMANENTLY.
AND YOU KILLED ALL THOSE PEOPLE, AT THE BANK. LIKE THEY WERE ANIMALS.
I JUST FELT LIKE SOMEONE HAD TO BRING THAT BACK ON YOU.
REVENGE IS GOOD. THE GODDESS UNDERSTANDS REVENGE.
WASH YOUR HANDS, REQUIEM.
THAT'S NOT MY NAME.
IT WAS YOUR NAME BEFORE, AND WILL BE AGAIN.
YOU SHOULD WASH YOUR HANDS BEFORE THE SACRIFICE. IT SHOWS SERIOUSNESS OF PURPOSE.

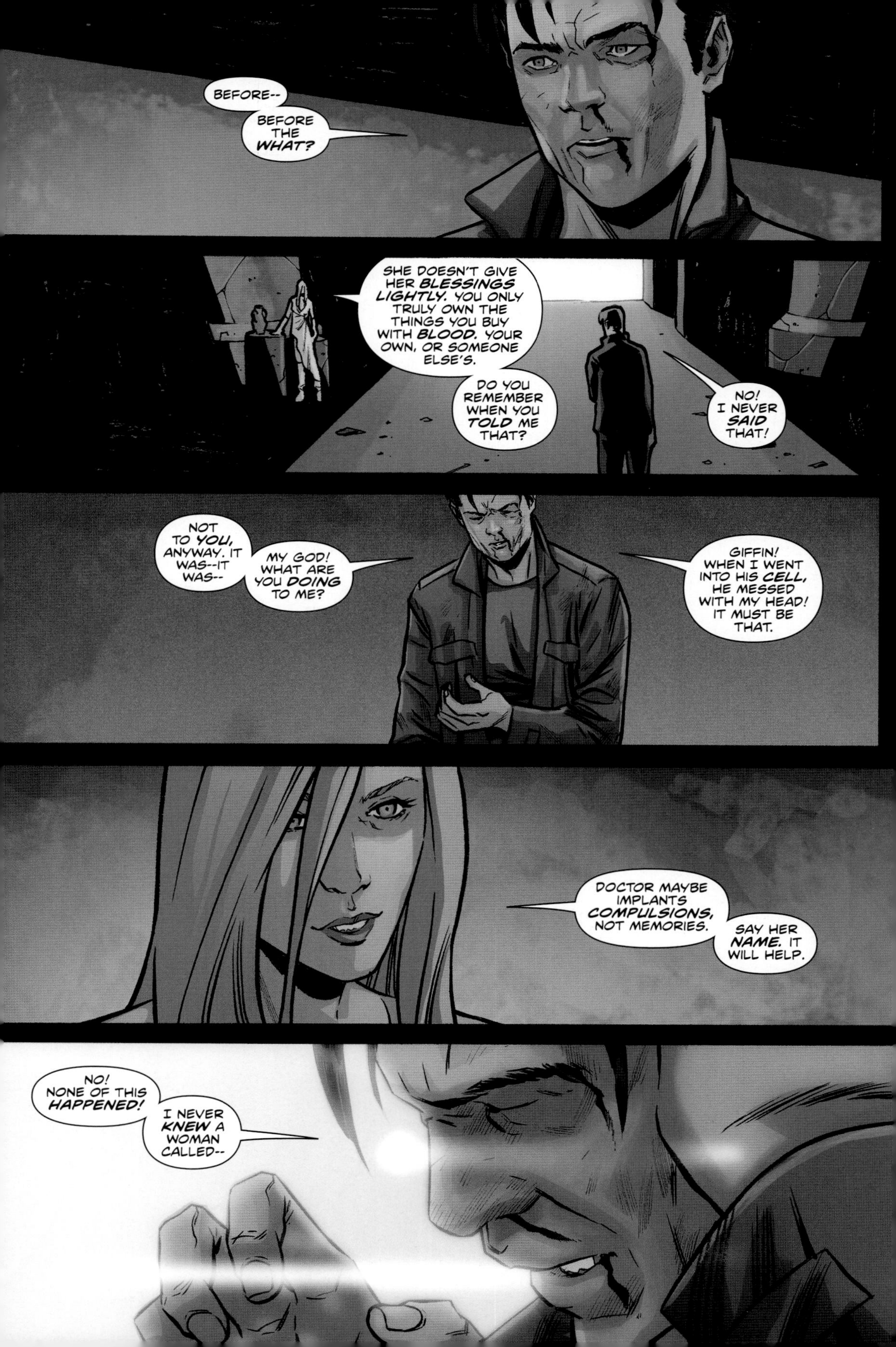
BEFORE--
BEFORE THE WHAT?
SHE DOESN'T GIVE HER BLESSINGS LIGHTLY. YOU ONLY TRULY OWN THE THINGS YOU BUY WITH BLOOD. YOUR OWN, OR SOMEONE ELSE'S.
DO YOU REMEMBER WHEN YOU TOLD ME THAT?
NO! I NEVER SAID THAT!
NOT TO YOU, ANYWAY. IT WAS--IT WAS--
MY GOD! WHAT ARE YOU DOING TO ME?
GIFFIN! WHEN I WENT INTO HIS CELL, HE MESSED WITH MY HEAD! IT MUST BE THAT.
DOCTOR MAYBE IMPLANTS COMPULSIONS, NOT MEMORIES.
SAY HER NAME. IT WILL HELP.
NO! NONE OF THIS HAPPENED!
I NEVER KNEW A WOMAN CALLED--

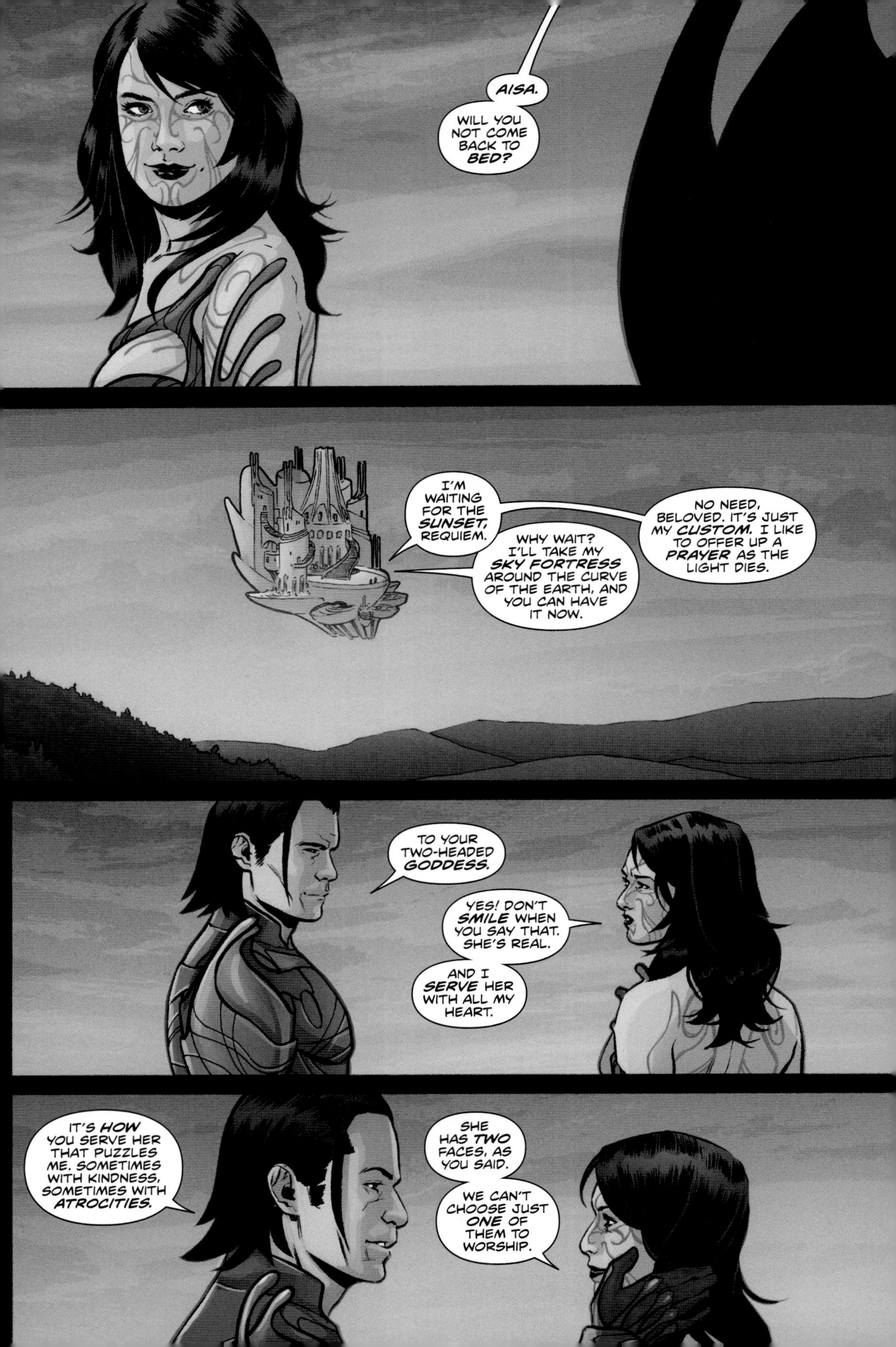
AISA.
WILL YOU NOT COME BACK TO BED?
I'M WAITING FOR THE SUNSET, REQUIEM.
WHY WAIT? I'LL TAKE MY SKY FORTRESS AROUND THE CURVE OF THE EARTH, AND YOU CAN HAVE IT NOW.
NO NEED, BELOVED. IT'S JUST MY CUSTOM. I LIKE TO OFFER UP A PRAYER AS THE LIGHT DIES.
TO YOUR TWO-HEADED GODDESS.
YES! DON'T SMILE WHEN YOU SAY THAT. SHE'S REAL.
AND I SERVE HER WITH ALL MY HEART.
IT'S HOW YOU SERVE HER THAT PUZZLES ME. SOMETIMES WITH KINDNESS, SOMETIMES WITH ATROCITIES.
SHE HAS TWO FACES, AS YOU SAID.
WE CAN'T CHOOSE JUST ONE OF THEM TO WORSHIP.

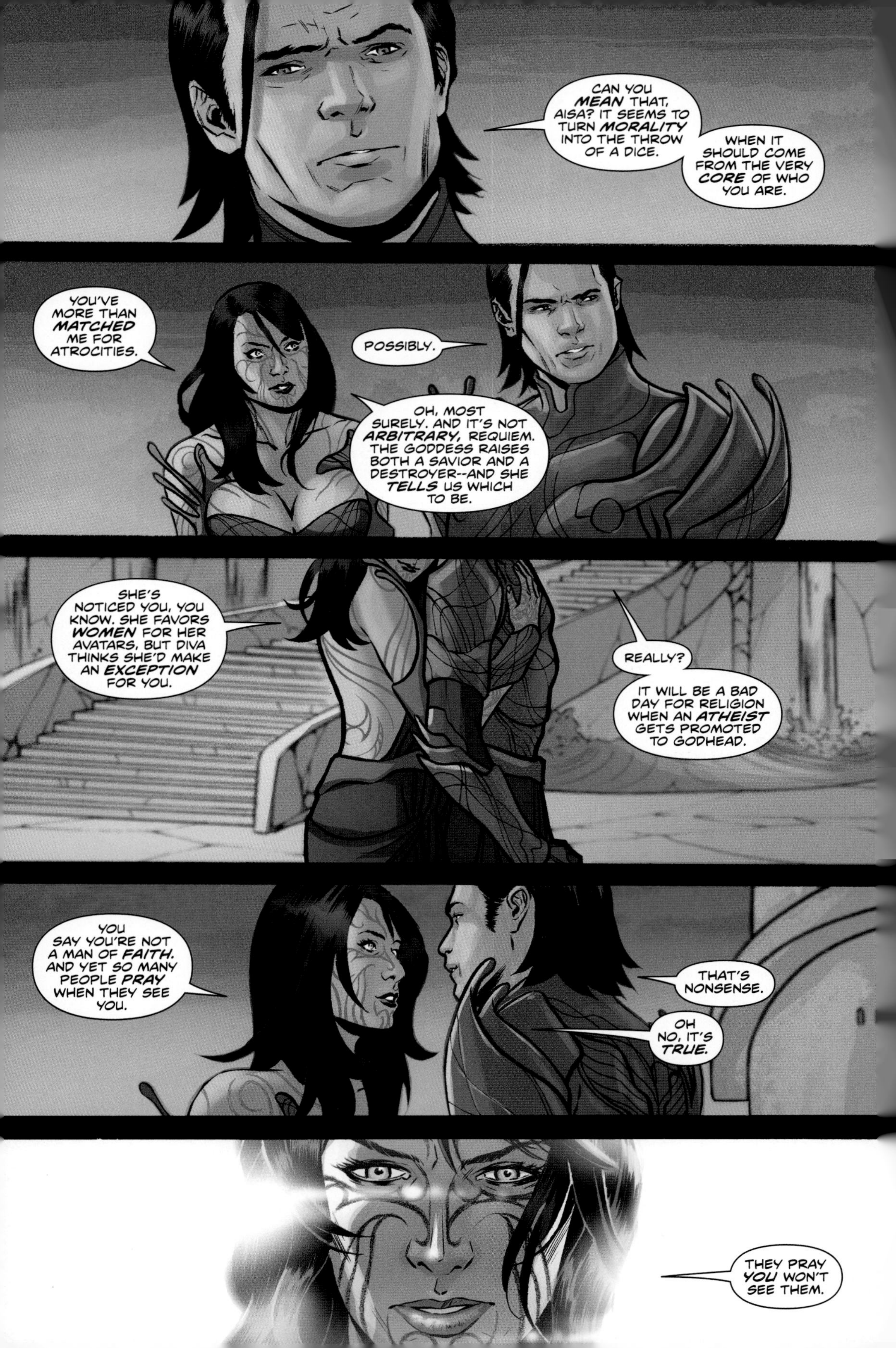

CAN YOU MEAN THAT, AISA? IT SEEMS TO TURN MORALITY INTO THE THROW OF A DICE.
WHEN IT SHOULD COME FROM THE VERY CORE OF WHO YOU ARE.
YOU'VE MORE THAN MATCHED ME FOR ATROCITIES.
POSSIBLY.
OH, MOST SURELY. AND IT'S NOT ARBITRARY, REQUIEM. THE GODDESS RAISES BOTH A SAVIOR AND A DESTROYER--AND SHE TELLS US WHICH TO BE.
SHE'S NOTICED YOU, YOU KNOW. SHE FAVORS WOMEN FOR HER AVATARS, BUT DIVA THINKS SHE'D MAKE AN EXCEPTION FOR YOU.
REALLY?
IT WILL BE A BAD DAY FOR RELIGION WHEN AN ATHEIST GETS PROMOTED TO GODHEAD.
YOU SAY YOU'RE NOT A MAN OF FAITH. AND YET SO MANY PEOPLE PRAY WHEN THEY SEE YOU.
THAT'S NONSENSE.
OH NO, IT'S TRUE.
THEY PRAY YOU WON'T SEE THEM.

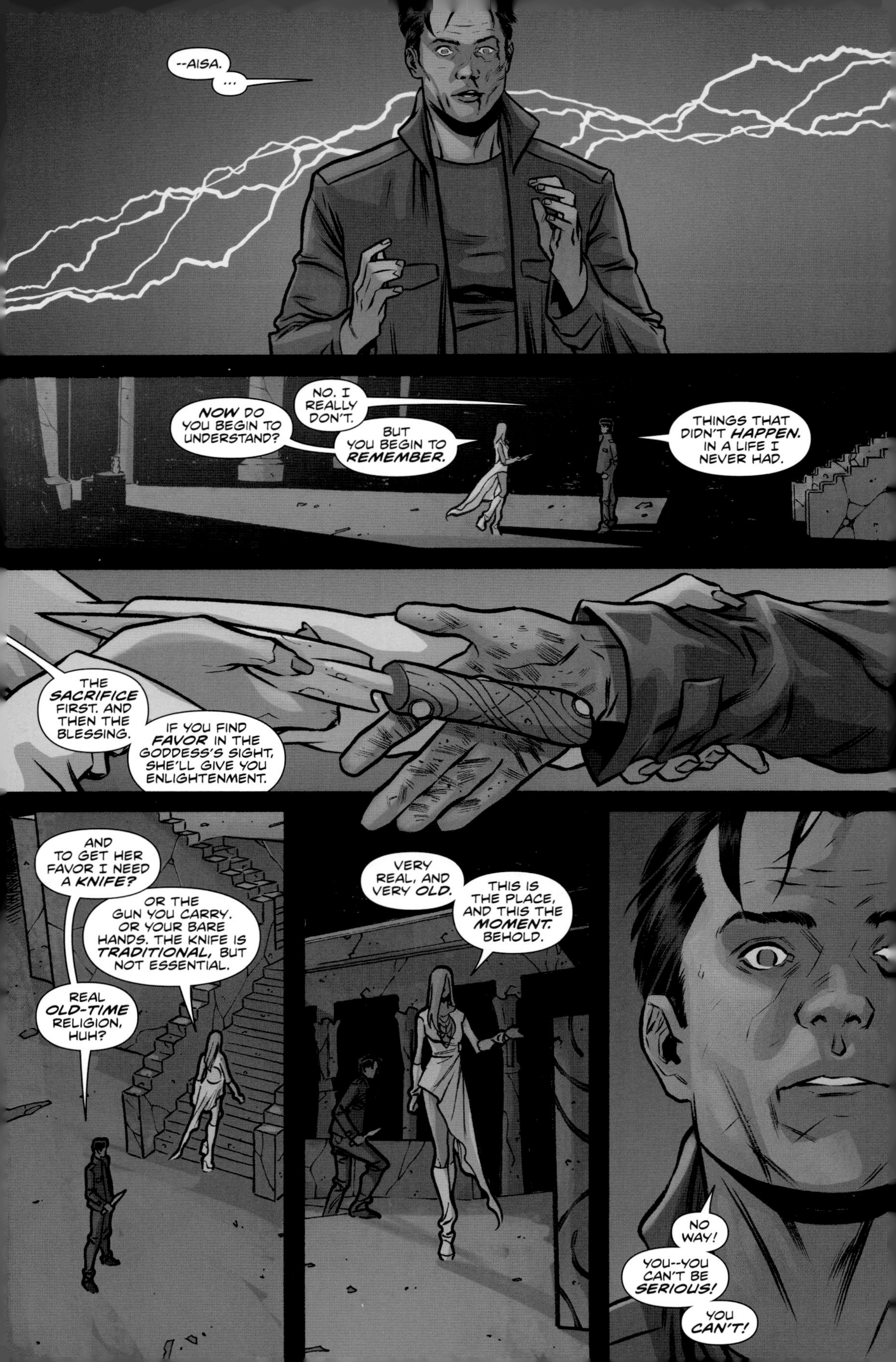
--AISA.
...
NO. I REALLY DON'T.
NOW DO YOU BEGIN TO UNDERSTAND?
BUT YOU BEGIN TO REMEMBER.
THINGS THAT DIDN'T HAPPEN. IN A LIFE I NEVER HAD.
THE SACRIFICE FIRST. AND THEN THE BLESSING.
IF YOU FIND FAVOR IN THE GODDESS'S SIGHT, SHE'LL GIVE YOU ENLIGHTENMENT.
AND TO GET HER FAVOR I NEED A KNIFE?
OR THE GUN YOU CARRY. OR YOUR BARE HANDS. THE KNIFE IS TRADITIONAL, BUT NOT ESSENTIAL.
REAL OLD-TIME RELIGION, HUH?
VERY REAL, AND VERY OLD.
THIS IS THE PLACE, AND THIS THE MOMENT. BEHOLD.
NO WAY!
YOU--YOU CAN'T BE SERIOUS!
YOU CAN'T!

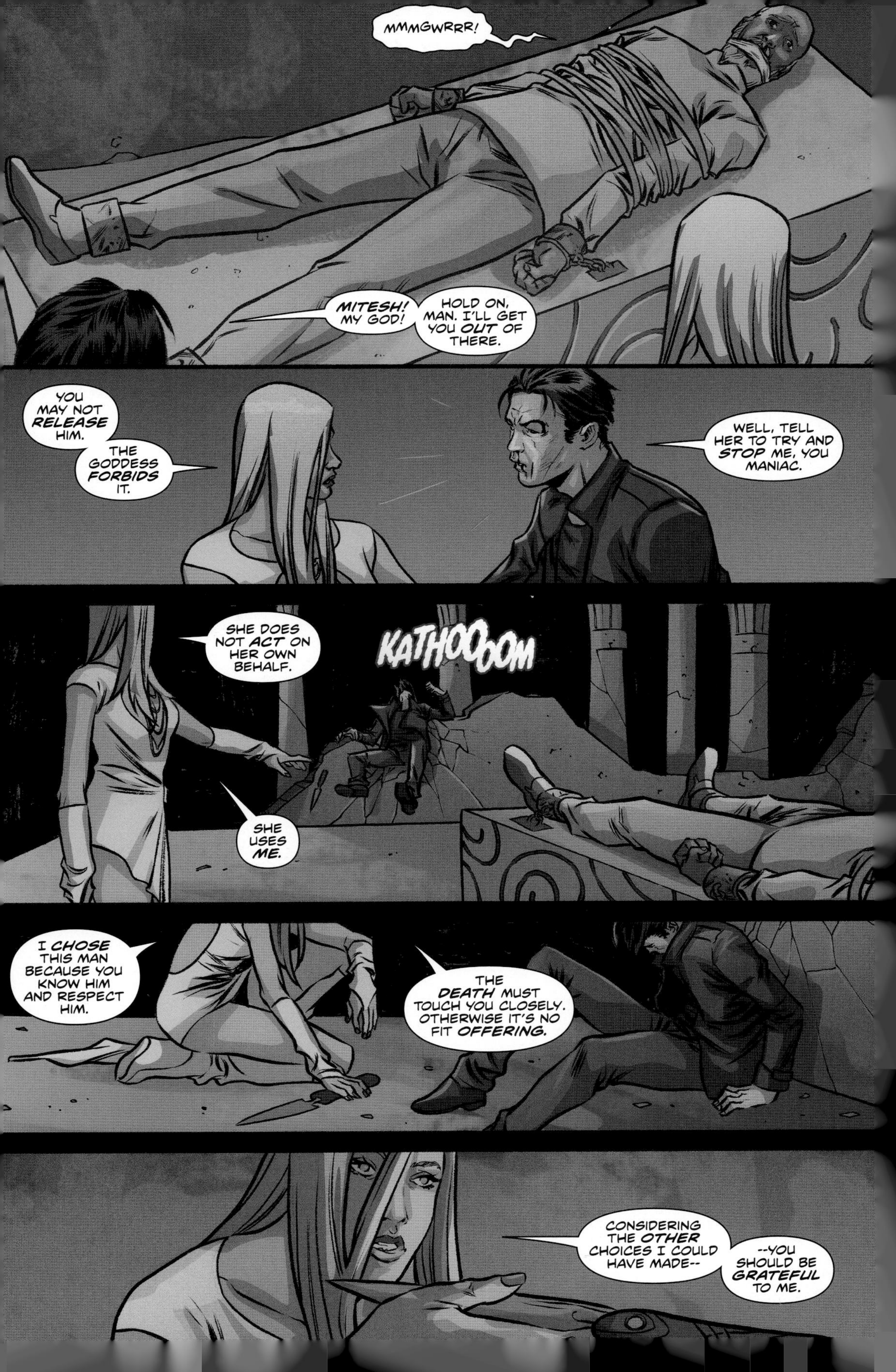
MMMGWRRR!
MITESH! MY GOD!
HOLD ON, MAN. I'LL GET YOU OUT OF THERE.
YOU MAY NOT RELEASE HIM.
THE GODDESS FORBIDS IT.
WELL, TELL HER TO TRY AND STOP ME, YOU MANIAC.
SHE DOES NOT ACT ON HER OWN BEHALF.
KATHOOOOM
SHE USES ME.
I CHOSE THIS MAN BECAUSE YOU KNOW HIM AND RESPECT HIM.
THE DEATH MUST TOUCH YOU CLOSELY. OTHERWISE IT'S NO FIT OFFERING.
CONSIDERING THE OTHER CHOICES I COULD HAVE MADE--
--YOU SHOULD BE GRATEFUL TO ME.

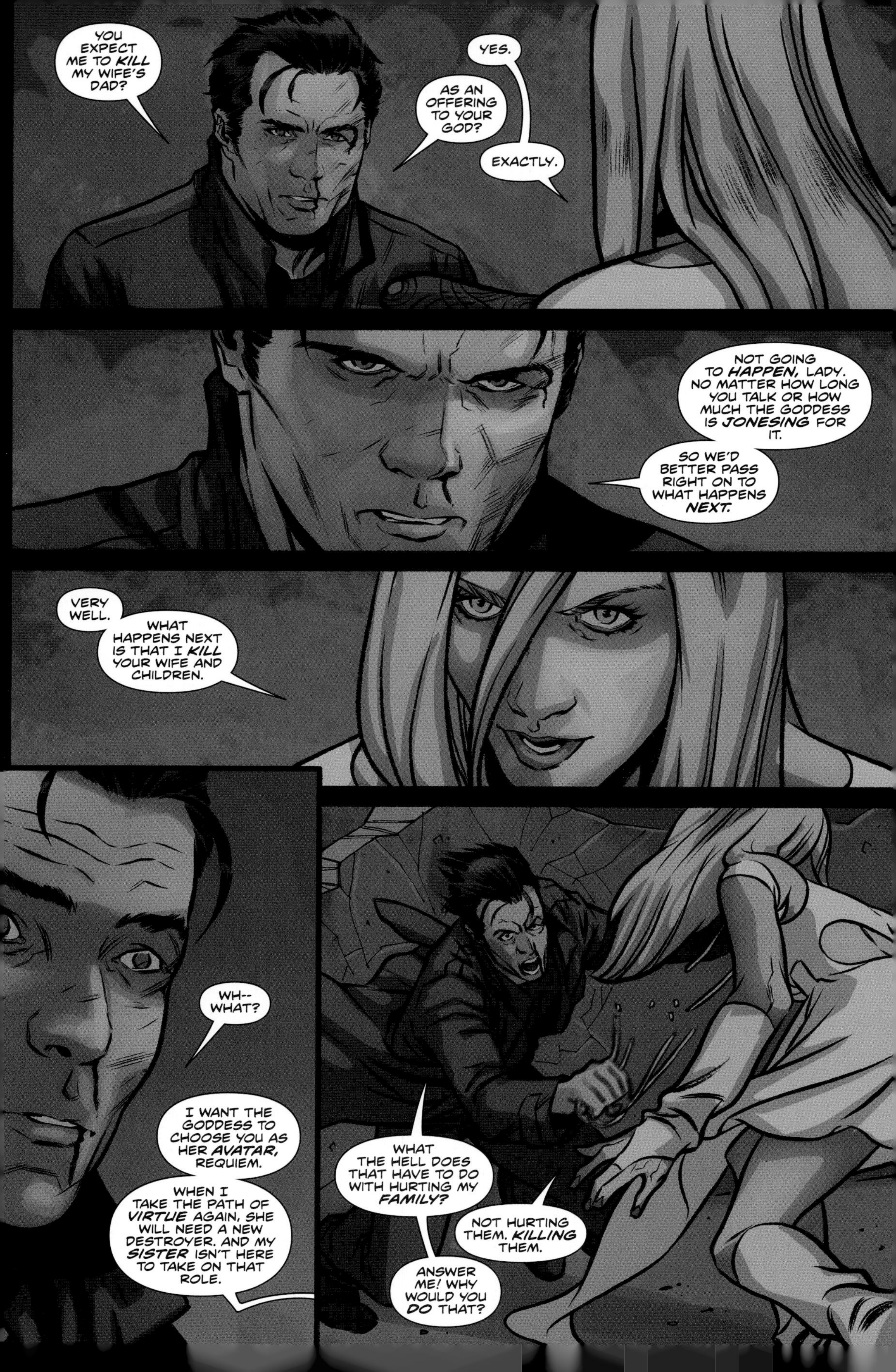
YOU EXPECT ME TO KILL MY WIFE'S DAD?
AS AN OFFERING TO YOUR GOD?
YES.
EXACTLY.
NOT GOING TO HAPPEN, LADY. NO MATTER HOW LONG YOU TALK OR HOW MUCH THE GODDESS IS JONESING FOR IT.
SO WE'D BETTER PASS RIGHT ON TO WHAT HAPPENS NEXT.
VERY WELL.
WHAT HAPPENS NEXT IS THAT I KILL YOUR WIFE AND CHILDREN.
WH-- WHAT?
I WANT THE GODDESS TO CHOOSE YOU AS HER AVATAR, REQUIEM.
WHEN I TAKE THE PATH OF VIRTUE AGAIN, SHE WILL NEED A NEW DESTROYER. AND MY SISTER ISN'T HERE TO TAKE ON THAT ROLE.
WHAT THE HELL DOES THAT HAVE TO DO WITH HURTING MY FAMILY?
NOT HURTING THEM. KILLING THEM.
ANSWER ME! WHY WOULD YOU DO THAT?

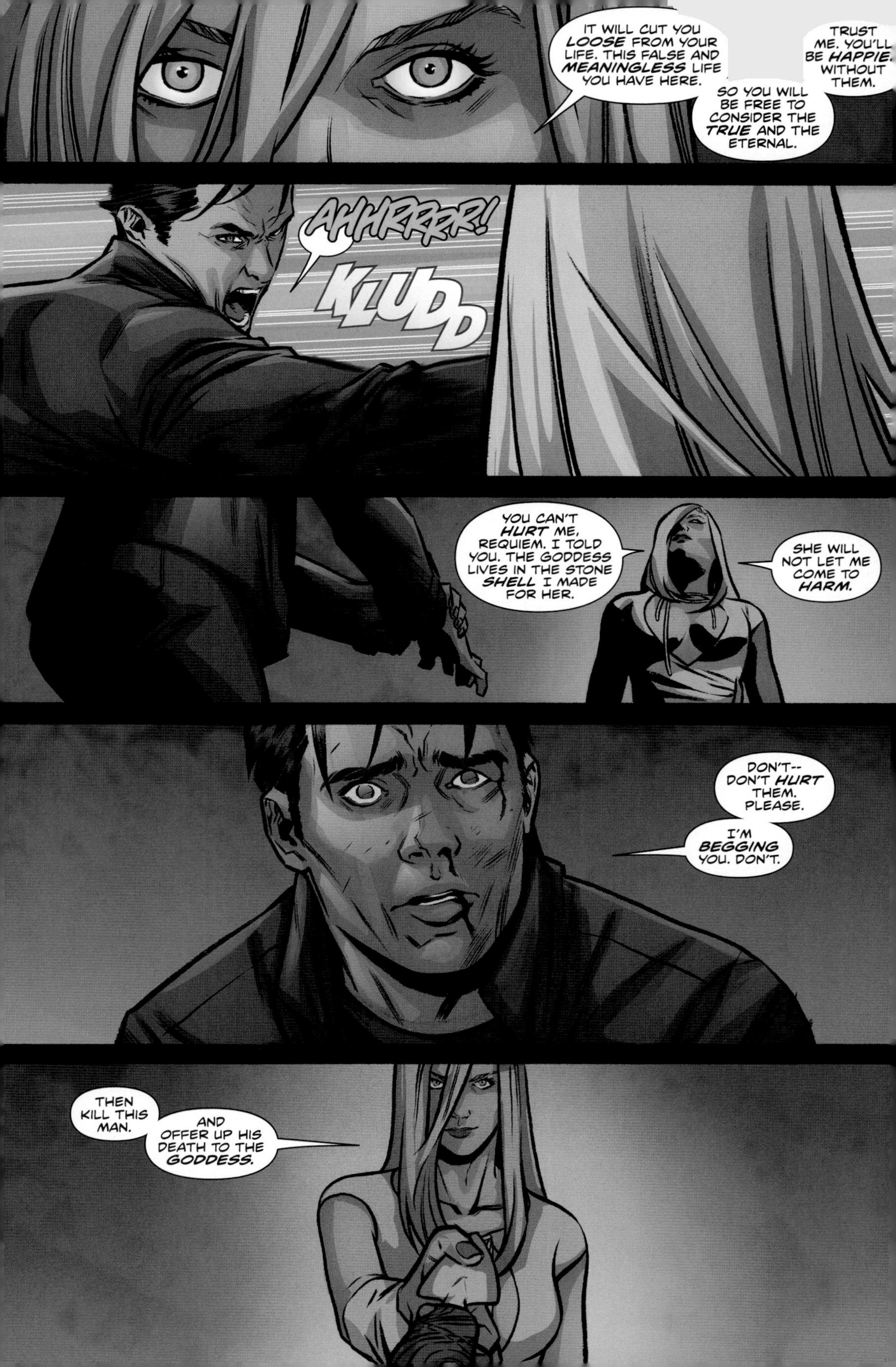
IT WILL CUT YOU LOOSE FROM YOUR LIFE. THIS FALSE AND MEANINGLESS LIFE YOU HAVE HERE.
SO YOU WILL BE FREE TO CONSIDER THE TRUE AND THE ETERNAL.
TRUST ME. YOU'LL BE HAPPIE. WITHOUT THEM.
AHHRRRR!
KLUDD
YOU CAN'T HURT ME, REQUIEM. I TOLD YOU. THE GODDESS LIVES IN THE STONE SHELL I MADE FOR HER.
SHE WILL NOT LET ME COME TO HARM.
DON'T-- DON'T HURT THEM. PLEASE.
I'M BEGGING YOU. DON'T.
THEN KILL THIS MAN.
AND OFFER UP HIS DEATH TO THE GODDESS.

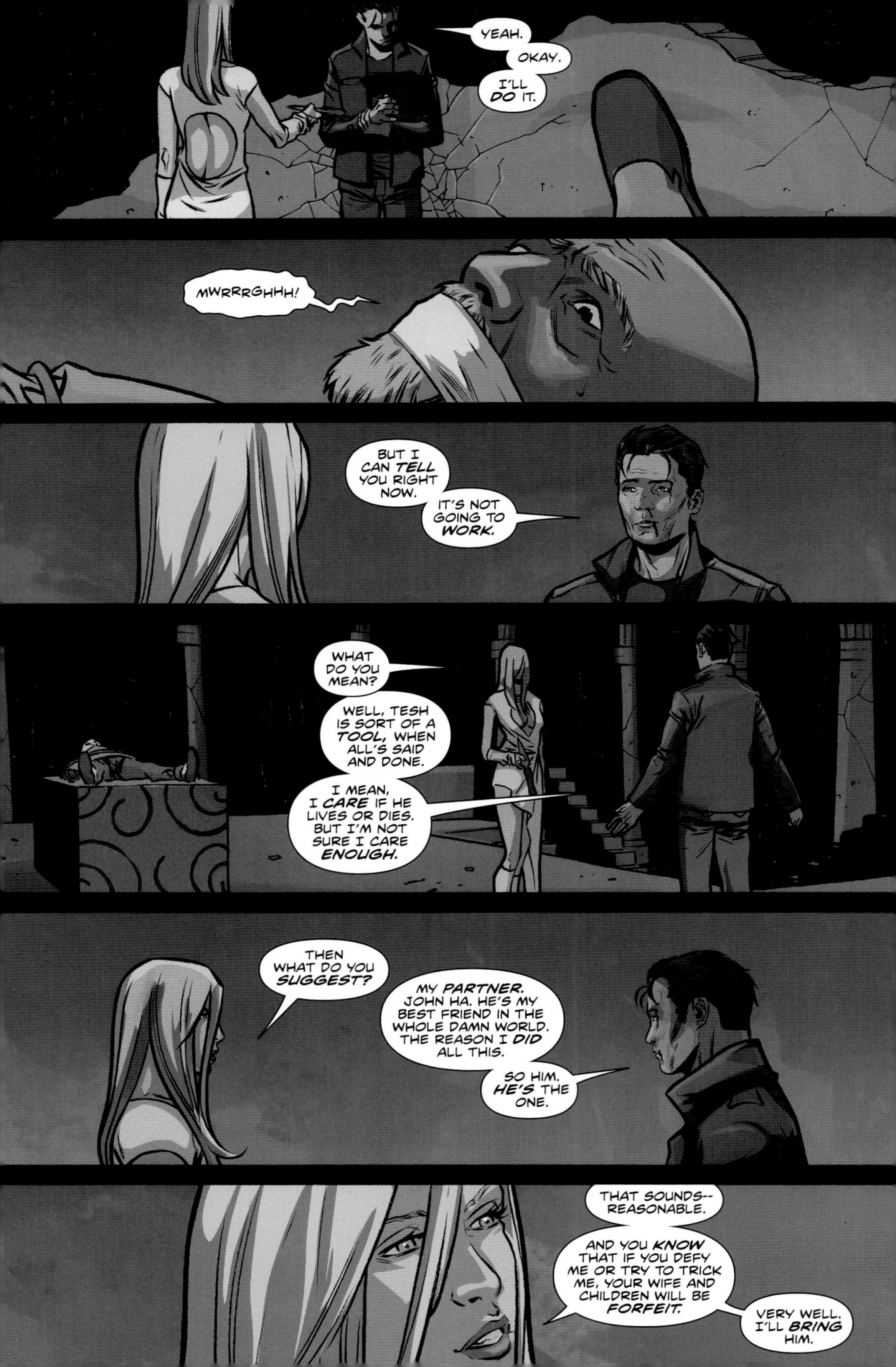
YEAH.
OKAY.
I'LL DO IT.
MWRRRGHHH!
BUT I CAN TELL YOU RIGHT NOW.
IT'S NOT GOING TO WORK.
WHAT DO YOU MEAN?
WELL, TESH IS SORT OF A TOOL, WHEN ALL'S SAID AND DONE.
I MEAN, I CARE IF HE LIVES OR DIES. BUT I'M NOT SURE I CARE ENOUGH.
THEN WHAT DO YOU SUGGEST?
MY PARTNER. JOHN HA. HE'S MY BEST FRIEND IN THE WHOLE DAMN WORLD. THE REASON I DID ALL THIS.
SO HIM. HE'S THE ONE.
THAT SOUNDS-- REASONABLE.
AND YOU KNOW THAT IF YOU DEFY ME OR TRY TO TRICK ME, YOUR WIFE AND CHILDREN WILL BE FORFEIT.
VERY WELL. I'LL BRING HIM.

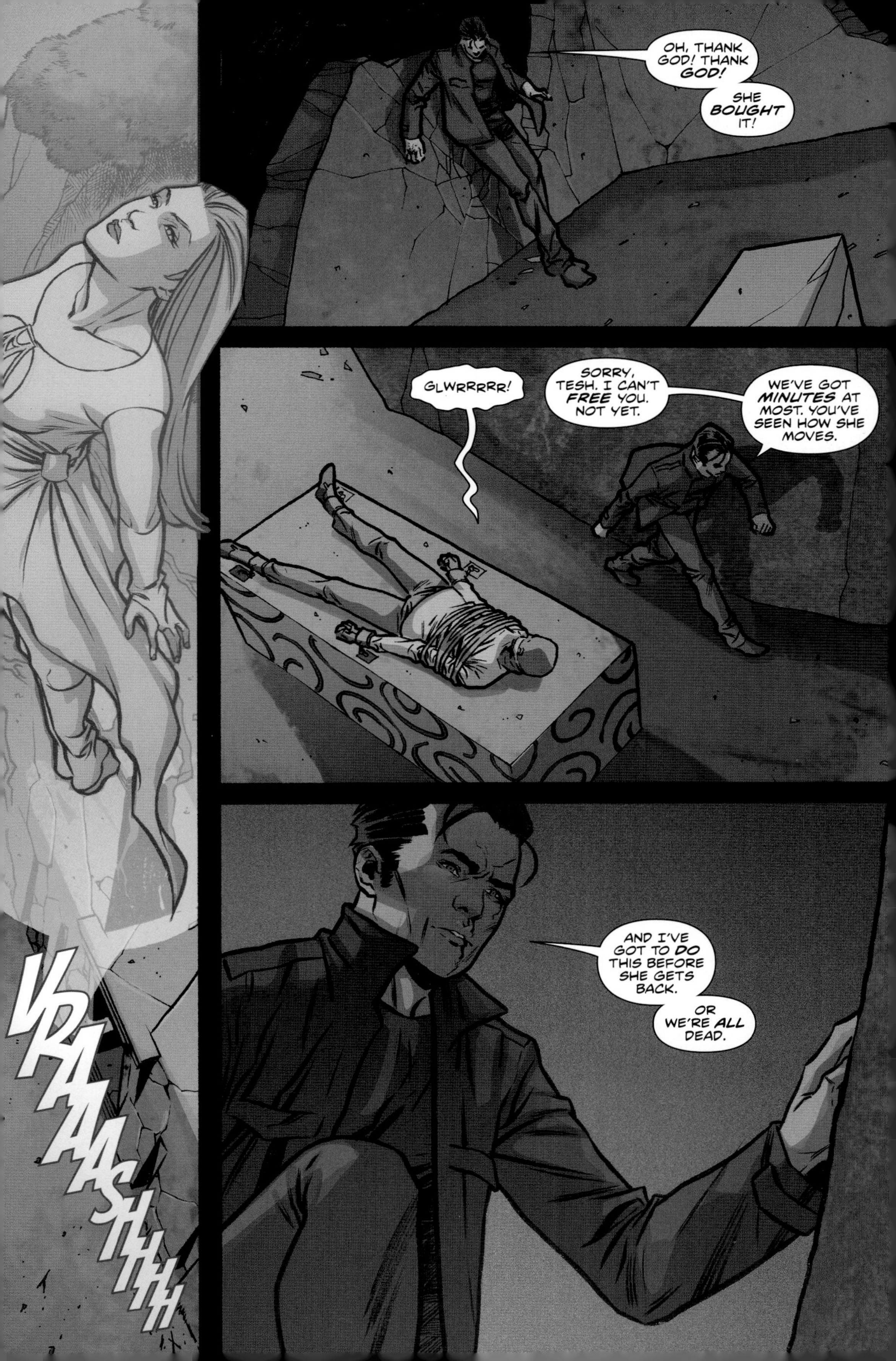
OH, THANK GOD! THANK GOD!
SHE BOUGHT IT!
GLWRRRRR!
SORRY, TESH. I CAN'T FREE YOU. NOT YET.
WE'VE GOT MINUTES AT MOST. YOU'VE SEEN HOW SHE MOVES.
VRAAASHHHH
AND I'VE GOT TO DO THIS BEFORE SHE GETS BACK.
OR WE'RE ALL DEAD.

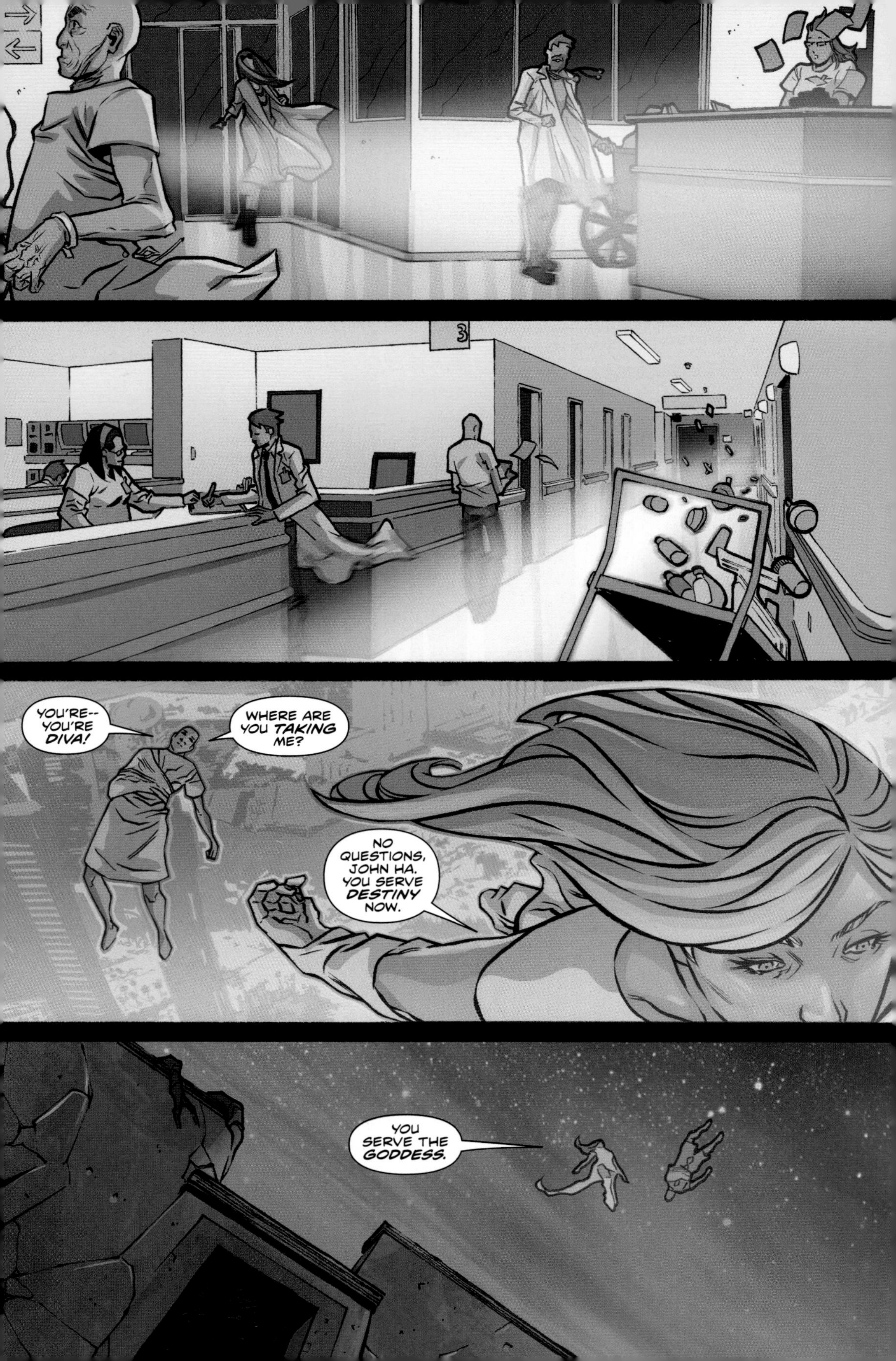
3
YOU'RE--
YOU'RE
DIVA!
WHERE ARE
YOU TAKING
ME?
NO
QUESTIONS,
JOHN HA.
YOU SERVE
DESTINY
NOW.
YOU
SERVE THE
GODDESS.

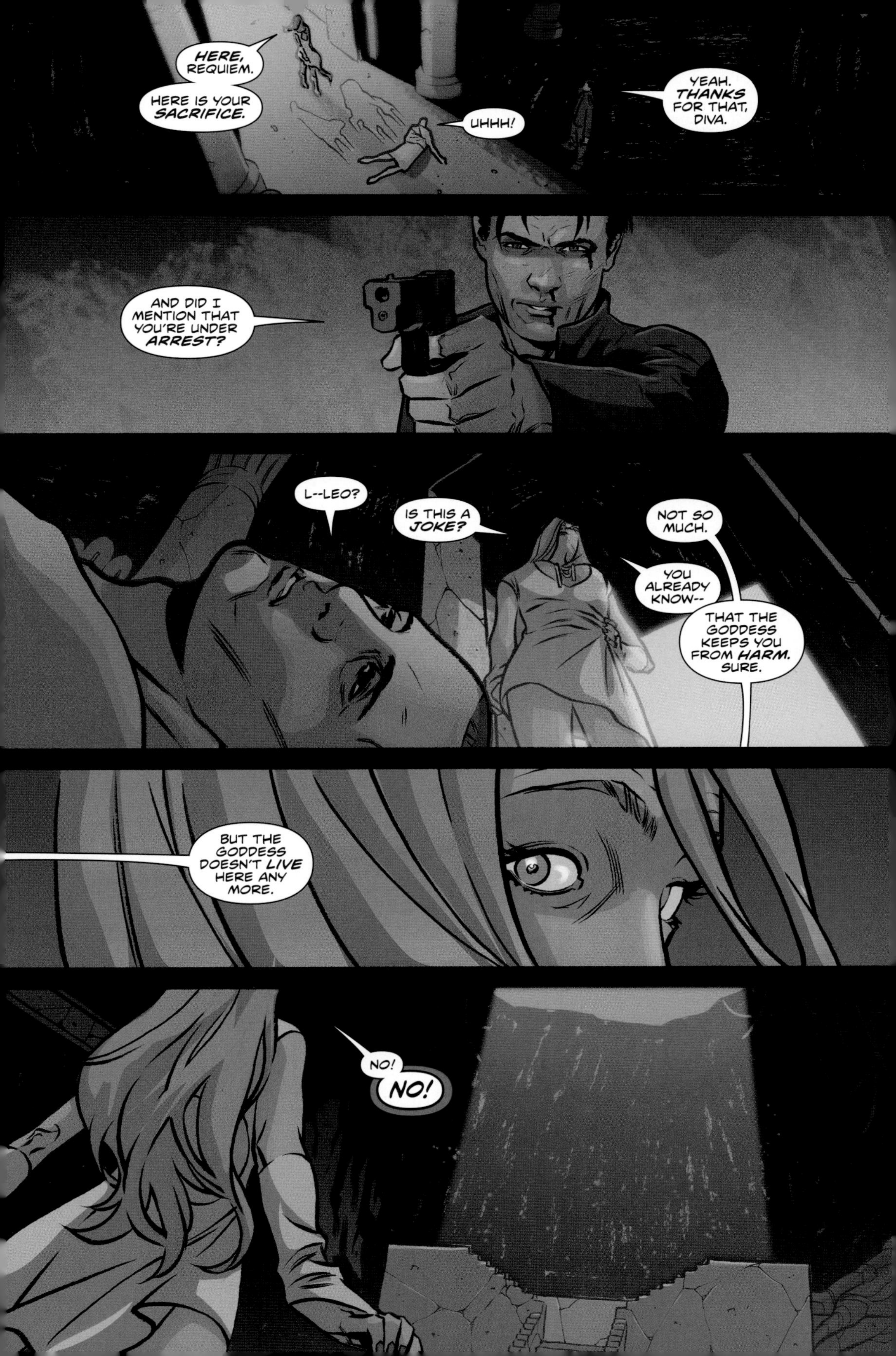
HERE, REQUIEM.
HERE IS YOUR SACRIFICE.
UHHH!
YEAH. THANKS FOR THAT, DIVA.
AND DID I MENTION THAT YOU'RE UNDER ARREST?
L--LEO?
IS THIS A JOKE?
NOT SO MUCH.
YOU ALREADY KNOW--
THAT THE GODDESS KEEPS YOU FROM HARM. SURE.
BUT THE GODDESS DOESN'T LIVE HERE ANY MORE.
NO!
NO!

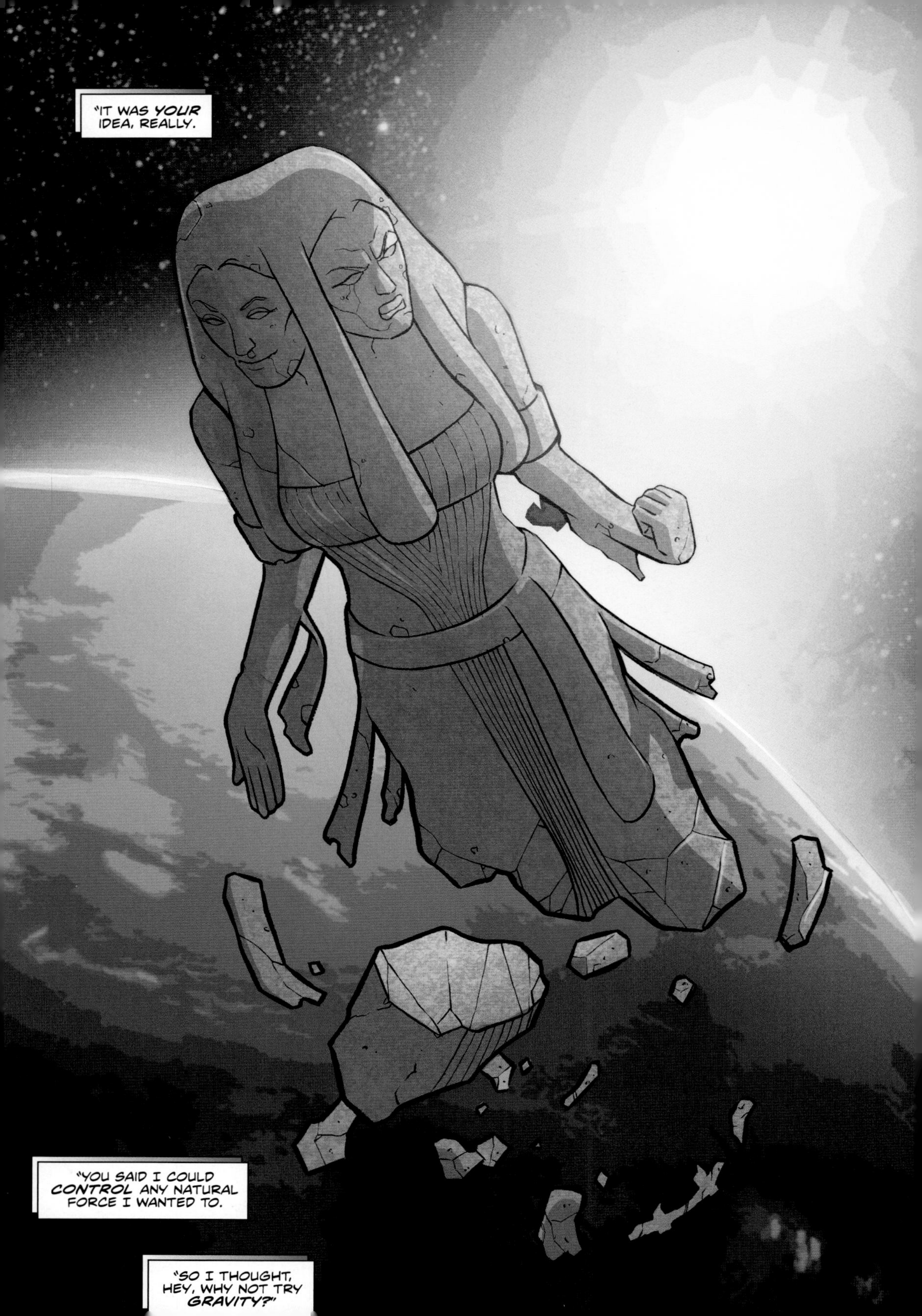
"IT WAS YOUR IDEA, REALLY.
"YOU SAID I COULD CONTROL ANY NATURAL FORCE I WANTED TO.
"SO I THOUGHT, HEY, WHY NOT TRY GRAVITY?"

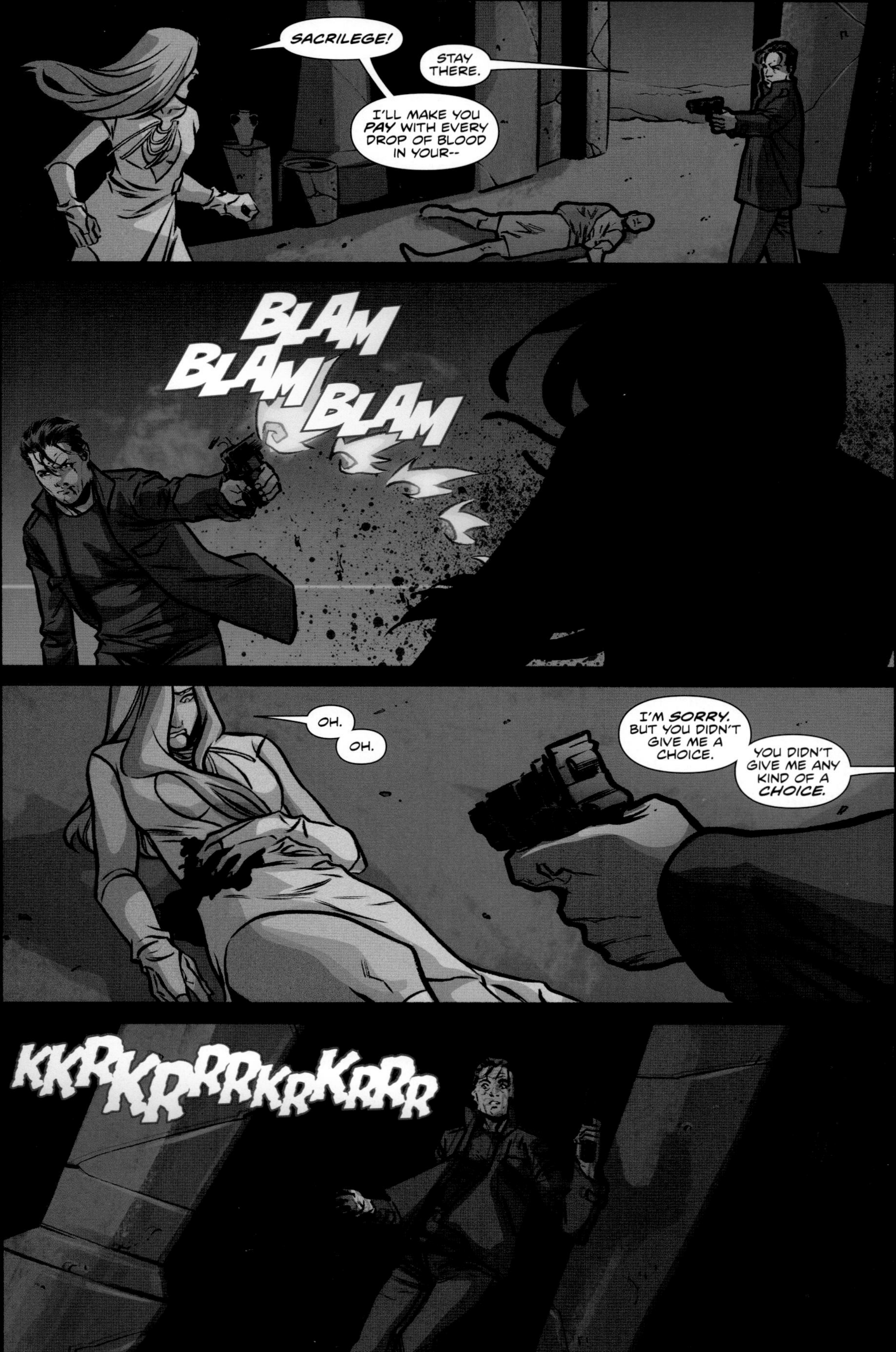
SACRILEGE!
STAY THERE.
I'LL MAKE YOU PAY WITH EVERY DROP OF BLOOD IN YOUR--
BLAM BLAM BLAM
OH.
OH.
I'M SORRY. BUT YOU DIDN'T GIVE ME A CHOICE.
YOU DIDN'T GIVE ME ANY KIND OF A CHOICE.
KKRKRRRKRKRRR

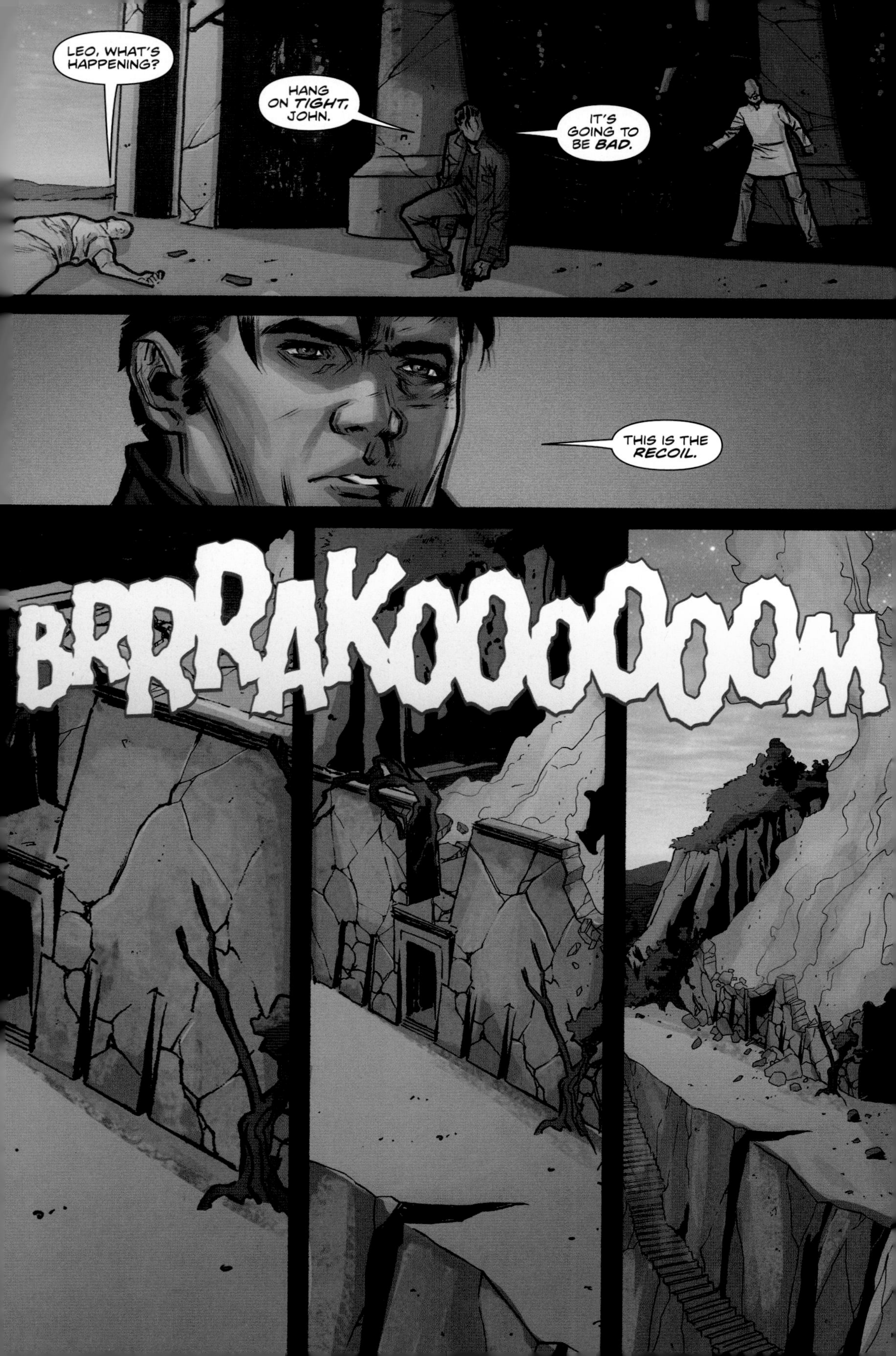
LEO, WHAT'S HAPPENING?
HANG ON *TIGHT,* JOHN.
IT'S GOING TO BE *BAD.*
THIS IS THE *RECOIL.*
BRRRAKOOOOOOM

COVER GALLERY

ISSUE ONE
TOMMY LEE EDWARDS

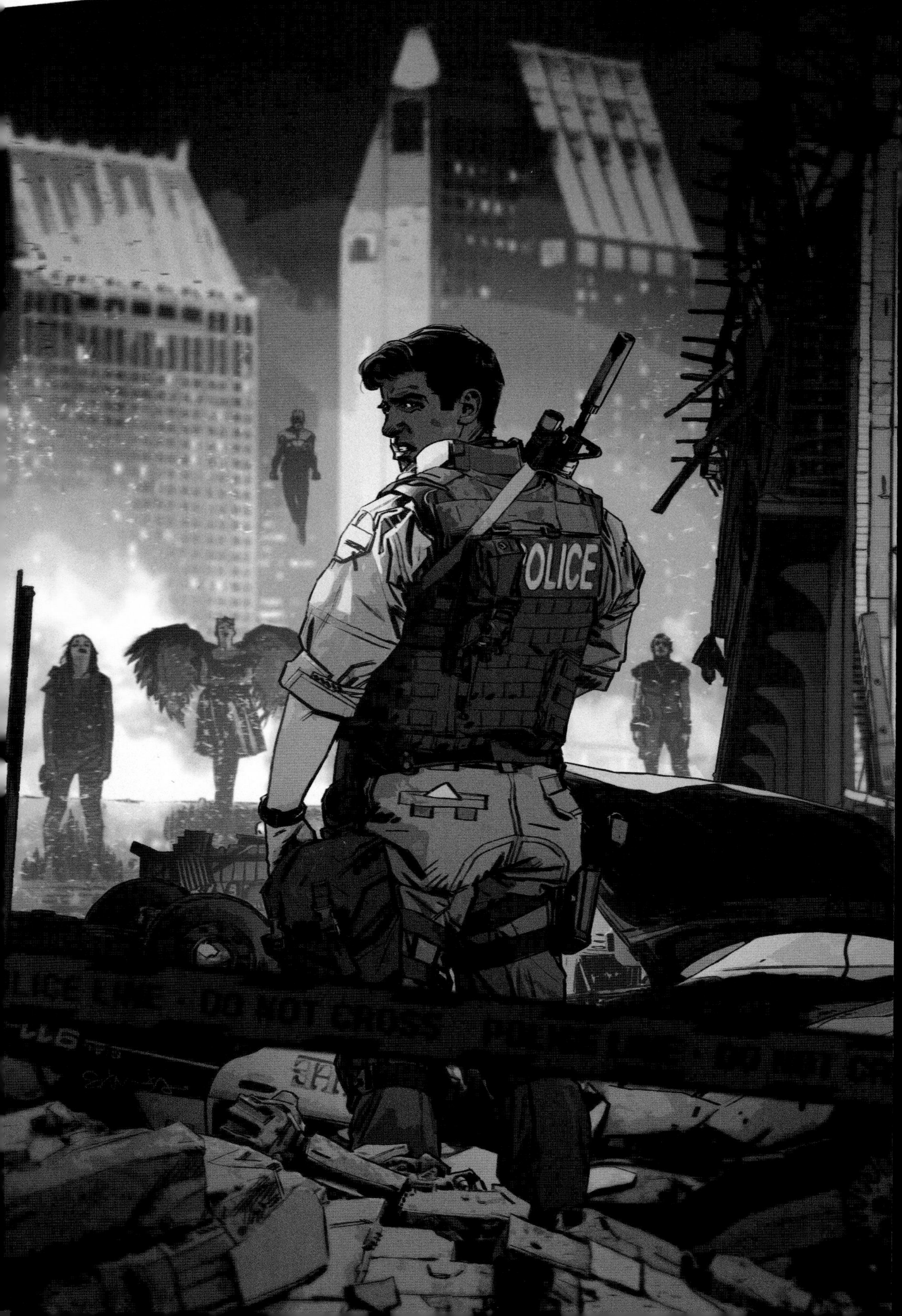
OLICE
DO NOT CROSS

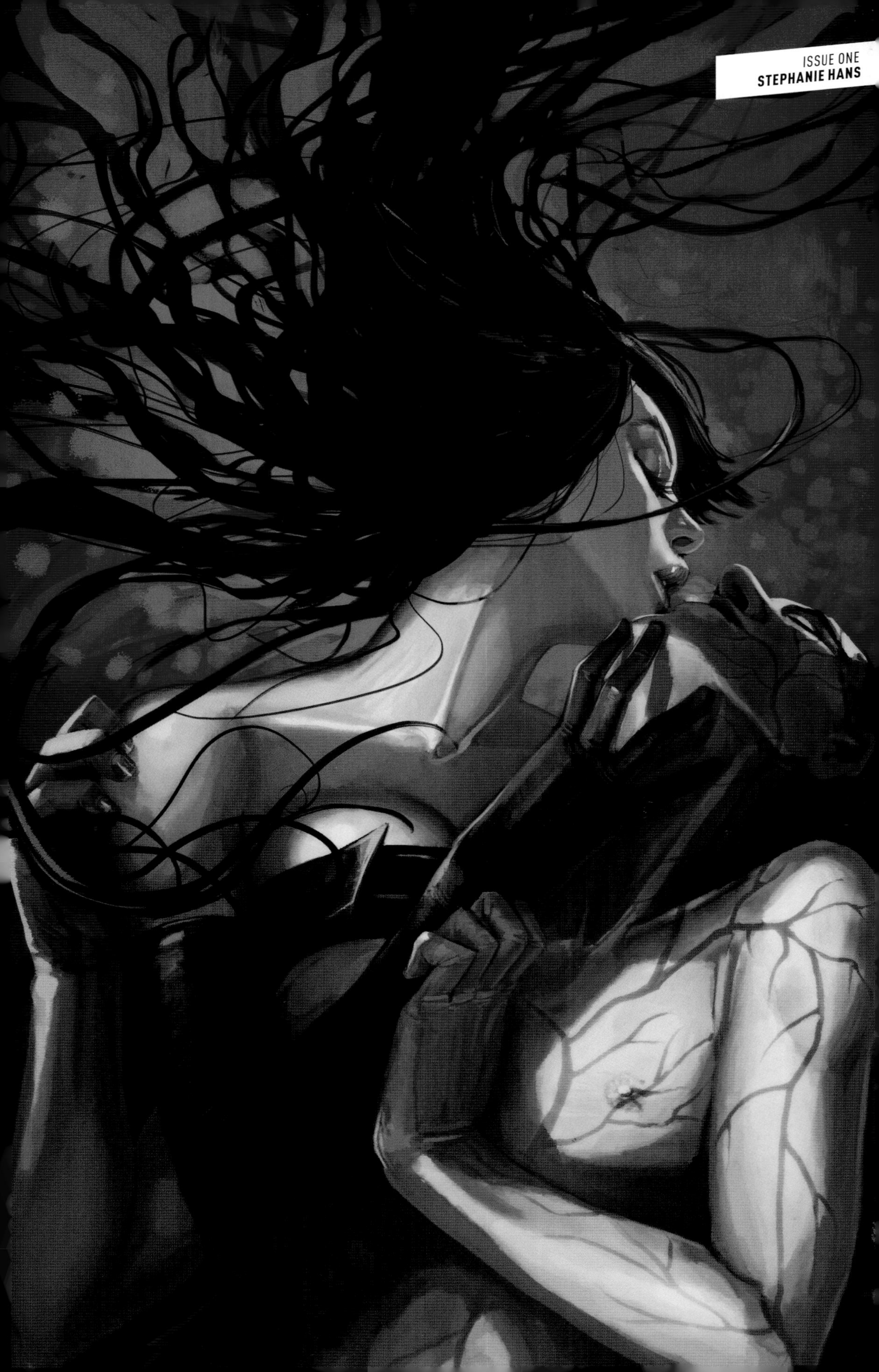
ISSUE ONE
STEPHANIE HANS

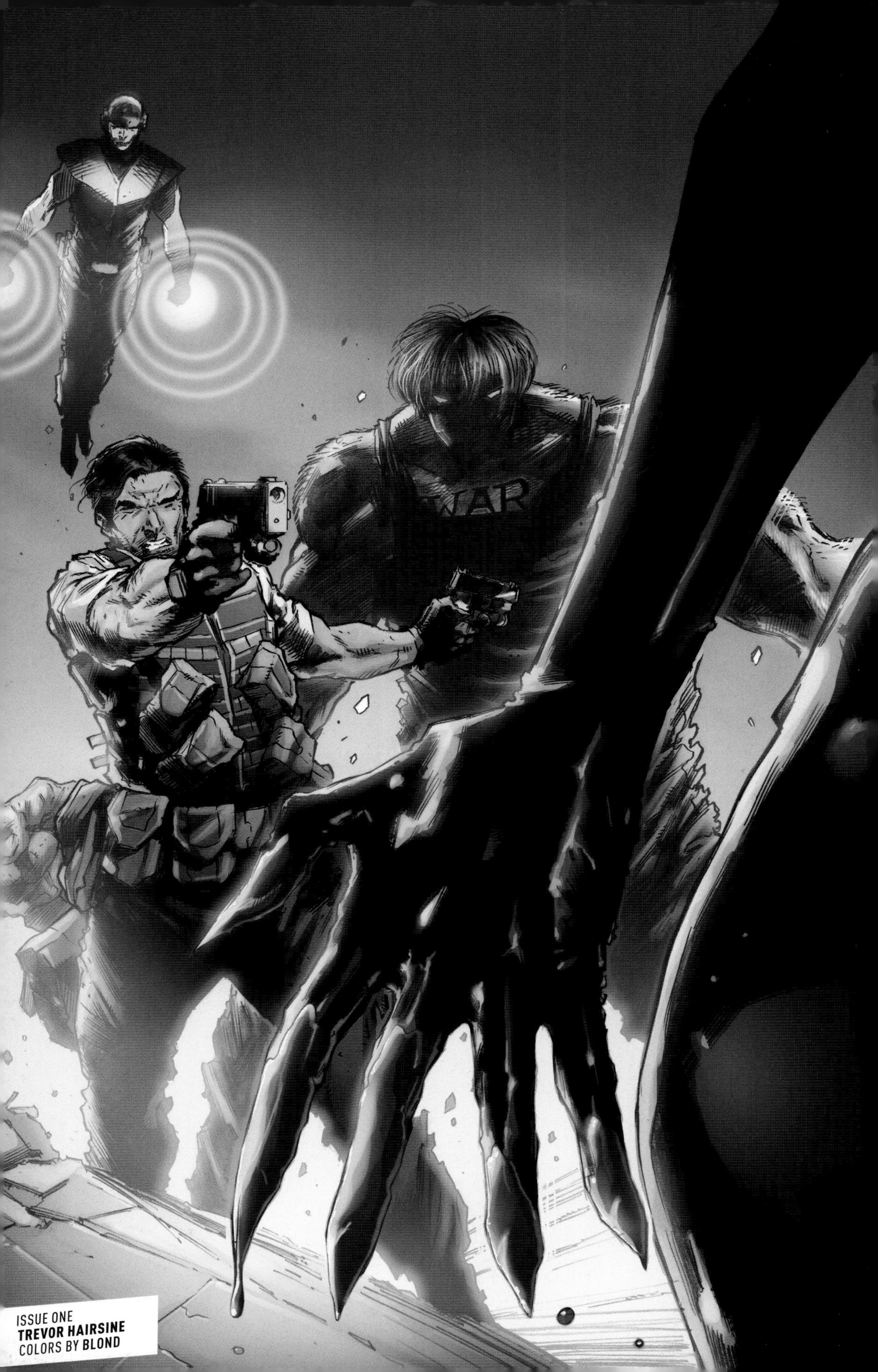
WAR

ISSUE ONE
TREVOR HAIRSINE
COLORS BY **BLOND**

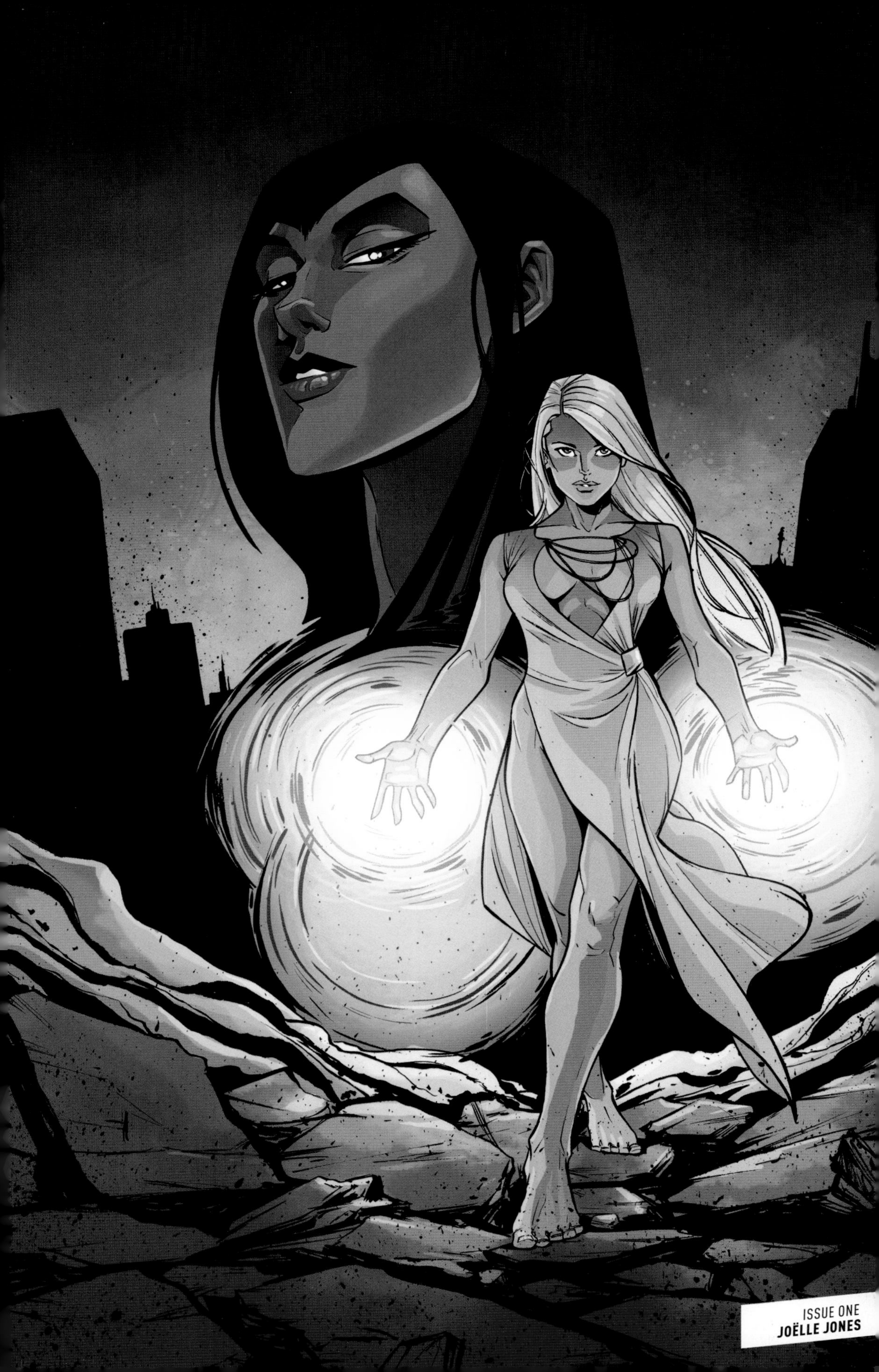

ISSUE ONE
JOËLLE JONES

ISSUE ONE
DAN PANOSIAN

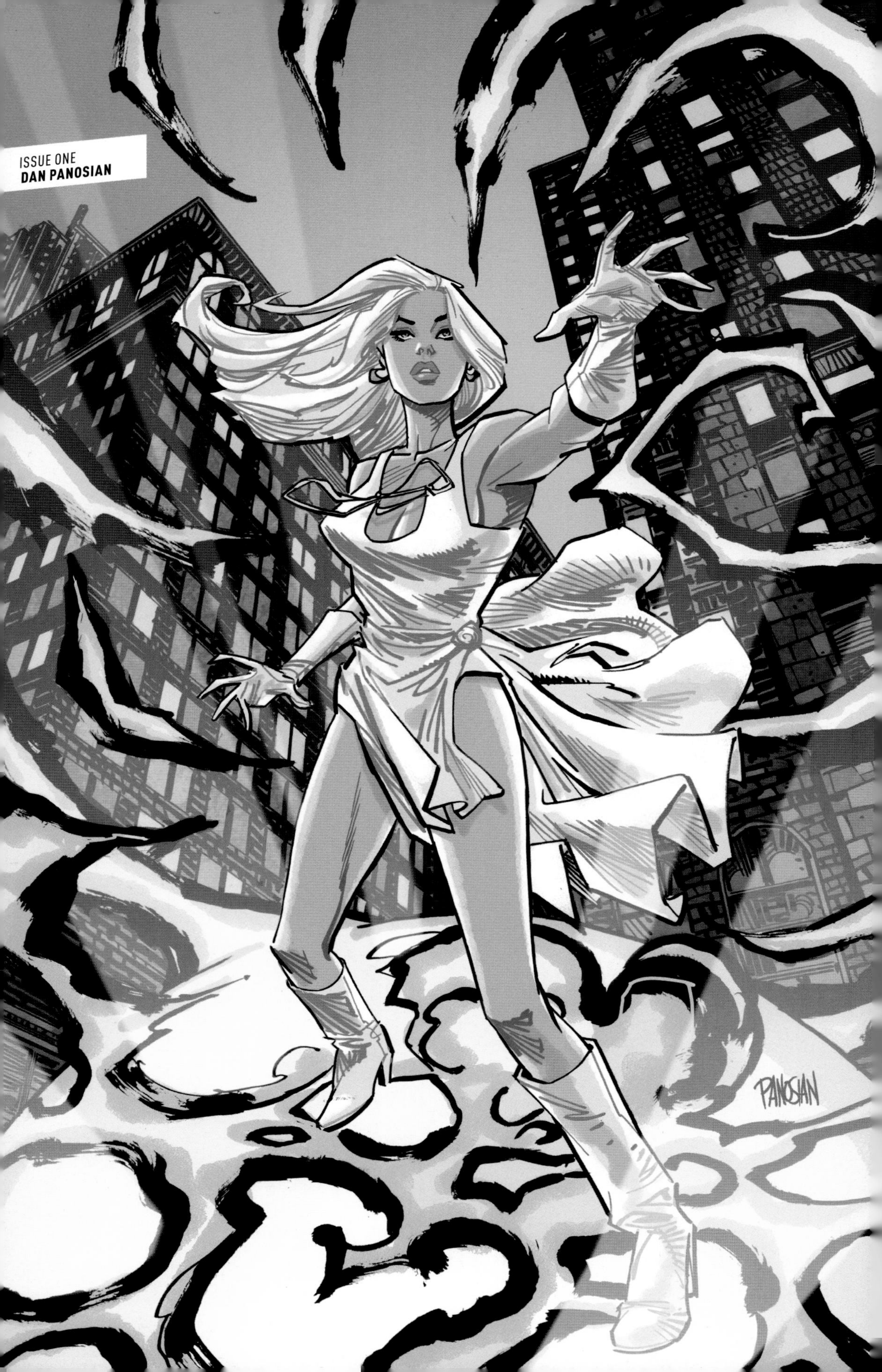
PANOSIAN

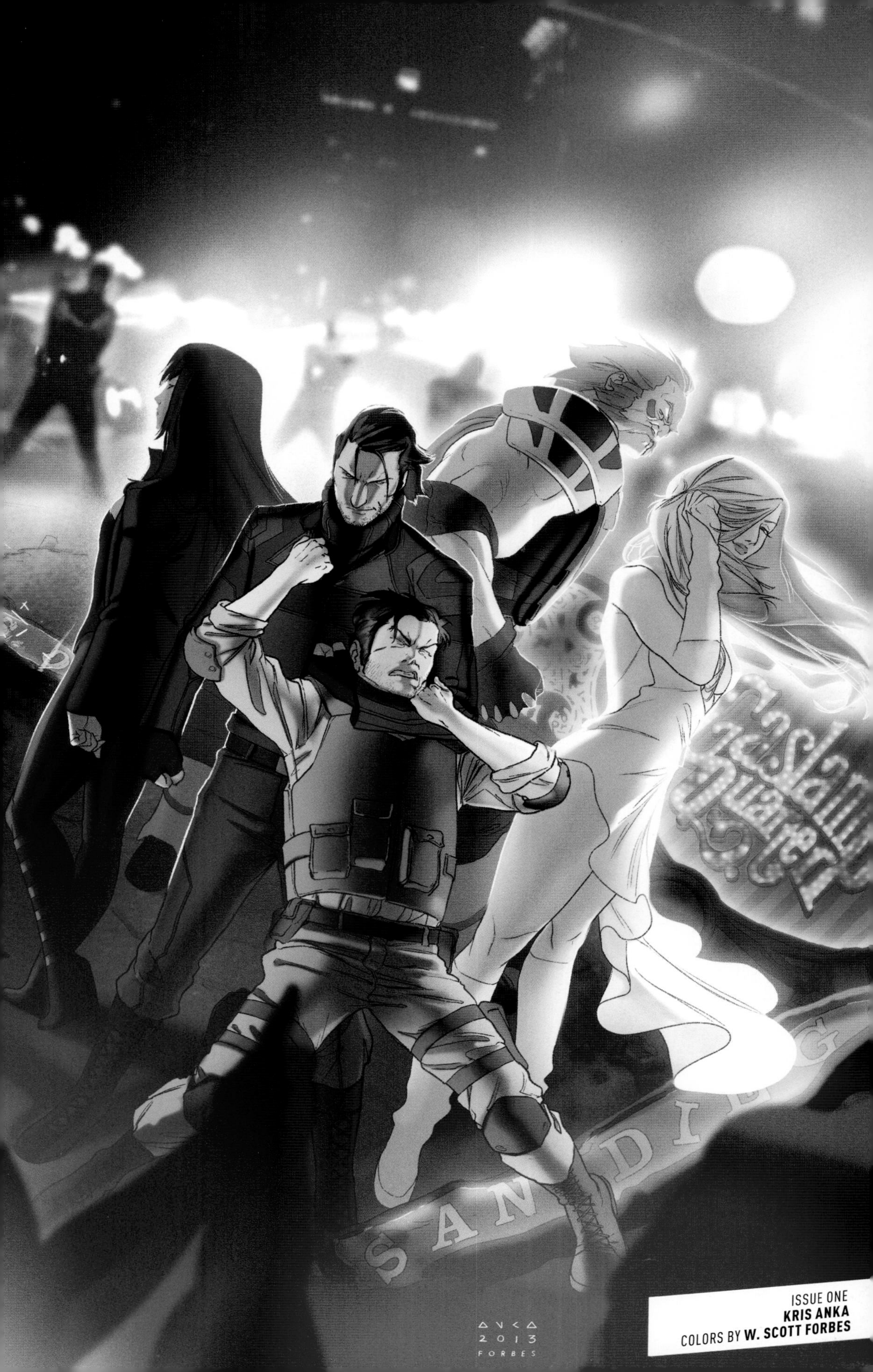
2013
FORBES

ISSUE ONE
KRIS ANKA
COLORS BY **W. SCOTT FORBES**

ISSUE ONE
GARRY BROWN

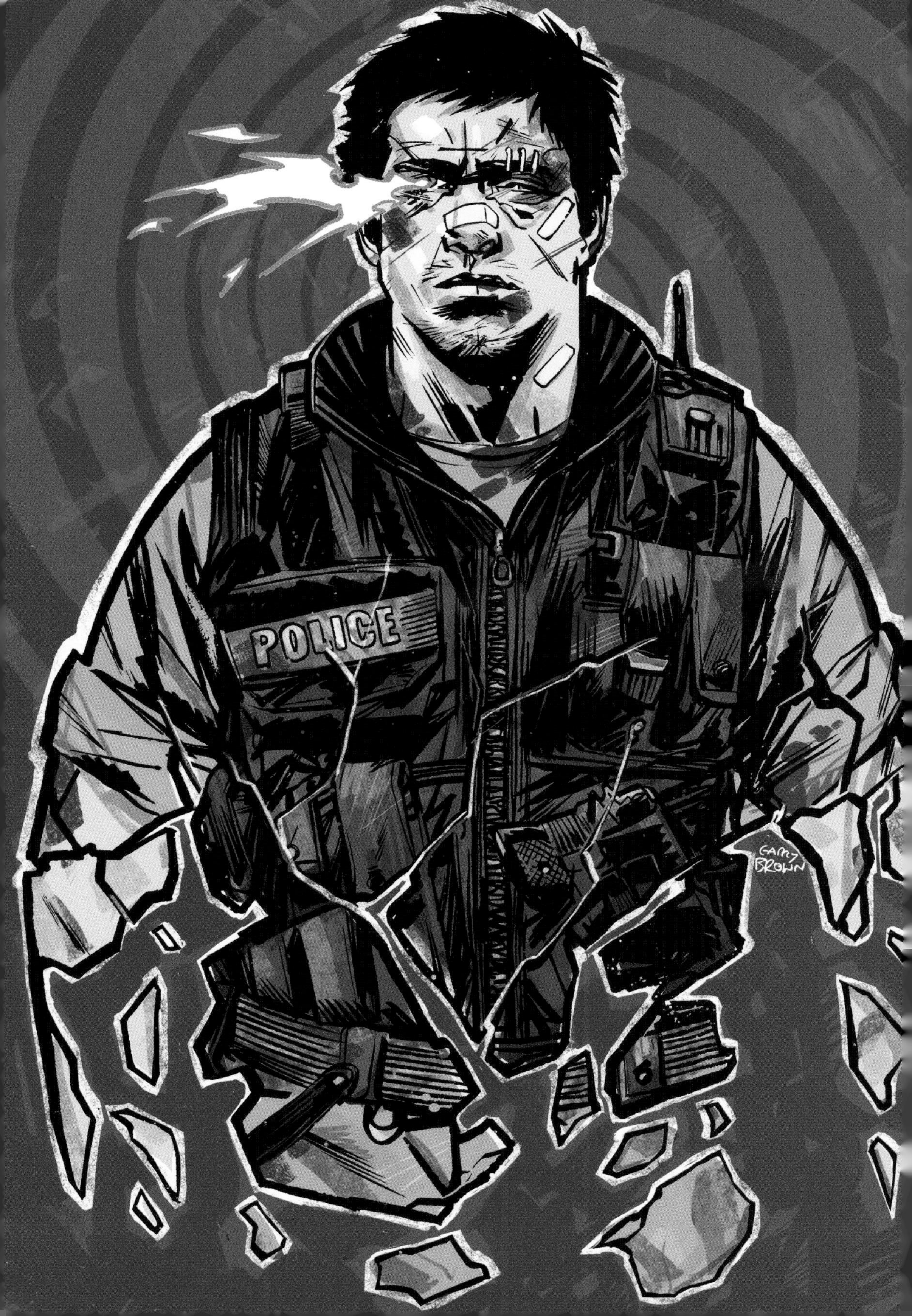
POLICE
GARRY BROWN

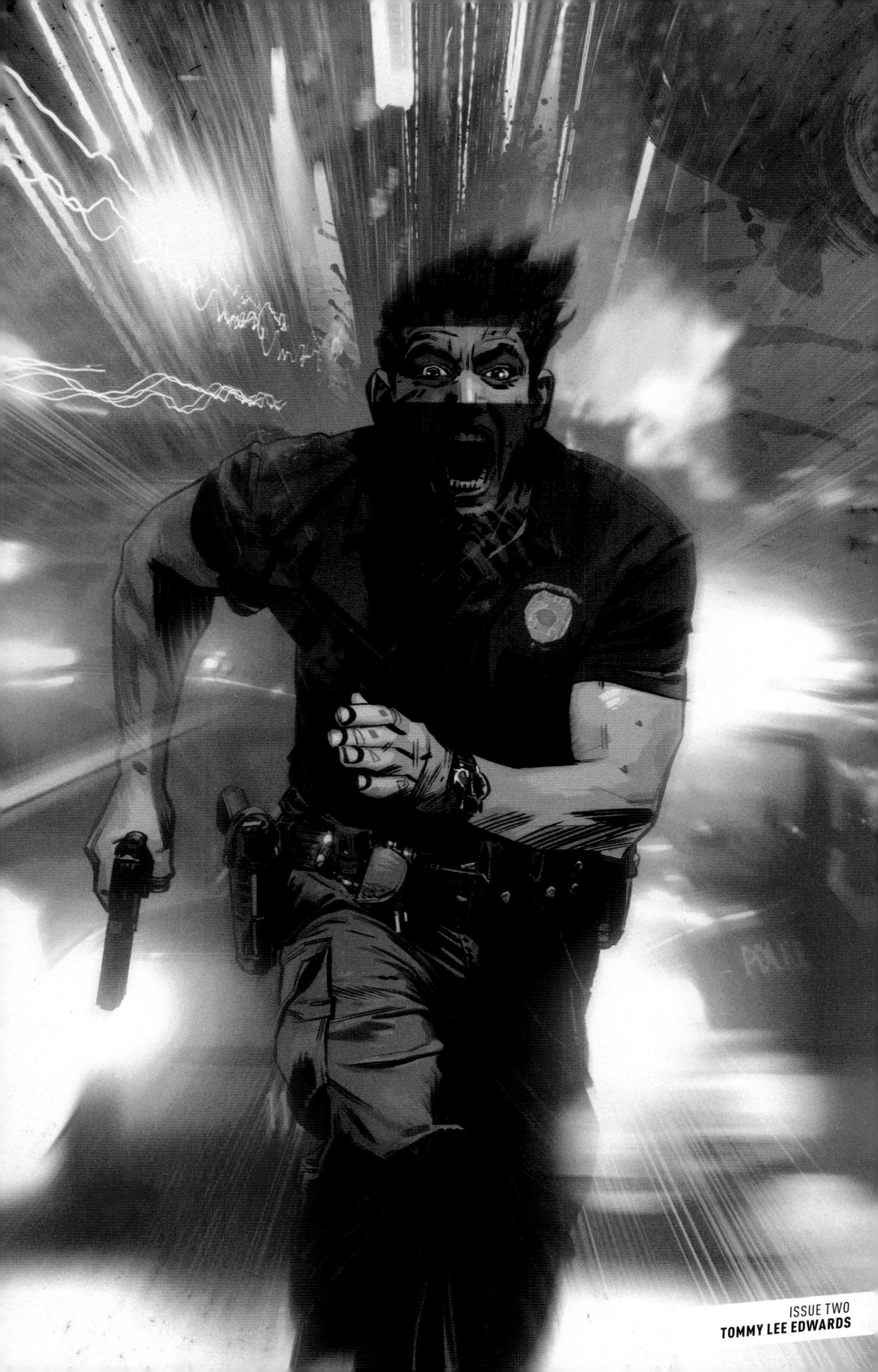

ISSUE TWO
TOMMY LEE EDWARDS

ISSUE TWO
STEPHANIE HANS

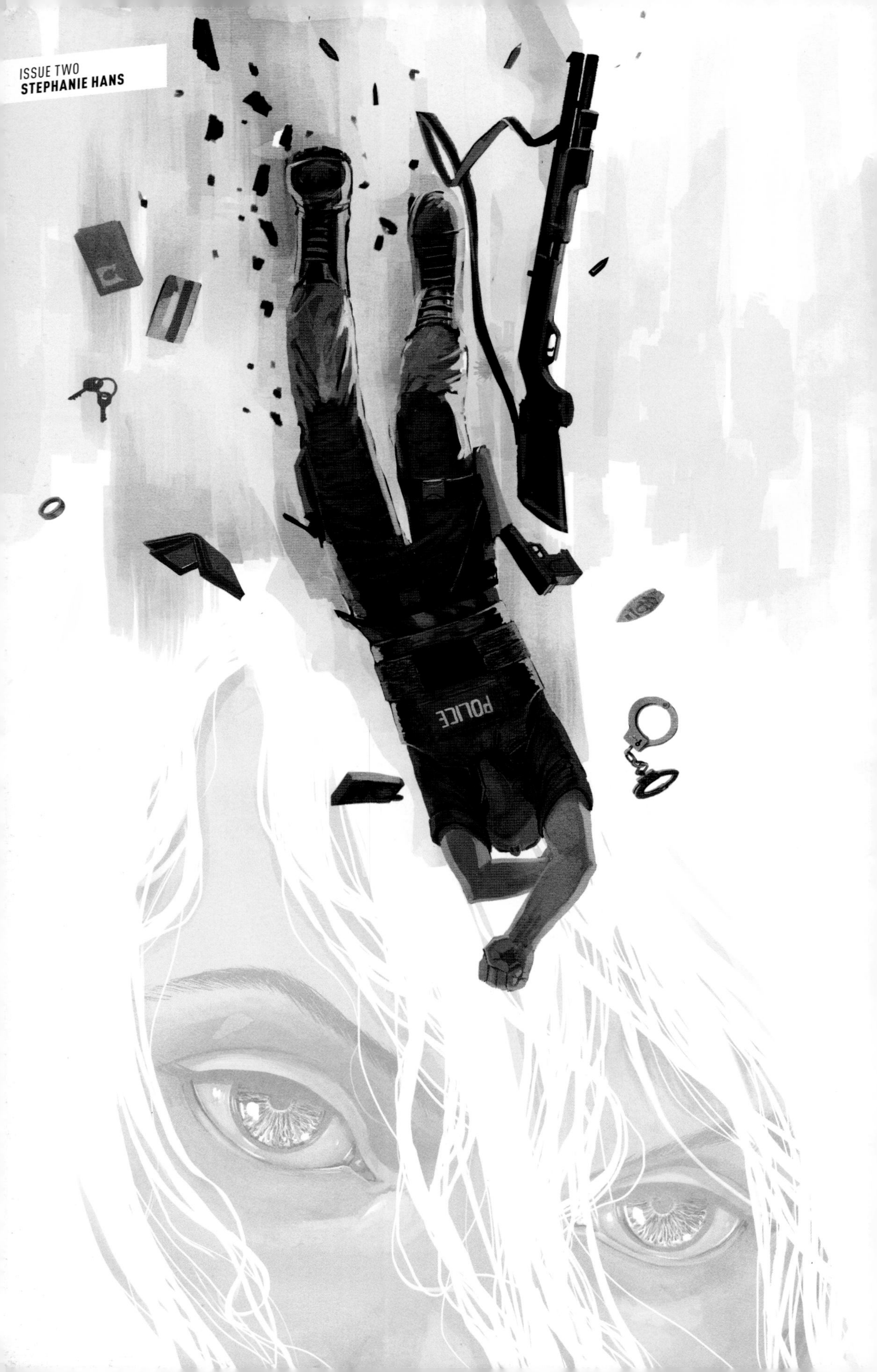
POLICE

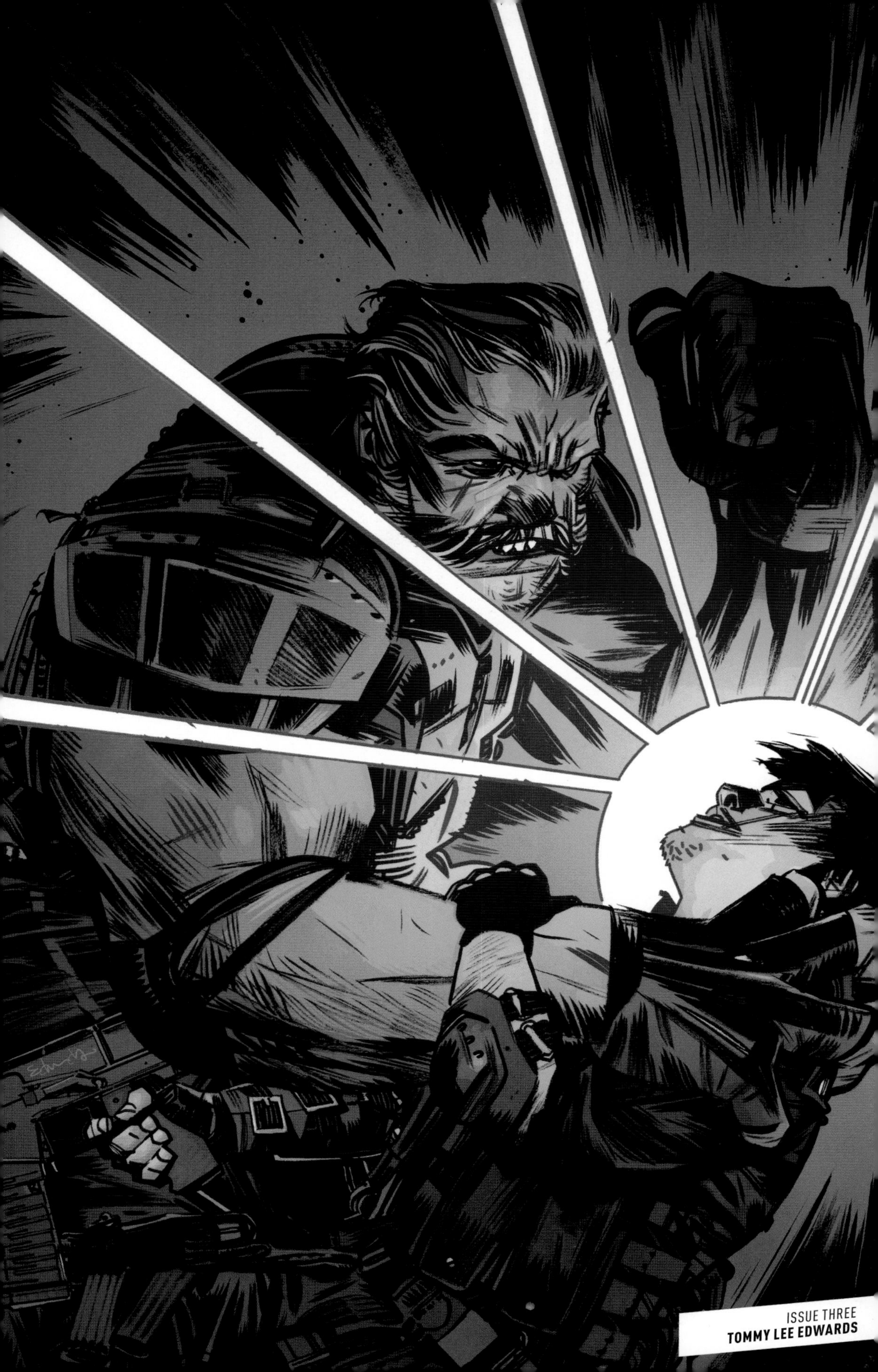

ISSUE THREE
TOMMY LEE EDWARDS

ISSUE THREE
STEPHANIE HANS

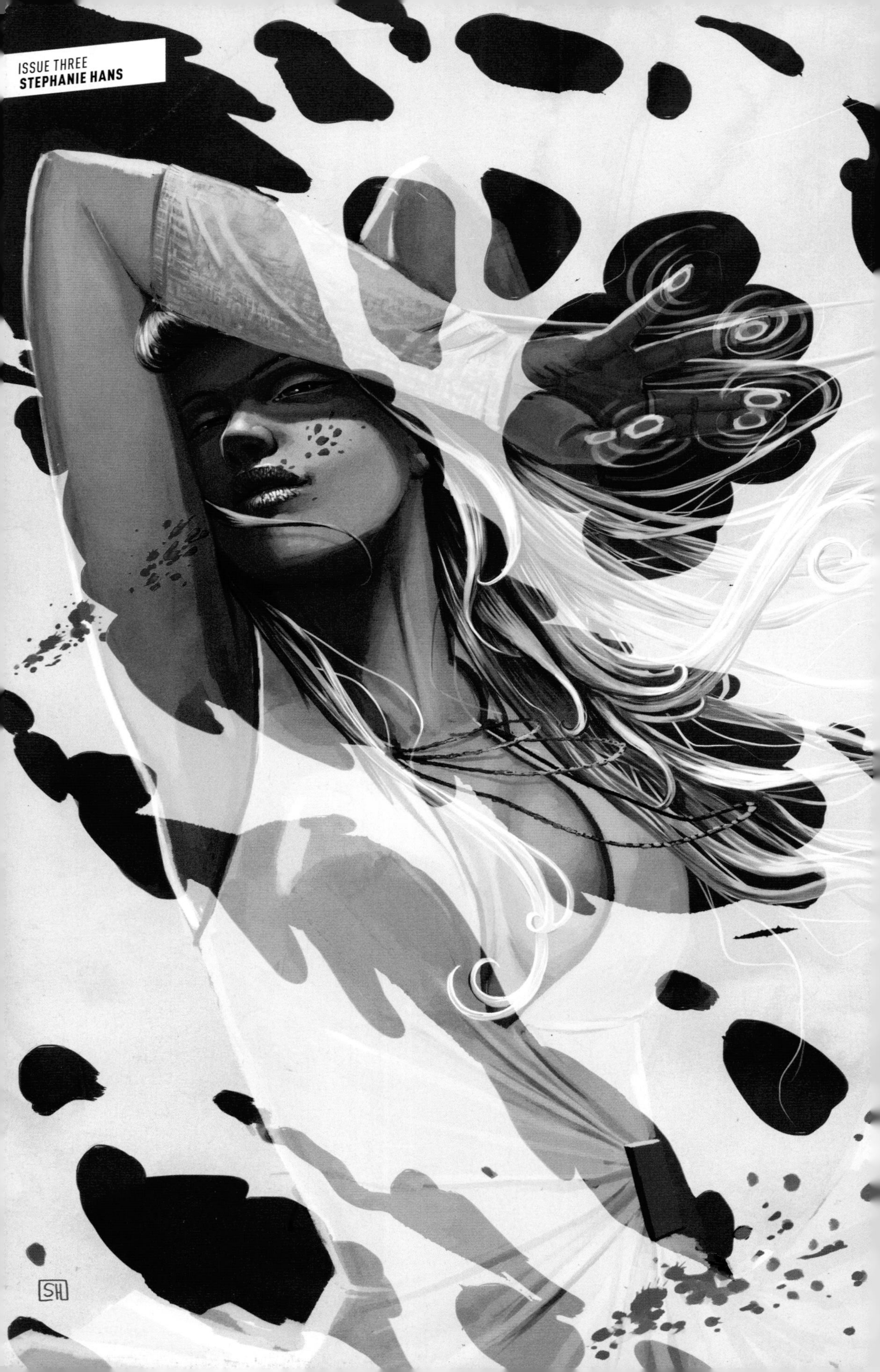
SH

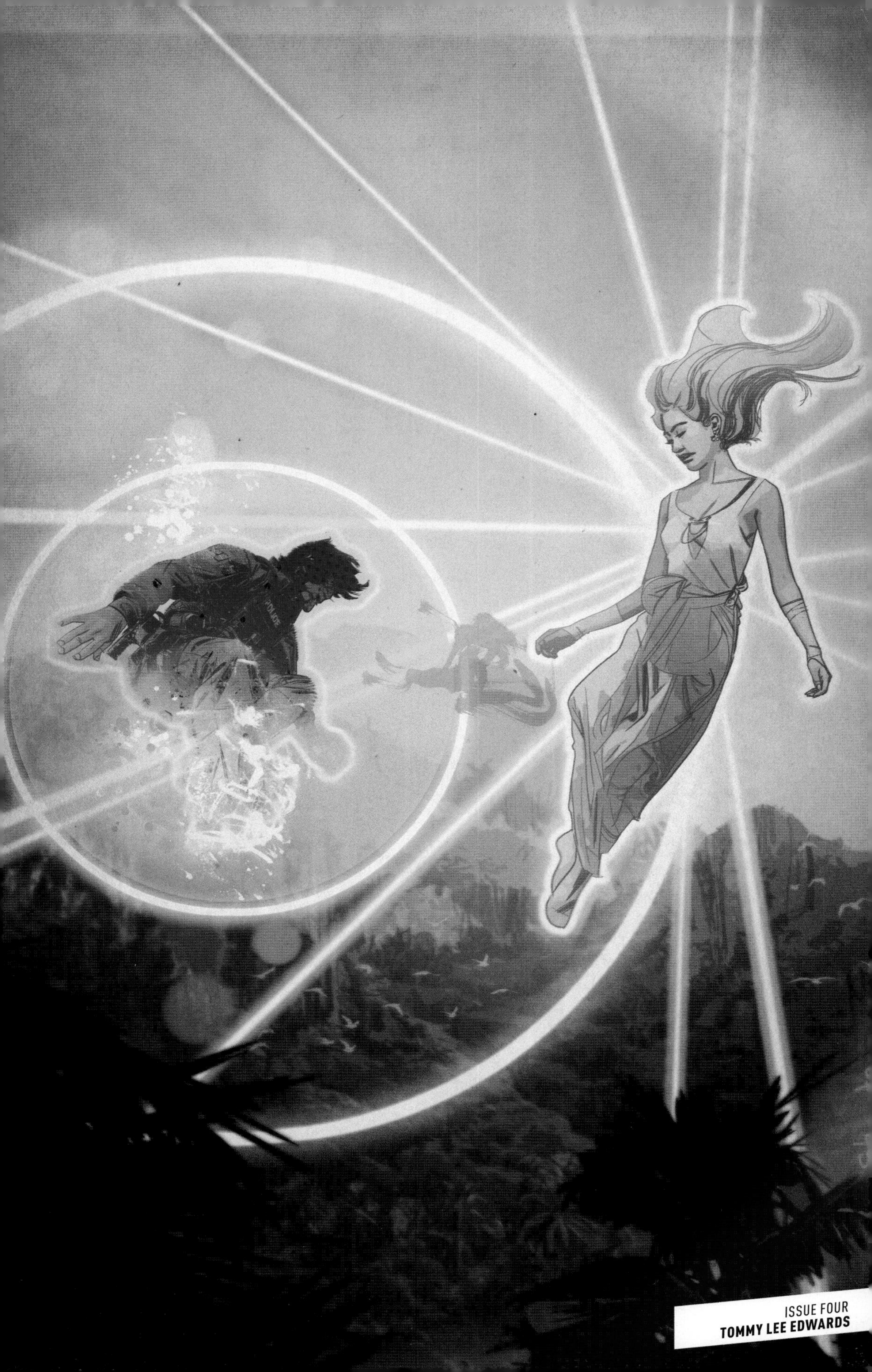

ISSUE FOUR
TOMMY LEE EDWARDS

ISSUE FOUR
STEPHANIE HANS

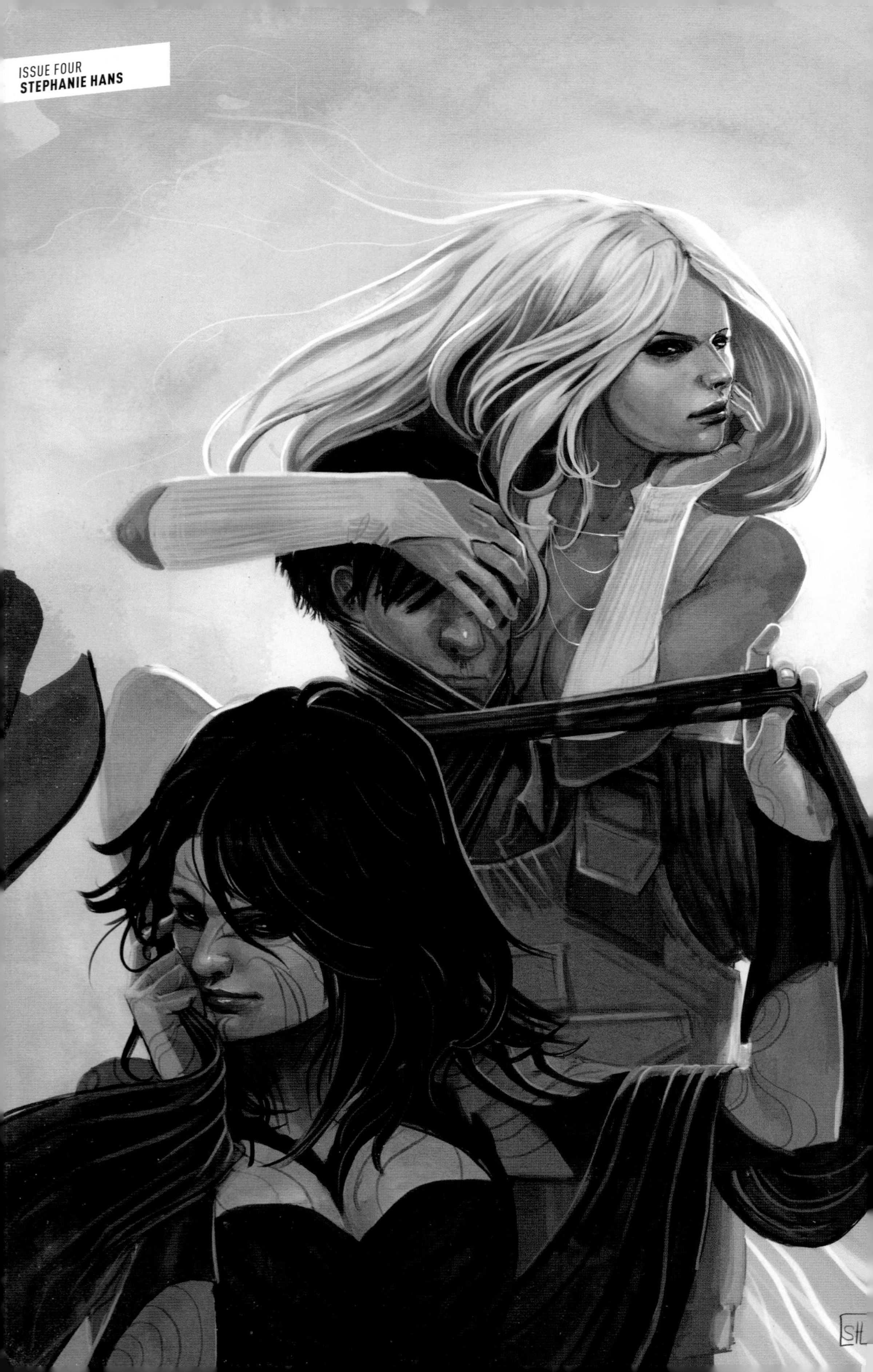